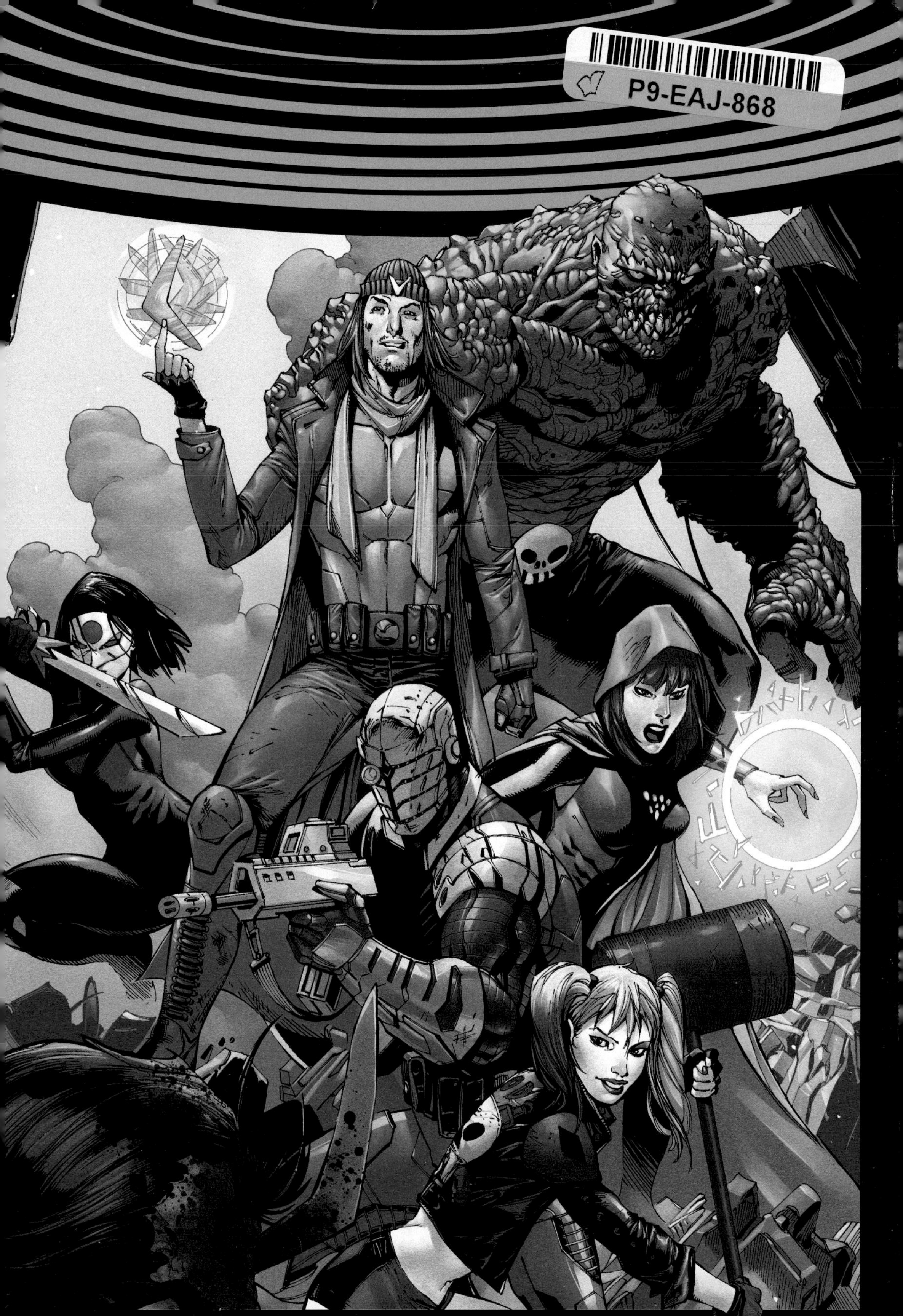

SUICIDE SQUAD

VOL. 4 EARTHLINGS ON FIRE

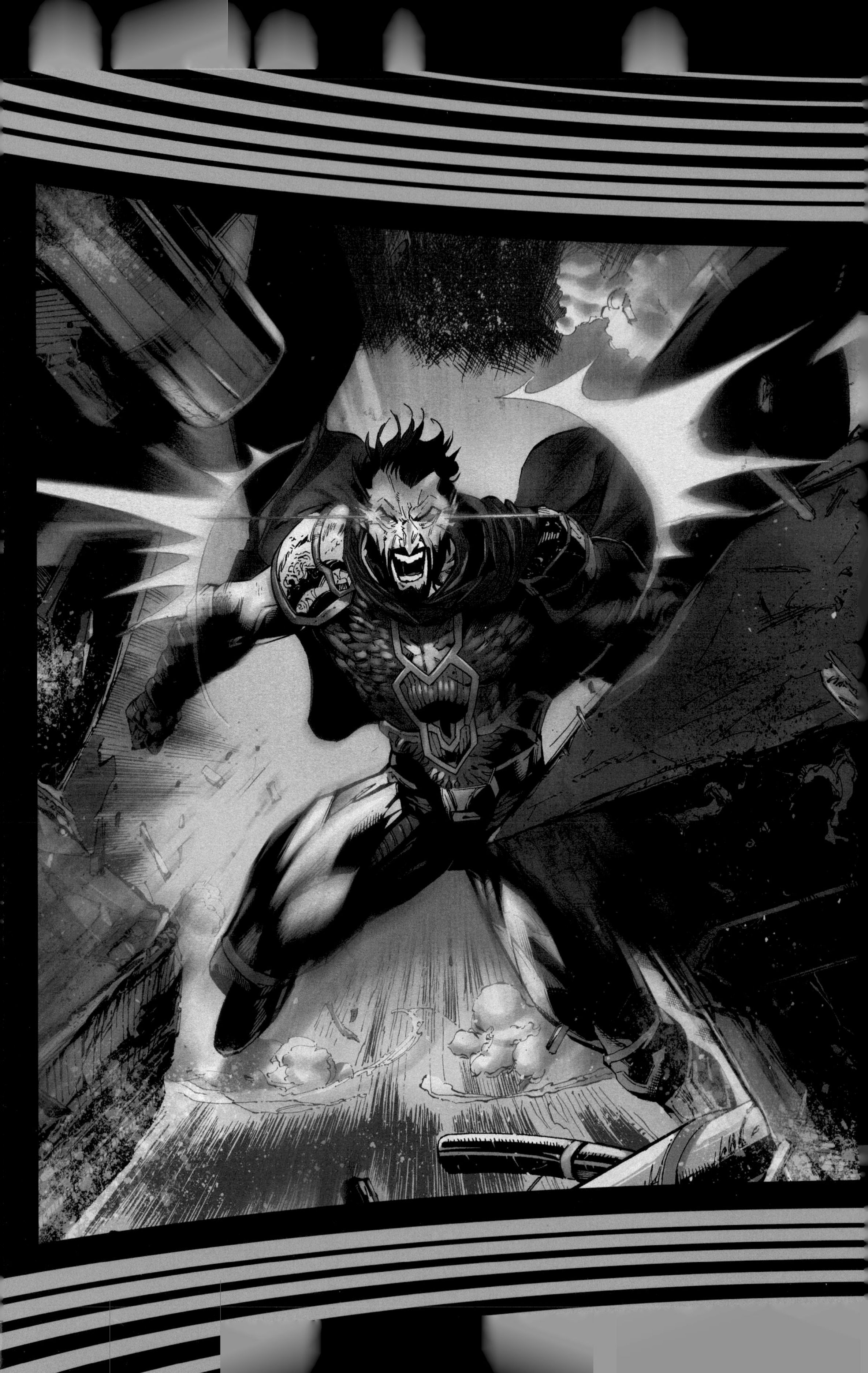

SUICIDE SQUAD
VOL.4 EARTHLINGS ON FIRE

ROB WILLIAMS
writer

TONY S. DANIEL ✳ **SANDU FLOREA**
NEIL EDWARDS ✳ **STJEPAN SEJIC**
artists

TOMEU MOREY ✳ **STJEPAN SEJIC**
colorists

PAT BROSSEAU
letterer

TONY S. DANIEL, SANDU FLOREA and TOMEU MOREY
collection cover art

TONY S. DANIEL, SANDU FLOREA and TOMEU MOREY
OTTO SCHMIDT
original series covers

ANDY KHOURI Editor - Original Series ✳ **HARVEY RICHARDS** Associate Editor - Original Series
JEB WOODARD Group Editor - Collected Editions ✳ **SCOTT NYBAKKEN** Editor - Collected Edition
STEVE COOK Design Director - Books ✳ **MONIQUE NARBONETA** Publication Design

BOB HARRAS Senior VP - Editor-in-Chief, DC Comics
PAT McCALLUM Executive Editor, DC Comics

DIANE NELSON President ✳ **DAN DiDIO** Publisher ✳ **JIM LEE** Publisher ✳ **GEOFF JOHNS** President & Chief Creative Officer
AMIT DESAI Executive VP - Business & Marketing Strategy, Direct to Consumer & Global Franchise Management
SAM ADES Senior VP & General Manager, Digital Services ✳ **BOBBIE CHASE** VP & Executive Editor, Young Reader & Talent Development
MARK CHIARELLO Senior VP - Art, Design & Collected Editions ✳ **JOHN CUNNINGHAM** Senior VP - Sales & Trade Marketing
ANNE DePIES Senior VP - Business Strategy, Finance & Administration ✳ **DON FALLETTI** VP - Manufacturing Operations
LAWRENCE GANEM VP - Editorial Administration & Talent Relations ✳ **ALISON GILL** Senior VP - Manufacturing & Operations
HANK KANALZ Senior VP - Editorial Strategy & Administration ✳ **JAY KOGAN** VP - Legal Affairs ✳ **JACK MAHAN** VP - Business Affairs
NICK J. NAPOLITANO VP - Manufacturing Administration ✳ **EDDIE SCANNELL** VP - Consumer Marketing
COURTNEY SIMMONS Senior VP - Publicity & Communications ✳ **JIM (SKI) SOKOLOWSKI** VP - Comic Book Specialty Sales & Trade Marketing
NANCY SPEARS VP - Mass, Book, Digital Sales & Trade Marketing ✳ **MICHELE R. WELLS** VP - Content Strategy

SUICIDE SQUAD VOL. 4: EARTHLINGS ON FIRE

DC Comics, 2900 West Alameda Ave., Burbank, CA 91505
Printed by LSC Communications, Kendallville, IN, USA. 11/10/17. First Printing.
ISBN: 978-1-4012-7539-6

Library of Congress Cataloging-in-Publication Data is available.

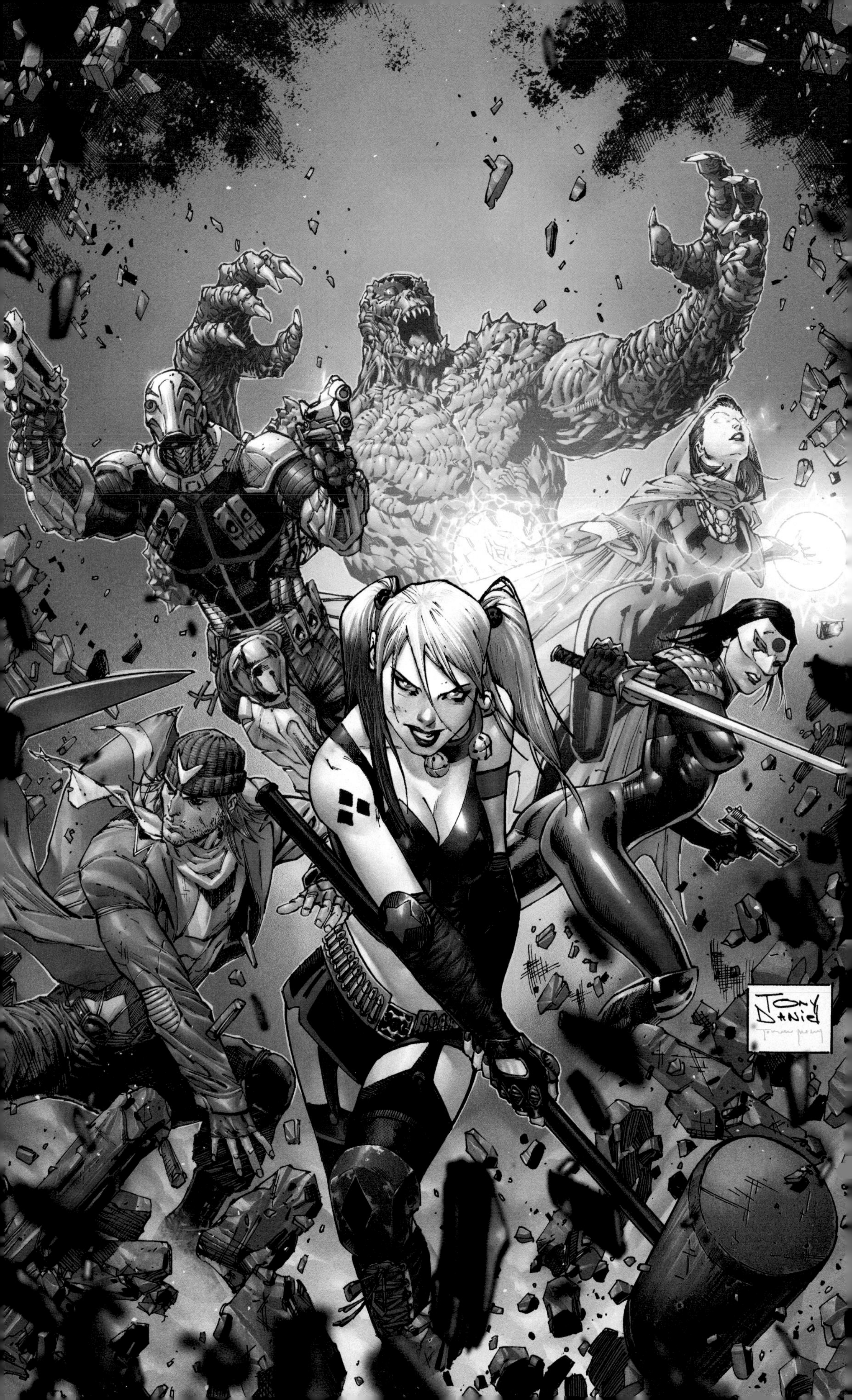

TONY DANIEL

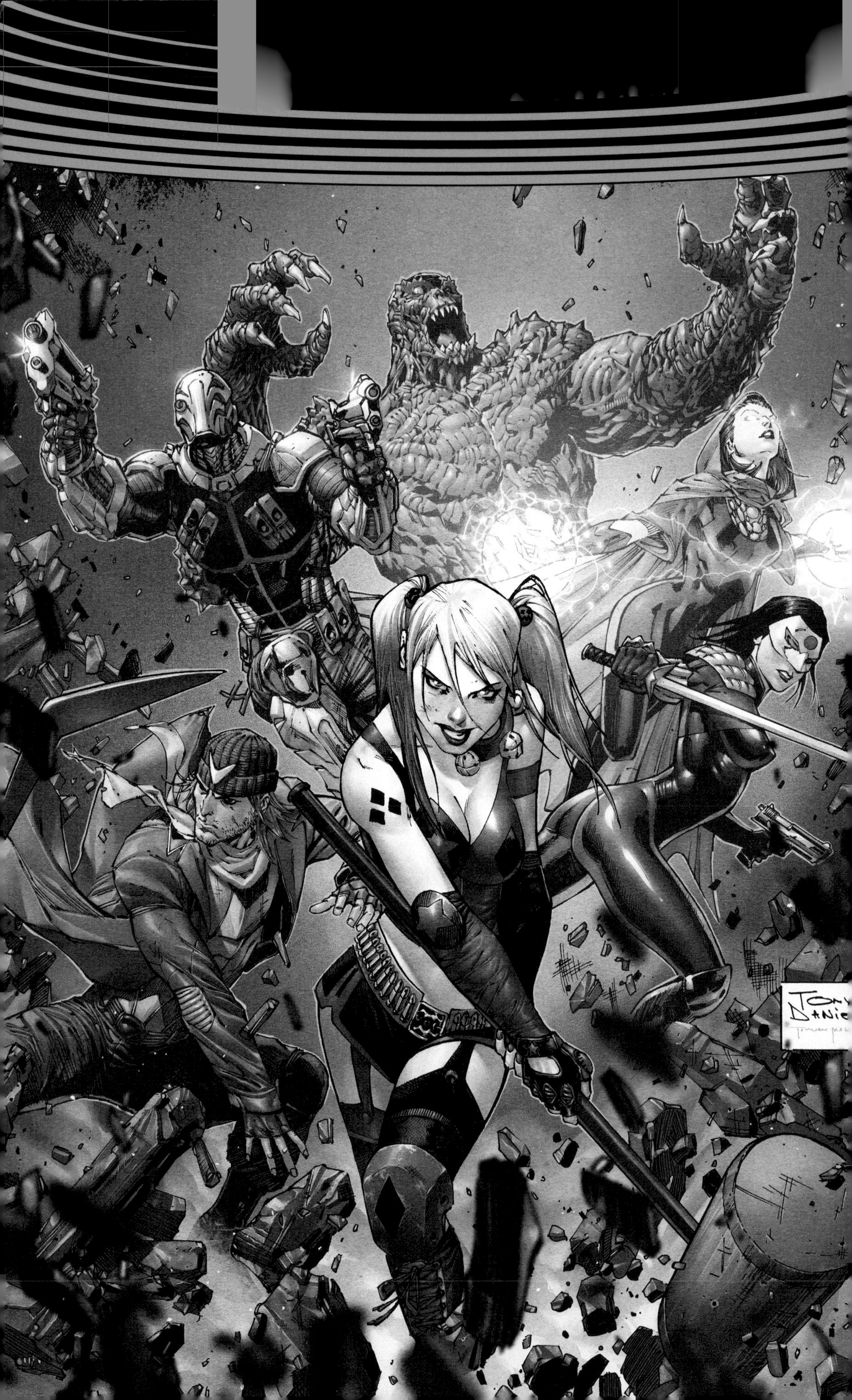

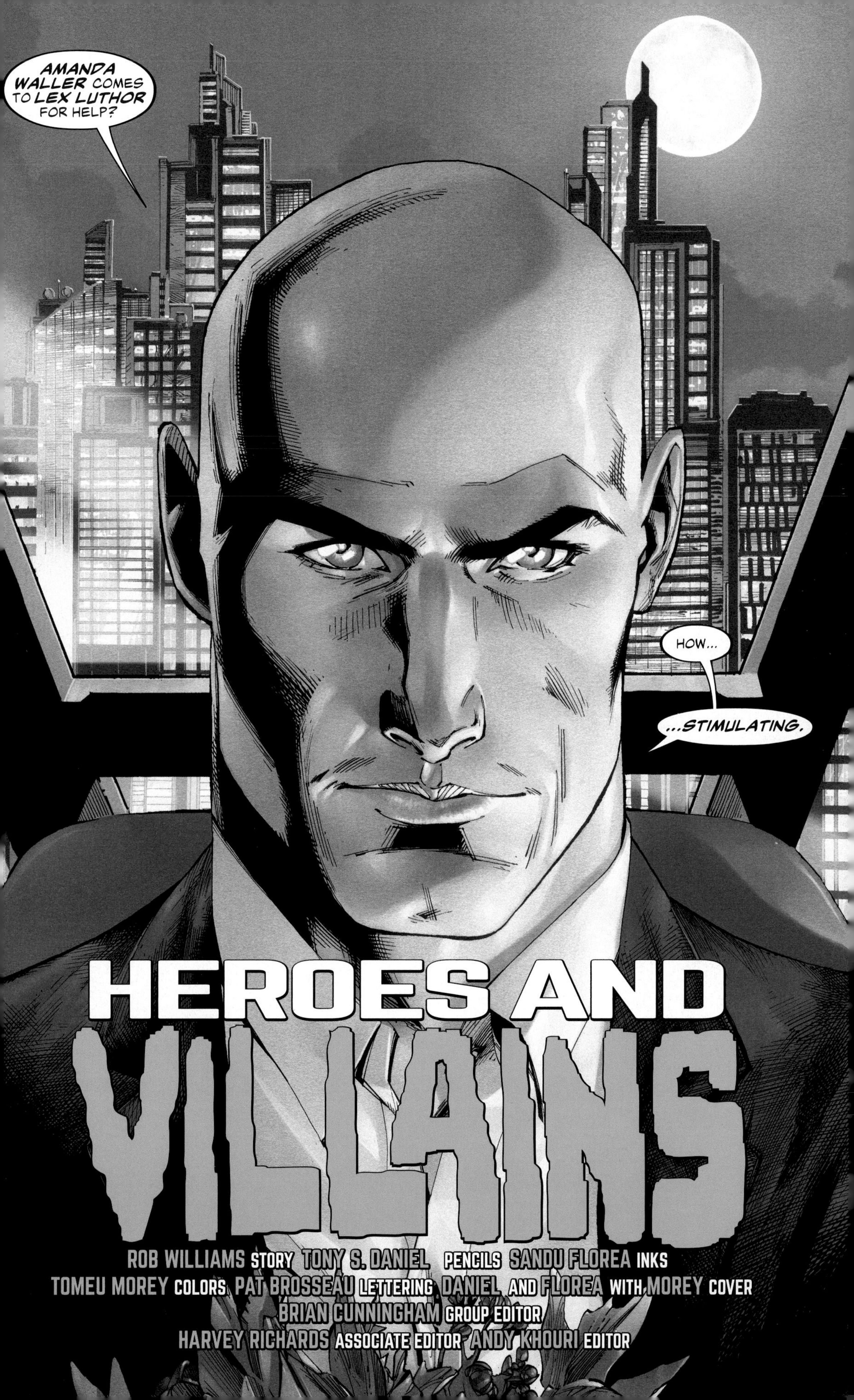
AMANDA WALLER COMES TO LEX LUTHOR FOR HELP?
HOW...
...STIMULATING.
HEROES AND VILLAINS
ROB WILLIAMS STORY TONY S. DANIEL PENCILS SANDU FLOREA INKS
TOMEU MOREY COLORS PAT BROSSEAU LETTERING DANIEL AND FLOREA WITH MOREY COVER
BRIAN CUNNINGHAM GROUP EDITOR
HARVEY RICHARDS ASSOCIATE EDITOR ANDY KHOURI EDITOR

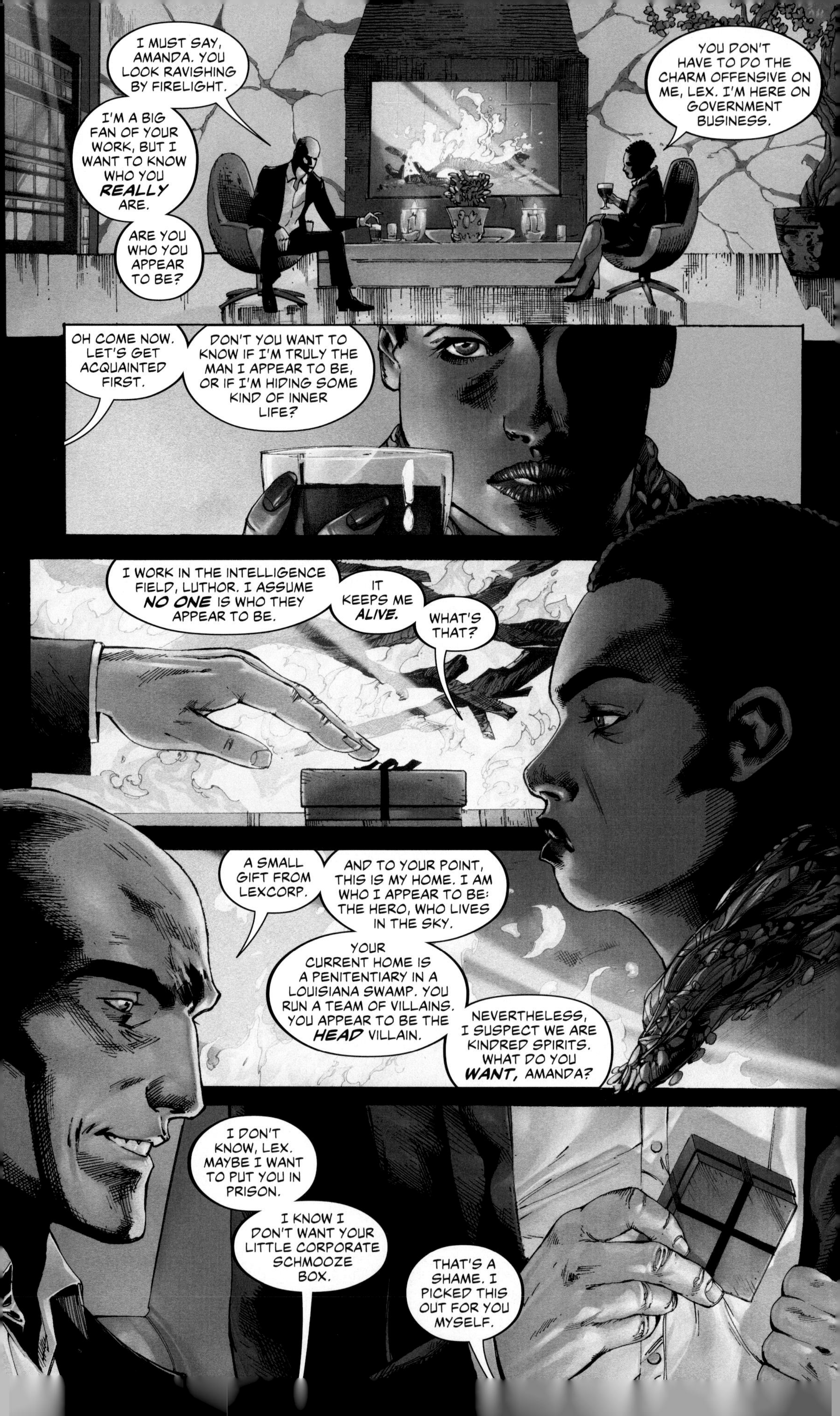
I MUST SAY, AMANDA. YOU LOOK RAVISHING BY FIRELIGHT.
I'M A BIG FAN OF YOUR WORK, BUT I WANT TO KNOW WHO YOU REALLY ARE.
ARE YOU WHO YOU APPEAR TO BE?
YOU DON'T HAVE TO DO THE CHARM OFFENSIVE ON ME, LEX. I'M HERE ON GOVERNMENT BUSINESS.
OH COME NOW. LET'S GET ACQUAINTED FIRST.
DON'T YOU WANT TO KNOW IF I'M TRULY THE MAN I APPEAR TO BE, OR IF I'M HIDING SOME KIND OF INNER LIFE?
I WORK IN THE INTELLIGENCE FIELD, LUTHOR. I ASSUME NO ONE IS WHO THEY APPEAR TO BE.
IT KEEPS ME ALIVE.
WHAT'S THAT?
A SMALL GIFT FROM LEXCORP.
AND TO YOUR POINT, THIS IS MY HOME. I AM WHO I APPEAR TO BE: THE HERO, WHO LIVES IN THE SKY.
YOUR CURRENT HOME IS A PENITENTIARY IN A LOUISIANA SWAMP. YOU RUN A TEAM OF VILLAINS. YOU APPEAR TO BE THE HEAD VILLAIN.
NEVERTHELESS, I SUSPECT WE ARE KINDRED SPIRITS. WHAT DO YOU WANT, AMANDA?
I DON'T KNOW, LEX. MAYBE I WANT TO PUT YOU IN PRISON.
I KNOW I DON'T WANT YOUR LITTLE CORPORATE SCHMOOZE BOX.
THAT'S A SHAME. I PICKED THIS OUT FOR YOU MYSELF.

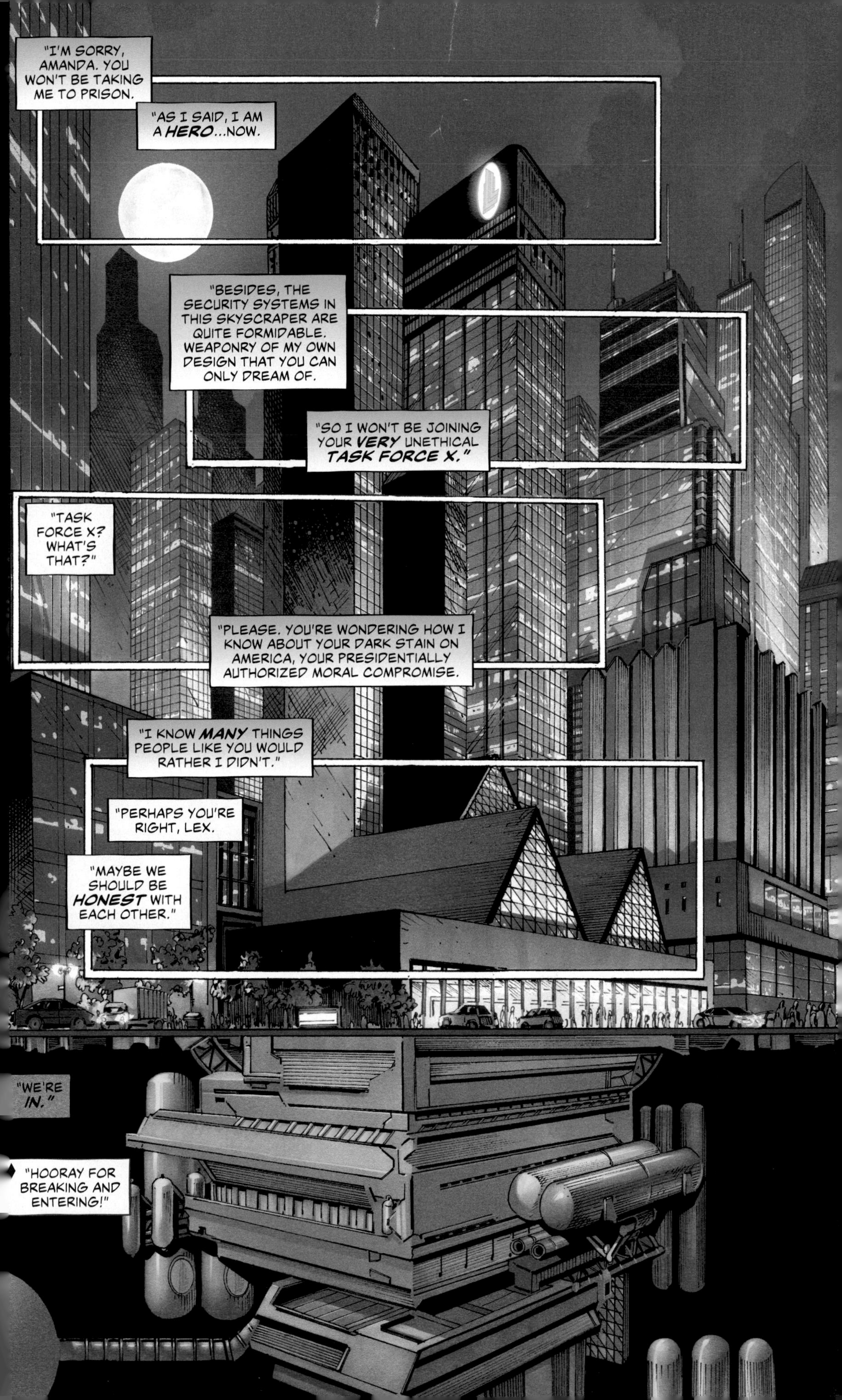
"I'M SORRY, AMANDA. YOU WON'T BE TAKING ME TO PRISON.
"AS I SAID, I AM A HERO...NOW.
"BESIDES, THE SECURITY SYSTEMS IN THIS SKYSCRAPER ARE QUITE FORMIDABLE. WEAPONRY OF MY OWN DESIGN THAT YOU CAN ONLY DREAM OF.
"SO I WON'T BE JOINING YOUR VERY UNETHICAL TASK FORCE X."
"TASK FORCE X? WHAT'S THAT?"
"PLEASE. YOU'RE WONDERING HOW I KNOW ABOUT YOUR DARK STAIN ON AMERICA, YOUR PRESIDENTIALLY AUTHORIZED MORAL COMPROMISE.
"I KNOW MANY THINGS PEOPLE LIKE YOU WOULD RATHER I DIDN'T."
"PERHAPS YOU'RE RIGHT, LEX.
"MAYBE WE SHOULD BE HONEST WITH EACH OTHER."
"WE'RE IN."
"HOORAY FOR BREAKING AND ENTERING!"

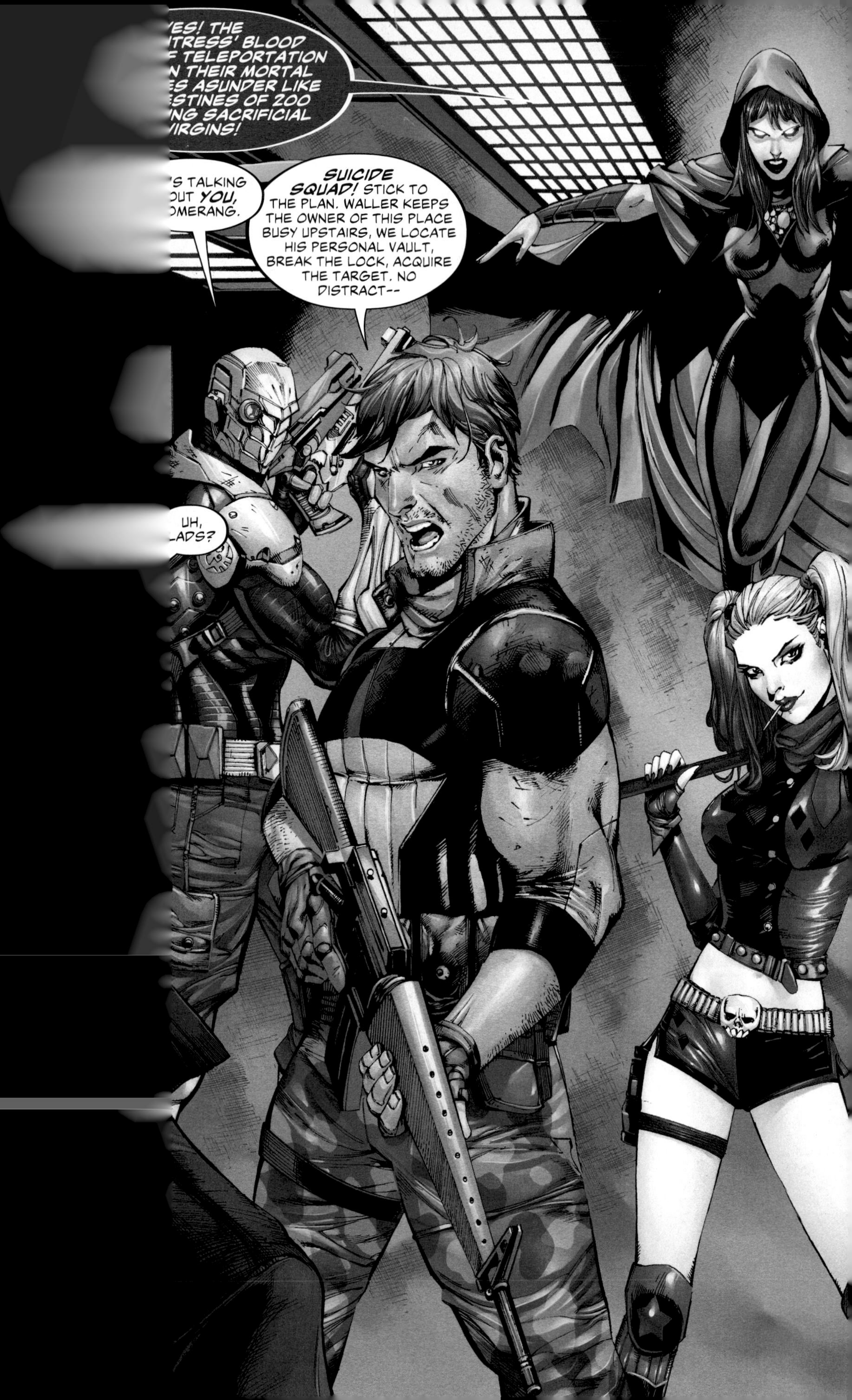

YES! THE
TRESS' BLOOD
F TELEPORTATION
N THEIR MORTAL
ES ASUNDER LIKE
ESTINES OF 200
NG SACRIFICIAL
VIRGINS!
'S TALKING
OUT YOU,
OMERANG.
SUICIDE SQUAD! STICK TO THE PLAN. WALLER KEEPS THE OWNER OF THIS PLACE BUSY UPSTAIRS, WE LOCATE HIS PERSONAL VAULT, BREAK THE LOCK, ACQUIRE THE TARGET. NO DISTRACT--
UH,
LADS?

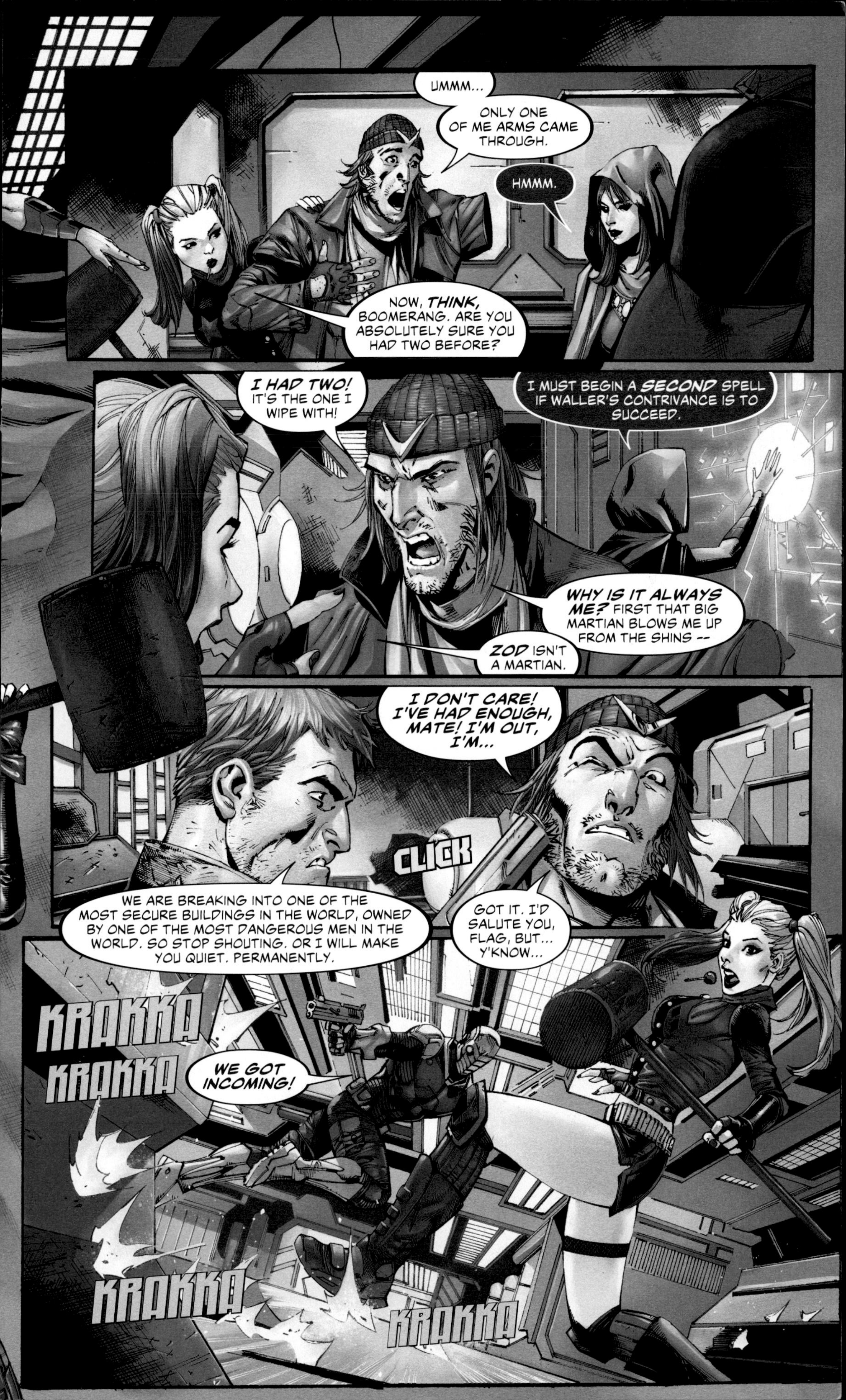
UMMM...
ONLY ONE OF ME ARMS CAME THROUGH.
HMMM.
NOW, THINK, BOOMERANG. ARE YOU ABSOLUTELY SURE YOU HAD TWO BEFORE?
I HAD TWO! IT'S THE ONE I WIPE WITH!
I MUST BEGIN A SECOND SPELL IF WALLER'S CONTRIVANCE IS TO SUCCEED.
WHY IS IT ALWAYS ME? FIRST THAT BIG MARTIAN BLOWS ME UP FROM THE SHINS --
ZOD ISN'T A MARTIAN.
I DON'T CARE! I'VE HAD ENOUGH, MATE! I'M OUT, I'M...
CLICK
WE ARE BREAKING INTO ONE OF THE MOST SECURE BUILDINGS IN THE WORLD, OWNED BY ONE OF THE MOST DANGEROUS MEN IN THE WORLD. SO STOP SHOUTING. OR I WILL MAKE YOU QUIET. PERMANENTLY.
GOT IT. I'D SALUTE YOU, FLAG, BUT... Y'KNOW...
KRAKKA
KRAKKA
WE GOT INCOMING!
KRAKKA
KRAKKA

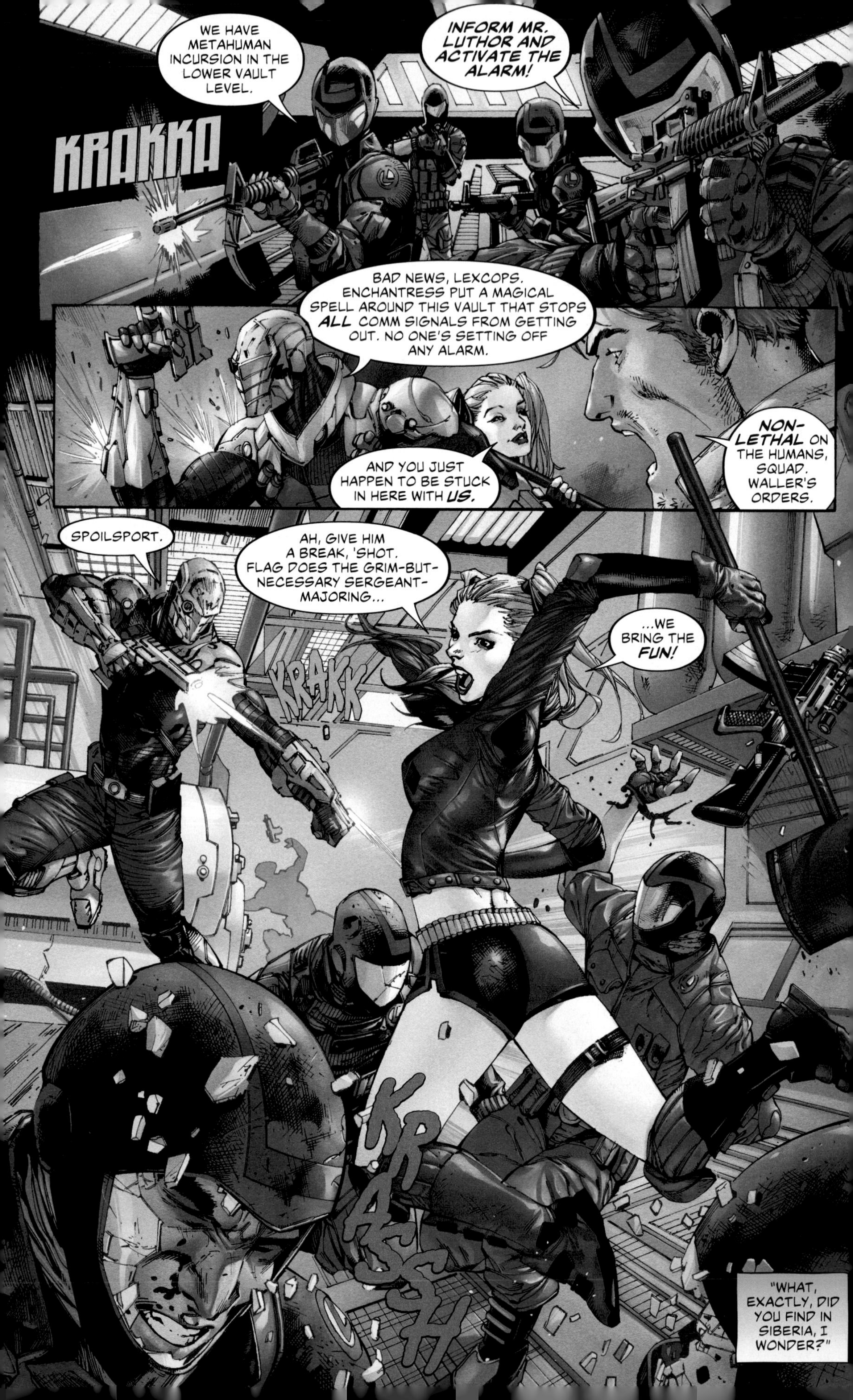

WE HAVE METAHUMAN INCURSION IN THE LOWER VAULT LEVEL.
INFORM MR. LUTHOR AND ACTIVATE THE ALARM!
KRAKKA
BAD NEWS, LEXCOPS. ENCHANTRESS PUT A MAGICAL SPELL AROUND THIS VAULT THAT STOPS ALL COMM SIGNALS FROM GETTING OUT. NO ONE'S SETTING OFF ANY ALARM.
AND YOU JUST HAPPEN TO BE STUCK IN HERE WITH US.
NON-LETHAL ON THE HUMANS, SQUAD. WALLER'S ORDERS.
SPOILSPORT.
AH, GIVE HIM A BREAK, 'SHOT. FLAG DOES THE GRIM-BUT-NECESSARY SERGEANT-MAJORING...
...WE BRING THE FUN!
KRAKK
KRASH
"WHAT, EXACTLY, DID YOU FIND IN SIBERIA, I WONDER?"

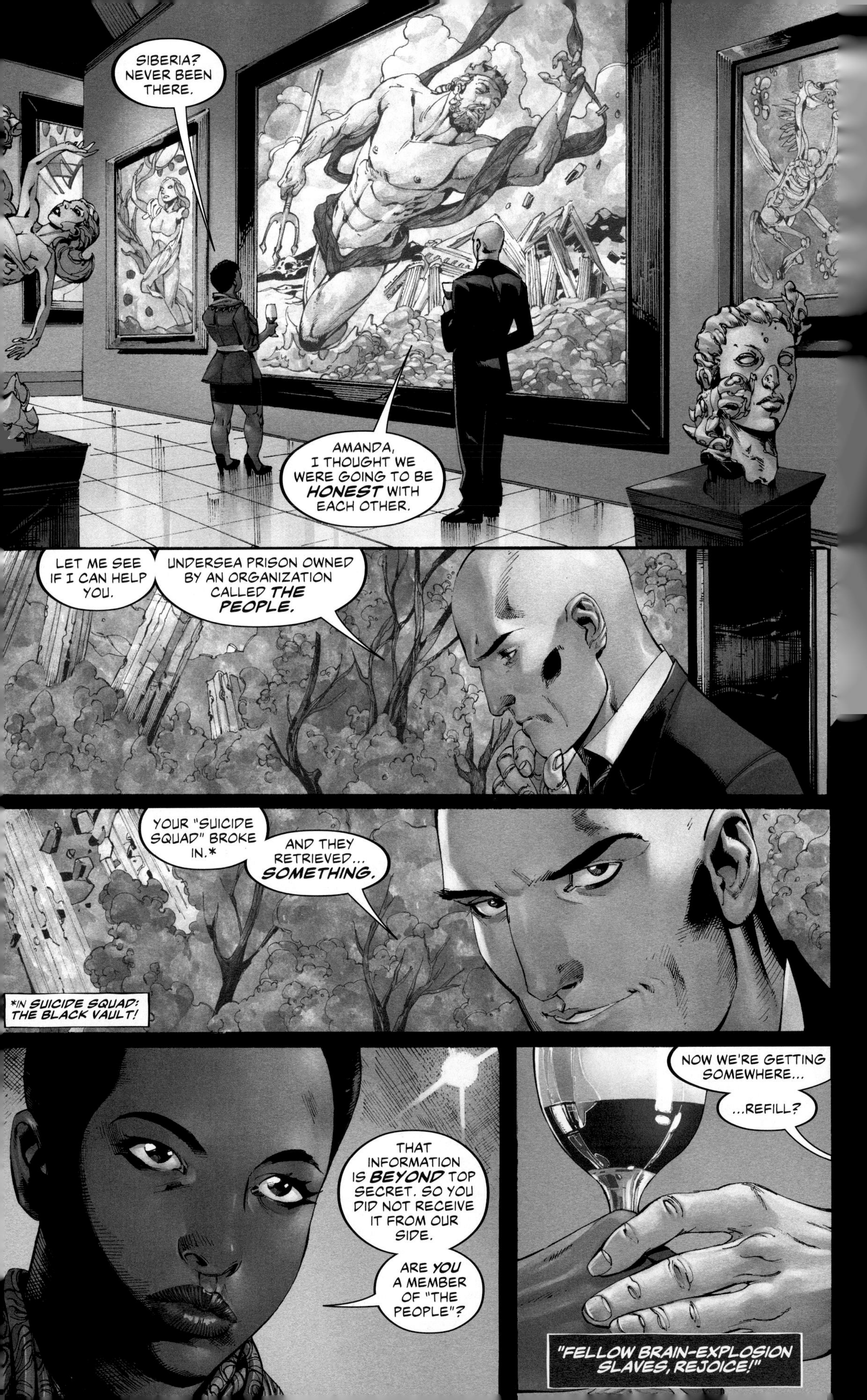
SIBERIA? NEVER BEEN THERE.
AMANDA, I THOUGHT WE WERE GOING TO BE HONEST WITH EACH OTHER.
LET ME SEE IF I CAN HELP YOU.
UNDERSEA PRISON OWNED BY AN ORGANIZATION CALLED THE PEOPLE.
YOUR "SUICIDE SQUAD" BROKE IN.*
AND THEY RETRIEVED... SOMETHING.
*IN SUICIDE SQUAD: THE BLACK VAULT!
THAT INFORMATION IS BEYOND TOP SECRET. SO YOU DID NOT RECEIVE IT FROM OUR SIDE.
ARE YOU A MEMBER OF "THE PEOPLE"?
NOW WE'RE GETTING SOMEWHERE...
...REFILL?
"FELLOW BRAIN-EXPLOSION SLAVES, REJOICE!"

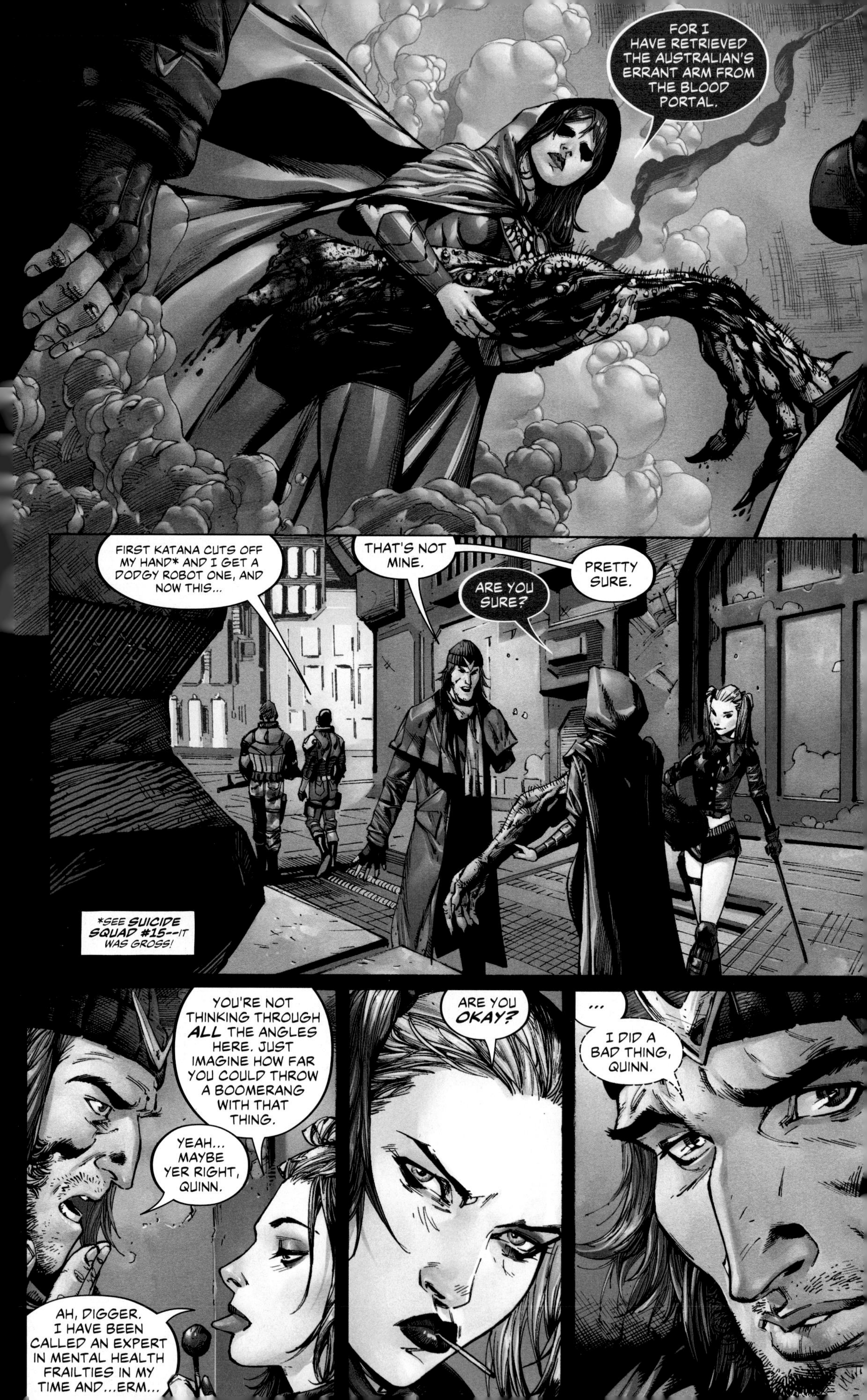
FOR I HAVE RETRIEVED THE AUSTRALIAN'S ERRANT ARM FROM THE BLOOD PORTAL.
FIRST KATANA CUTS OFF MY HAND* AND I GET A DODGY ROBOT ONE, AND NOW THIS...
THAT'S NOT MINE.
ARE YOU SURE?
PRETTY SURE.
*SEE SUICIDE SQUAD #15--IT WAS GROSS!
YOU'RE NOT THINKING THROUGH ALL THE ANGLES HERE. JUST IMAGINE HOW FAR YOU COULD THROW A BOOMERANG WITH THAT THING.
YEAH... MAYBE YER RIGHT, QUINN.
AH, DIGGER. I HAVE BEEN CALLED AN EXPERT IN MENTAL HEALTH FRAILTIES IN MY TIME AND...ERM...
ARE YOU OKAY?
...
I DID A BAD THING, QUINN.

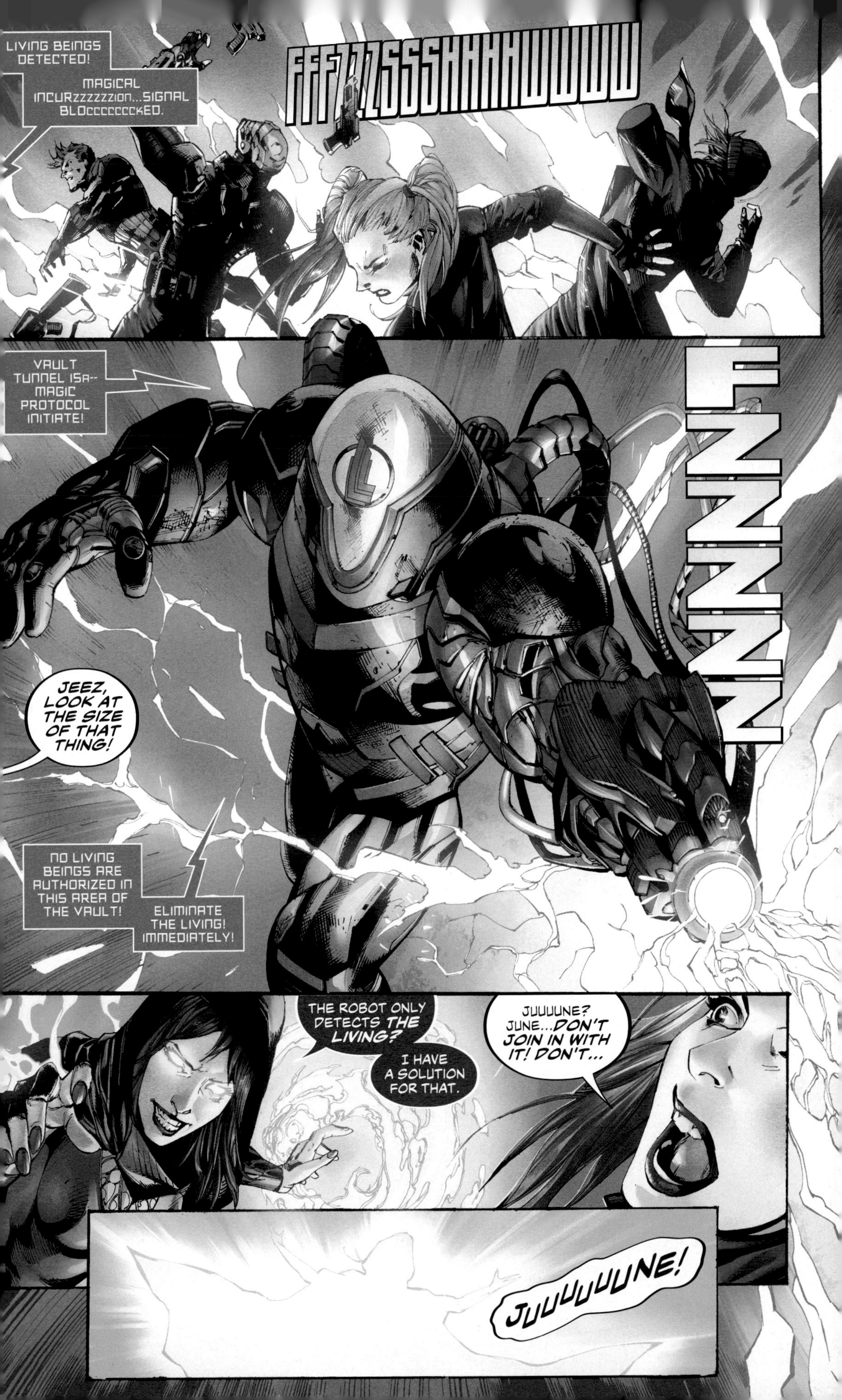
LIVING BEINGS DETECTED!
MAGICAL INCURzzzzzzion...SIGNAL BLOcccccccKED.
FFFZZZSSSHHHWWWW
VAULT TUNNEL ISa-- MAGIC PROTOCOL INITIATE!
FNNN
JEEZ, LOOK AT THE SIZE OF THAT THING!
NO LIVING BEINGS ARE AUTHORIZED IN THIS AREA OF THE VAULT!
ELIMINATE THE LIVING! IMMEDIATELY!
THE ROBOT ONLY DETECTS THE LIVING?
I HAVE A SOLUTION FOR THAT.
JUUUUNE? JUNE...DON'T JOIN IN WITH IT! DON'T...
JUUUUUUNE!

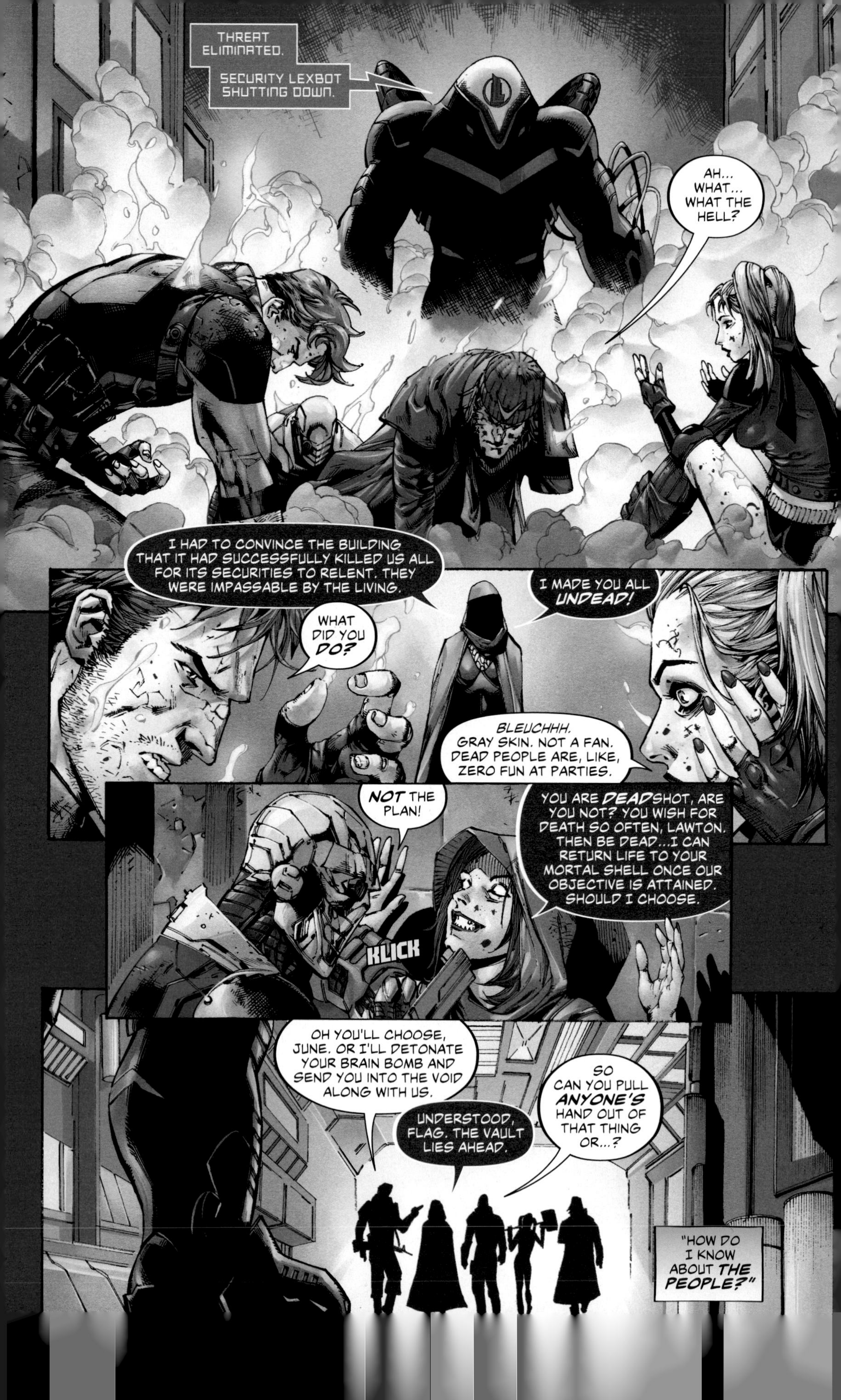
THREAT ELIMINATED.
SECURITY LEXBOT SHUTTING DOWN.
AH... WHAT... WHAT THE HELL?
I HAD TO CONVINCE THE BUILDING THAT IT HAD SUCCESSFULLY KILLED US ALL FOR ITS SECURITIES TO RELENT. THEY WERE IMPASSABLE BY THE LIVING.
WHAT DID YOU DO?
I MADE YOU ALL UNDEAD!
BLEUCHHH. GRAY SKIN. NOT A FAN. DEAD PEOPLE ARE, LIKE, ZERO FUN AT PARTIES.
NOT THE PLAN!
YOU ARE DEADSHOT, ARE YOU NOT? YOU WISH FOR DEATH SO OFTEN, LAWTON. THEN BE DEAD...I CAN RETURN LIFE TO YOUR MORTAL SHELL ONCE OUR OBJECTIVE IS ATTAINED. SHOULD I CHOOSE.
KLICK
OH YOU'LL CHOOSE, JUNE. OR I'LL DETONATE YOUR BRAIN BOMB AND SEND YOU INTO THE VOID ALONG WITH US.
UNDERSTOOD, FLAG. THE VAULT LIES AHEAD.
SO CAN YOU PULL ANYONE'S HAND OUT OF THAT THING OR...?
"HOW DO I KNOW ABOUT THE PEOPLE?"

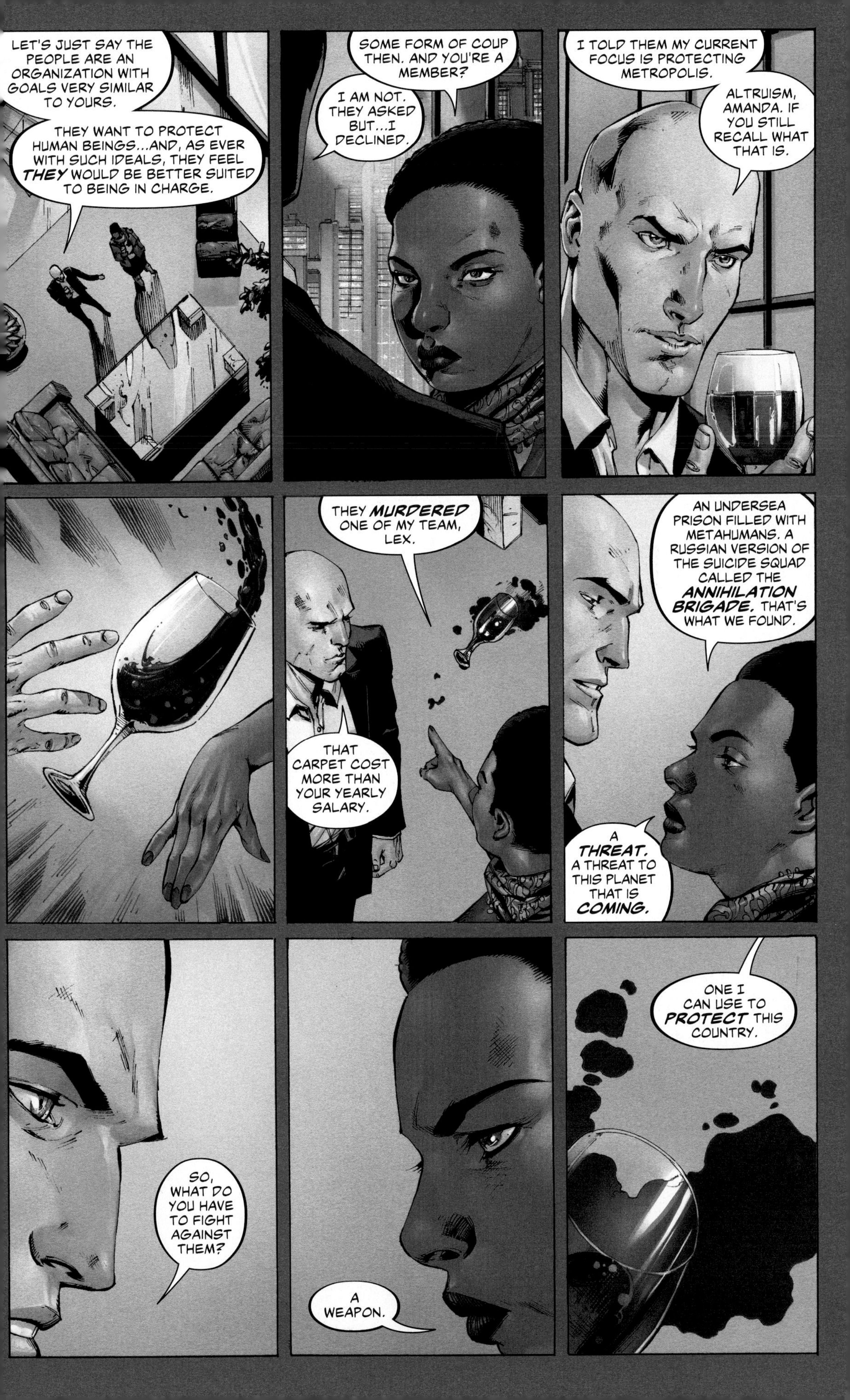
LET'S JUST SAY THE PEOPLE ARE AN ORGANIZATION WITH GOALS VERY SIMILAR TO YOURS.
THEY WANT TO PROTECT HUMAN BEINGS...AND, AS EVER WITH SUCH IDEALS, THEY FEEL *THEY* WOULD BE BETTER SUITED TO BEING IN CHARGE.
SOME FORM OF COUP THEN. AND YOU'RE A MEMBER?
I AM NOT. THEY ASKED BUT...I DECLINED.
I TOLD THEM MY CURRENT FOCUS IS PROTECTING METROPOLIS.
ALTRUISM, AMANDA. IF YOU STILL RECALL WHAT THAT IS.
THEY *MURDERED* ONE OF MY TEAM, LEX.
THAT CARPET COST MORE THAN YOUR YEARLY SALARY.
AN UNDERSEA PRISON FILLED WITH METAHUMANS. A RUSSIAN VERSION OF THE SUICIDE SQUAD CALLED THE *ANNIHILATION BRIGADE.* THAT'S WHAT WE FOUND.
A *THREAT.* A THREAT TO THIS PLANET THAT IS *COMING.*
SO, WHAT DO YOU HAVE TO FIGHT AGAINST THEM?
A WEAPON.
ONE I CAN USE TO *PROTECT* THIS COUNTRY.

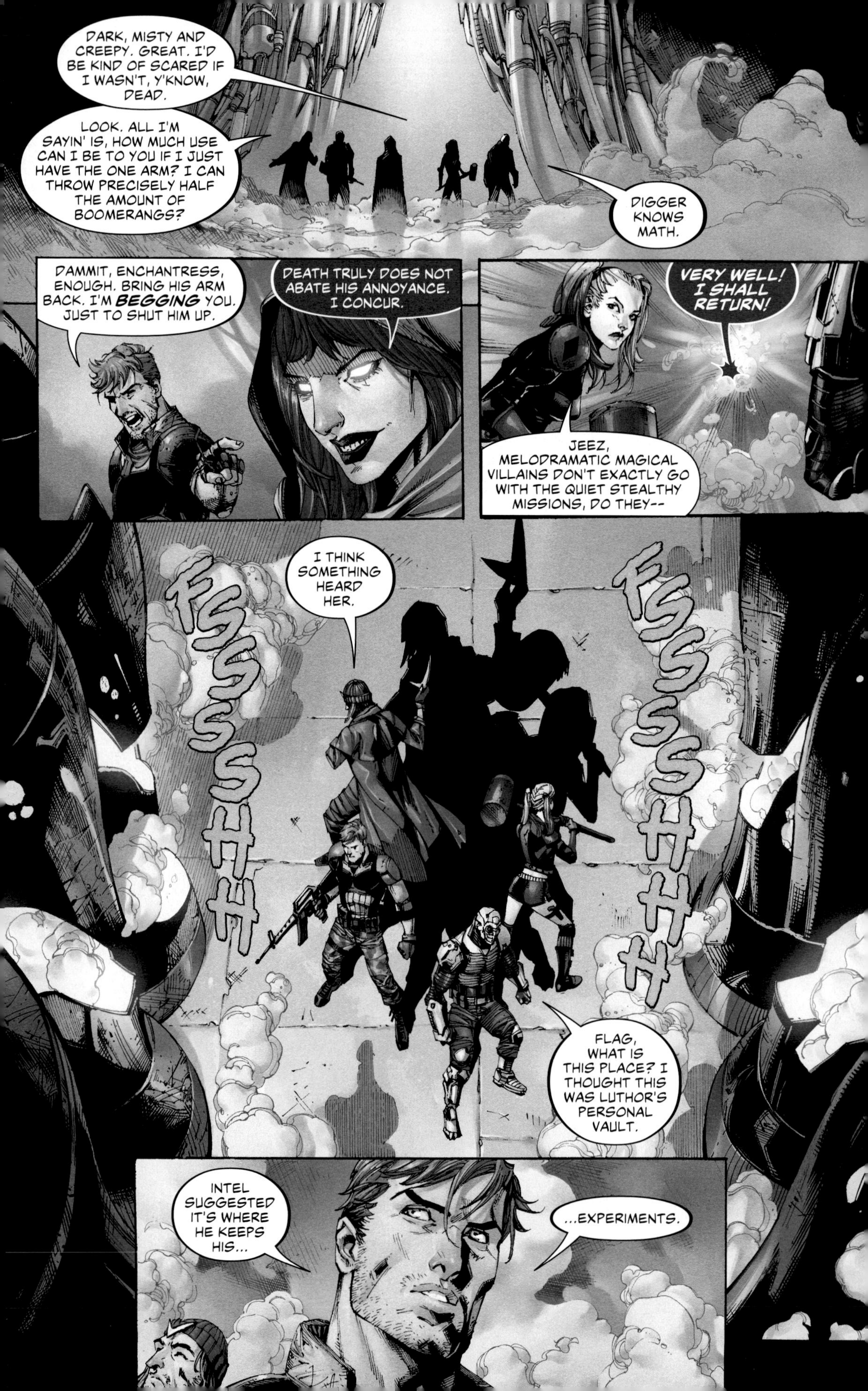
DARK, MISTY AND CREEPY. GREAT. I'D BE KIND OF SCARED IF I WASN'T, Y'KNOW, DEAD.
LOOK. ALL I'M SAYIN' IS, HOW MUCH USE CAN I BE TO YOU IF I JUST HAVE THE ONE ARM? I CAN THROW PRECISELY HALF THE AMOUNT OF BOOMERANGS?
DIGGER KNOWS MATH.
DAMMIT, ENCHANTRESS, ENOUGH. BRING HIS ARM BACK. I'M BEGGING YOU. JUST TO SHUT HIM UP.
DEATH TRULY DOES NOT ABATE HIS ANNOYANCE. I CONCUR.
VERY WELL! I SHALL RETURN!
JEEZ, MELODRAMATIC MAGICAL VILLAINS DON'T EXACTLY GO WITH THE QUIET STEALTHY MISSIONS, DO THEY--
FSSSHH
I THINK SOMETHING HEARD HER.
FSSSHHH
FLAG, WHAT IS THIS PLACE? I THOUGHT THIS WAS LUTHOR'S PERSONAL VAULT.
INTEL SUGGESTED IT'S WHERE HE KEEPS HIS...
...EXPERIMENTS.

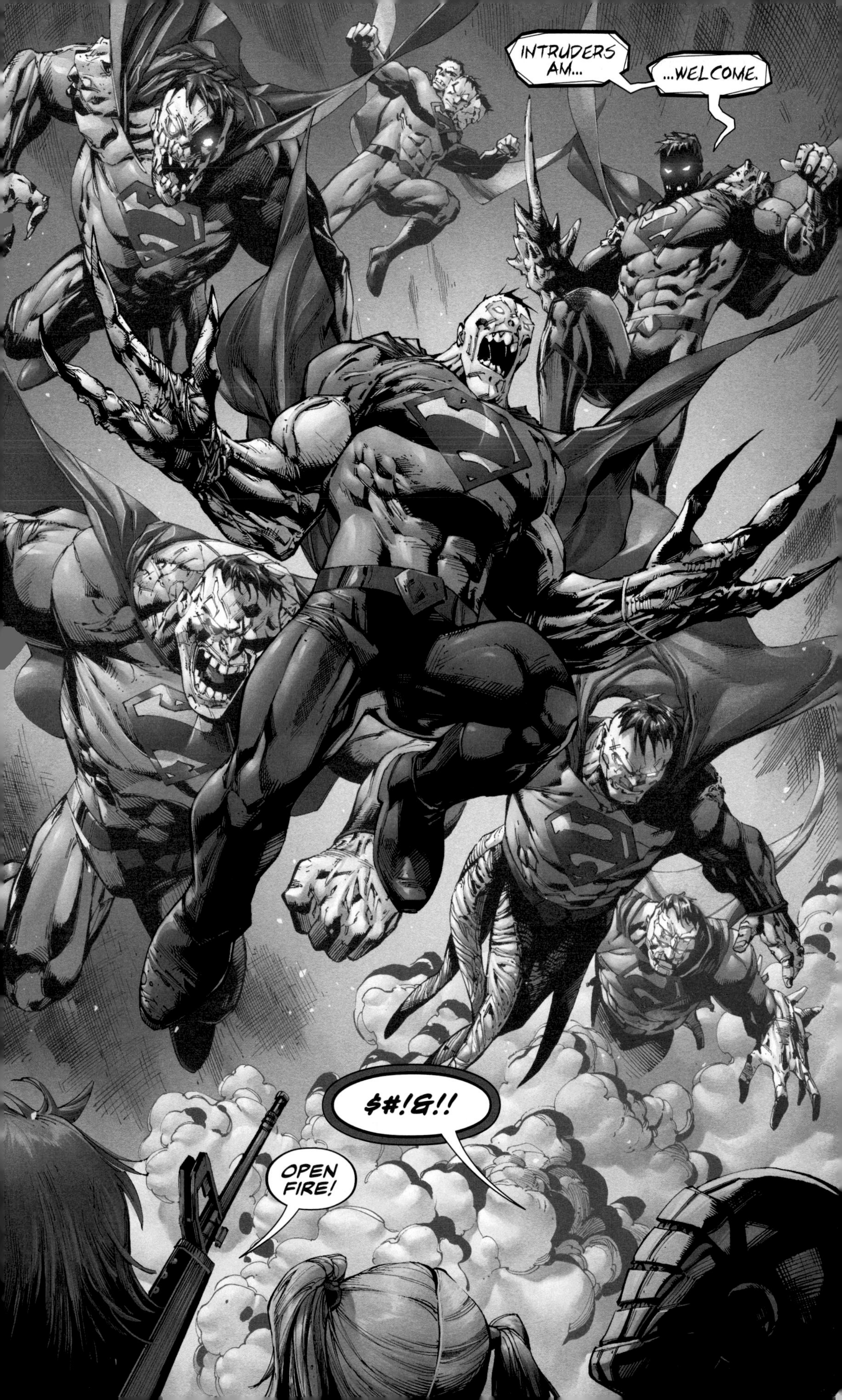

INTRUDERS AM...
...WELCOME.
OPEN FIRE!
$#!&!!

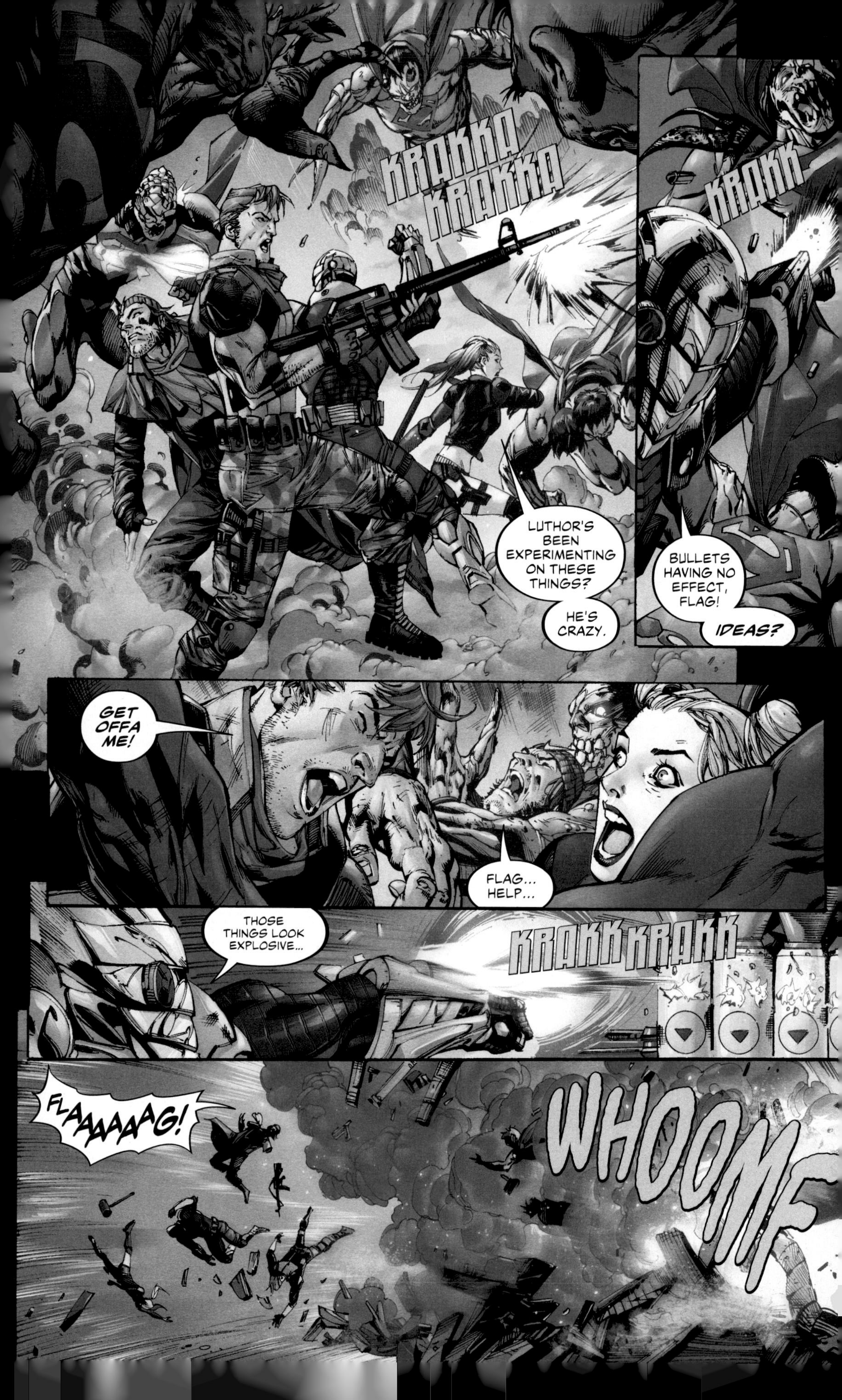
KRAKKA KRAKKA
LUTHOR'S BEEN EXPERIMENTING ON THESE THINGS?
HE'S CRAZY.
KRAKK
BULLETS HAVING NO EFFECT, FLAG!
IDEAS?
GET OFFA ME!
FLAG... HELP...
THOSE THINGS LOOK EXPLOSIVE...
KRAKK KRAKK
FLAAAAAAG!
WHOOMF

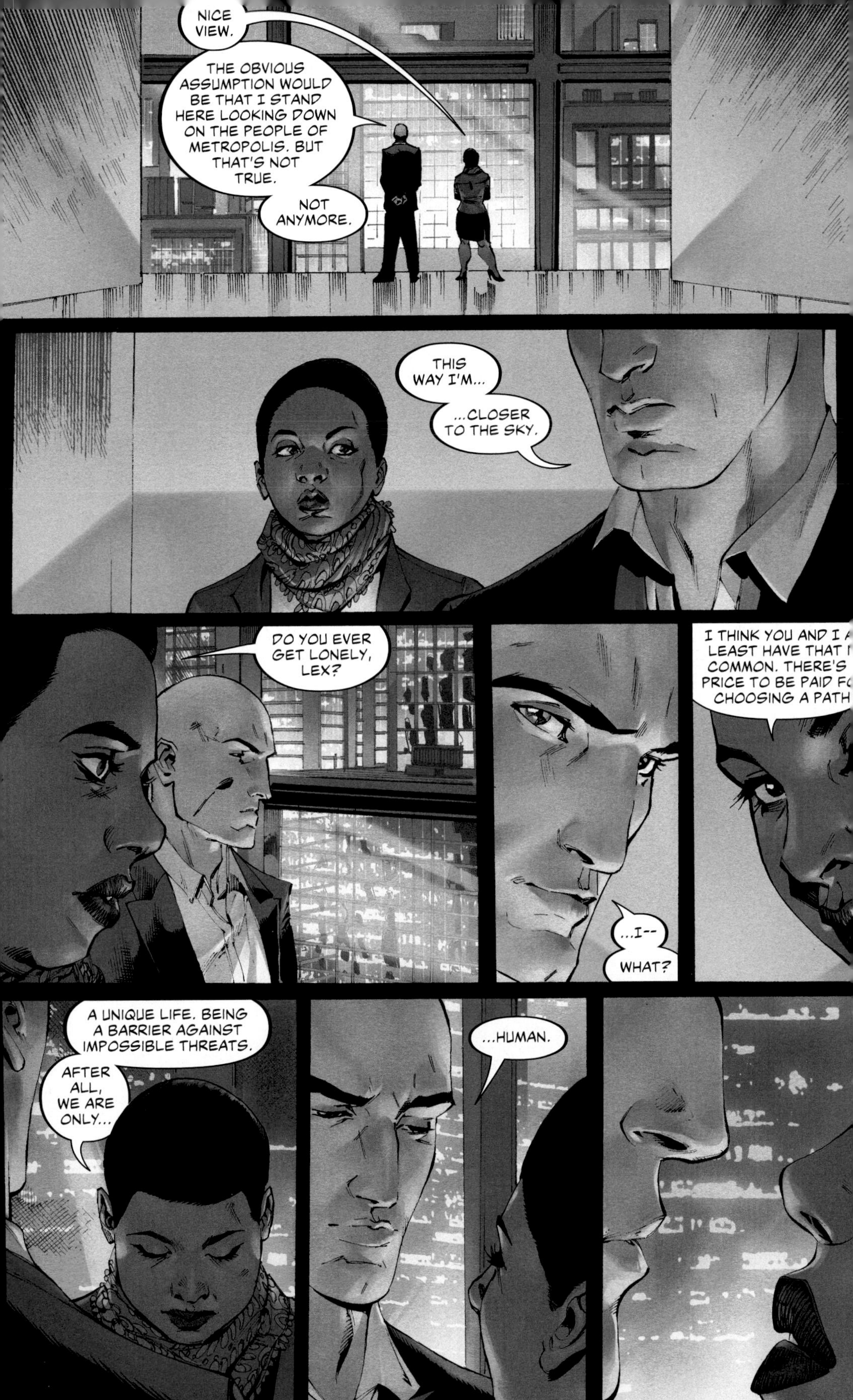
NICE VIEW.
THE OBVIOUS ASSUMPTION WOULD BE THAT I STAND HERE LOOKING DOWN ON THE PEOPLE OF METROPOLIS. BUT THAT'S NOT TRUE.
NOT ANYMORE.
THIS WAY I'M...
...CLOSER TO THE SKY.
DO YOU EVER GET LONELY, LEX?
I THINK YOU AND I AT LEAST HAVE THAT IN COMMON. THERE'S A PRICE TO BE PAID FOR CHOOSING A PATH
...I--
WHAT?
A UNIQUE LIFE. BEING A BARRIER AGAINST IMPOSSIBLE THREATS.
AFTER ALL, WE ARE ONLY...
...HUMAN.

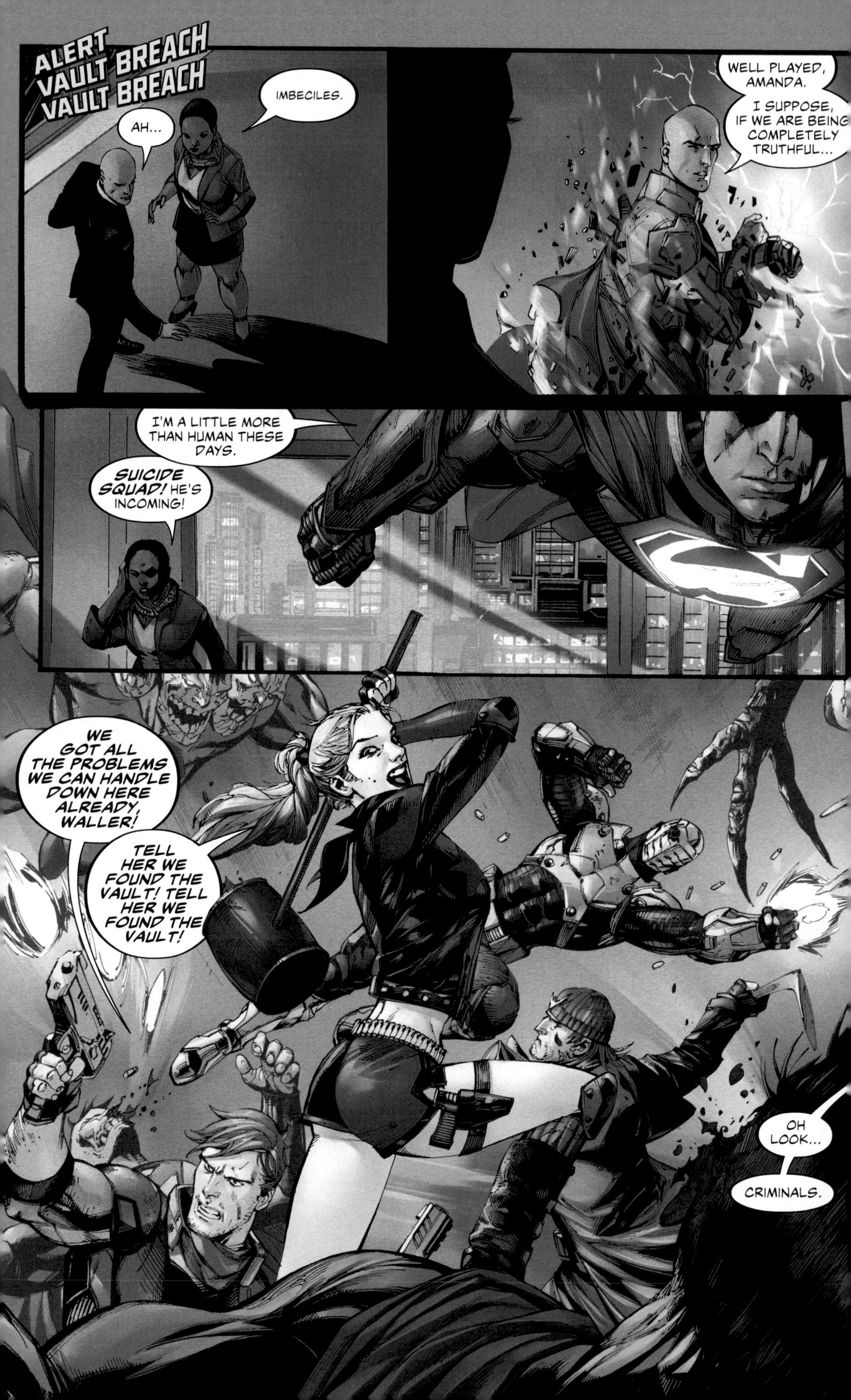
ALERT
VAULT BREACH
VAULT BREACH
AH...
IMBECILES.
WELL PLAYED, AMANDA.
I SUPPOSE, IF WE ARE BEING COMPLETELY TRUTHFUL...
I'M A LITTLE MORE THAN HUMAN THESE DAYS.
SUICIDE SQUAD! HE'S INCOMING!
WE GOT ALL THE PROBLEMS WE CAN HANDLE DOWN HERE ALREADY, WALLER!
TELL HER WE FOUND THE VAULT! TELL HER WE FOUND THE VAULT!
OH LOOK...
CRIMINALS.

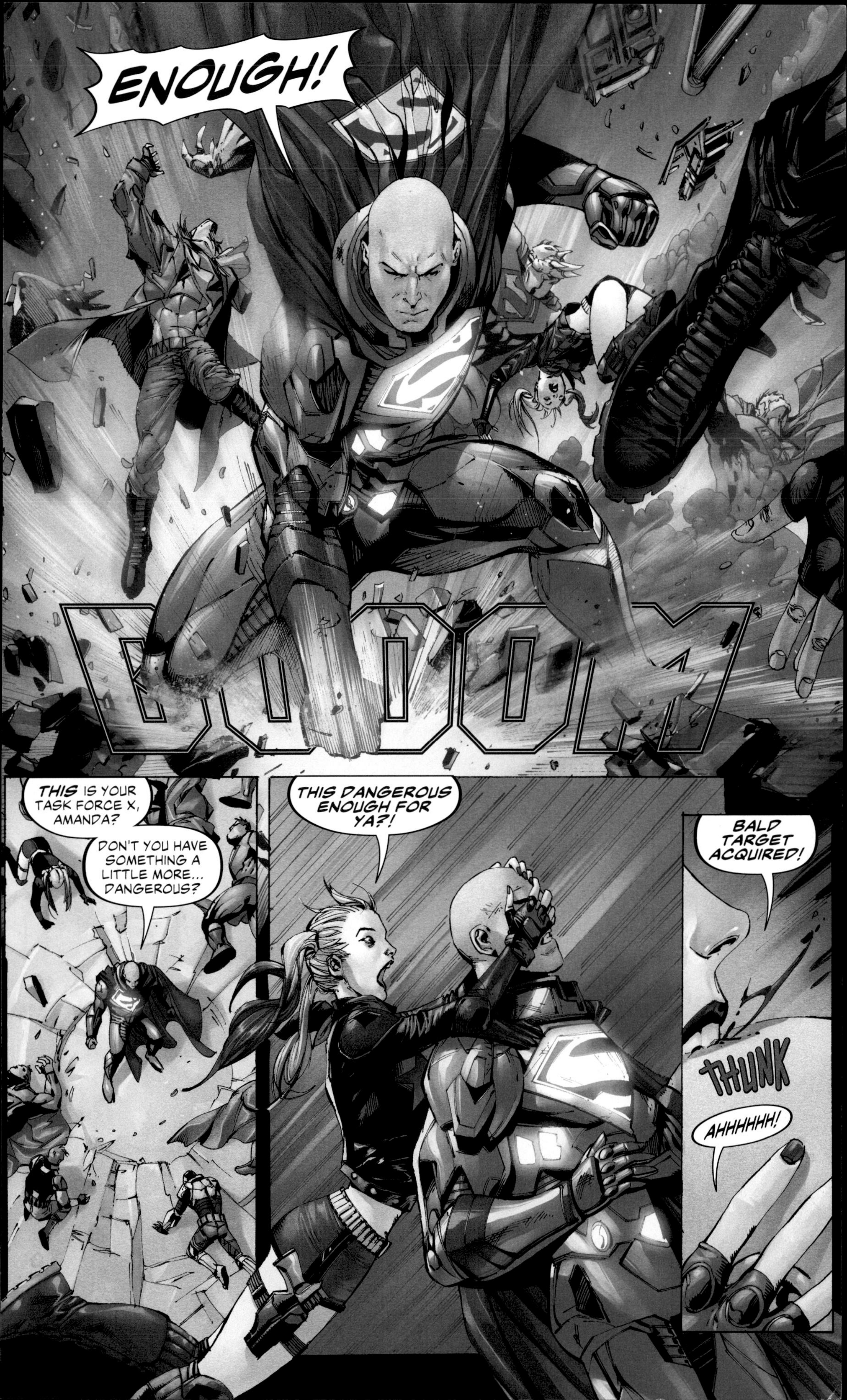
ENOUGH!
BOOOM
THIS IS YOUR TASK FORCE X, AMANDA?
DON'T YOU HAVE SOMETHING A LITTLE MORE... DANGEROUS?
THIS DANGEROUS ENOUGH FOR YA?!
BALD TARGET ACQUIRED!
THUNK
AHHHHHH!

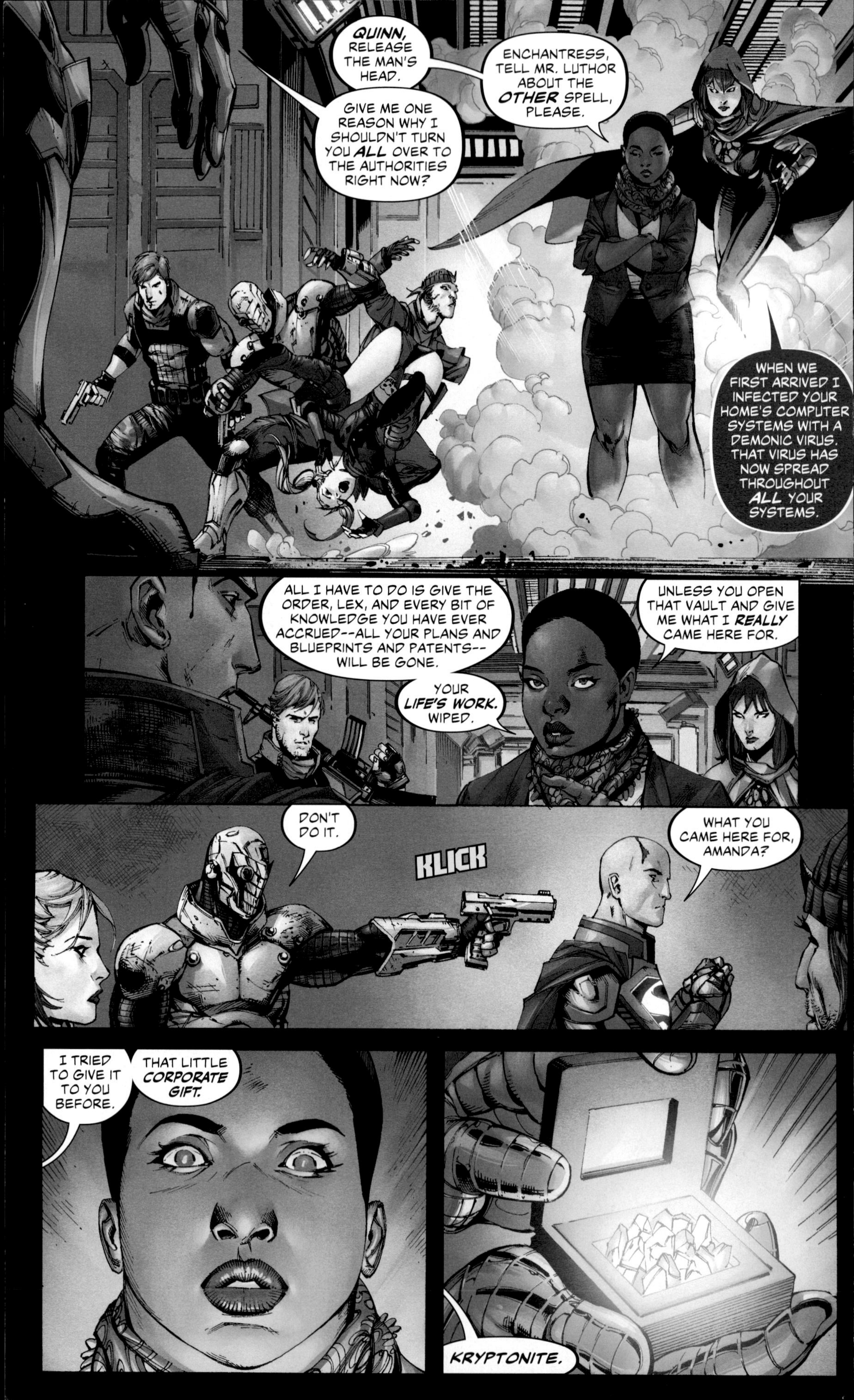

QUINN, RELEASE THE MAN'S HEAD.
ENCHANTRESS, TELL MR. LUTHOR ABOUT THE OTHER SPELL, PLEASE.
GIVE ME ONE REASON WHY I SHOULDN'T TURN YOU ALL OVER TO THE AUTHORITIES RIGHT NOW?
WHEN WE FIRST ARRIVED I INFECTED YOUR HOME'S COMPUTER SYSTEMS WITH A DEMONIC VIRUS. THAT VIRUS HAS NOW SPREAD THROUGHOUT ALL YOUR SYSTEMS.
ALL I HAVE TO DO IS GIVE THE ORDER, LEX, AND EVERY BIT OF KNOWLEDGE YOU HAVE EVER ACCRUED--ALL YOUR PLANS AND BLUEPRINTS AND PATENTS--WILL BE GONE.
YOUR LIFE'S WORK. WIPED.
UNLESS YOU OPEN THAT VAULT AND GIVE ME WHAT I REALLY CAME HERE FOR.
DON'T DO IT.
KLICK
WHAT YOU CAME HERE FOR, AMANDA?
I TRIED TO GIVE IT TO YOU BEFORE.
THAT LITTLE CORPORATE GIFT.
KRYPTONITE.

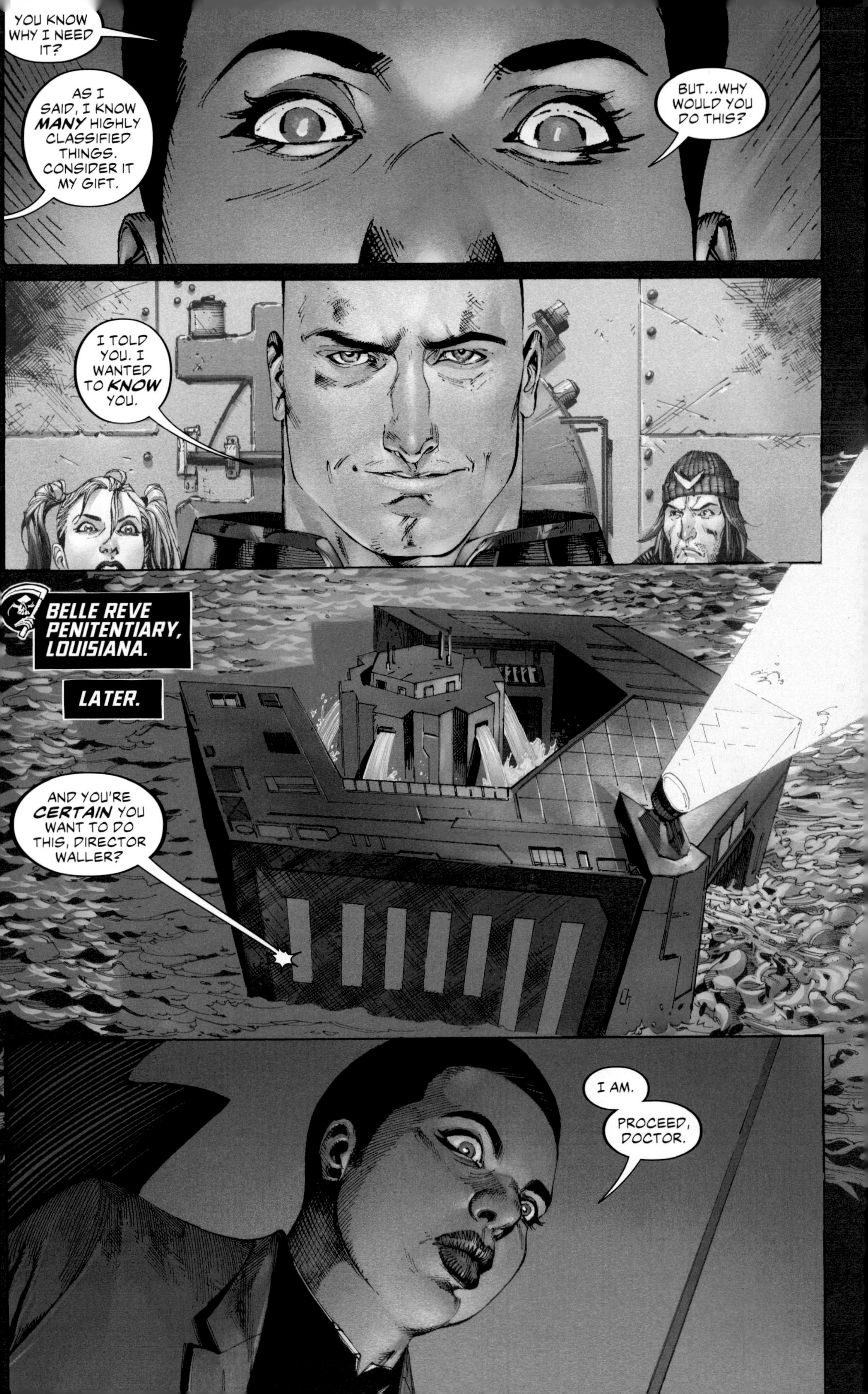
YOU KNOW WHY I NEED IT?
AS I SAID, I KNOW MANY HIGHLY CLASSIFIED THINGS. CONSIDER IT MY GIFT.
BUT...WHY WOULD YOU DO THIS?
I TOLD YOU. I WANTED TO KNOW YOU.
BELLE REVE PENITENTIARY, LOUISIANA.
LATER.
AND YOU'RE CERTAIN YOU WANT TO DO THIS, DIRECTOR WALLER?
I AM.
PROCEED, DOCTOR.

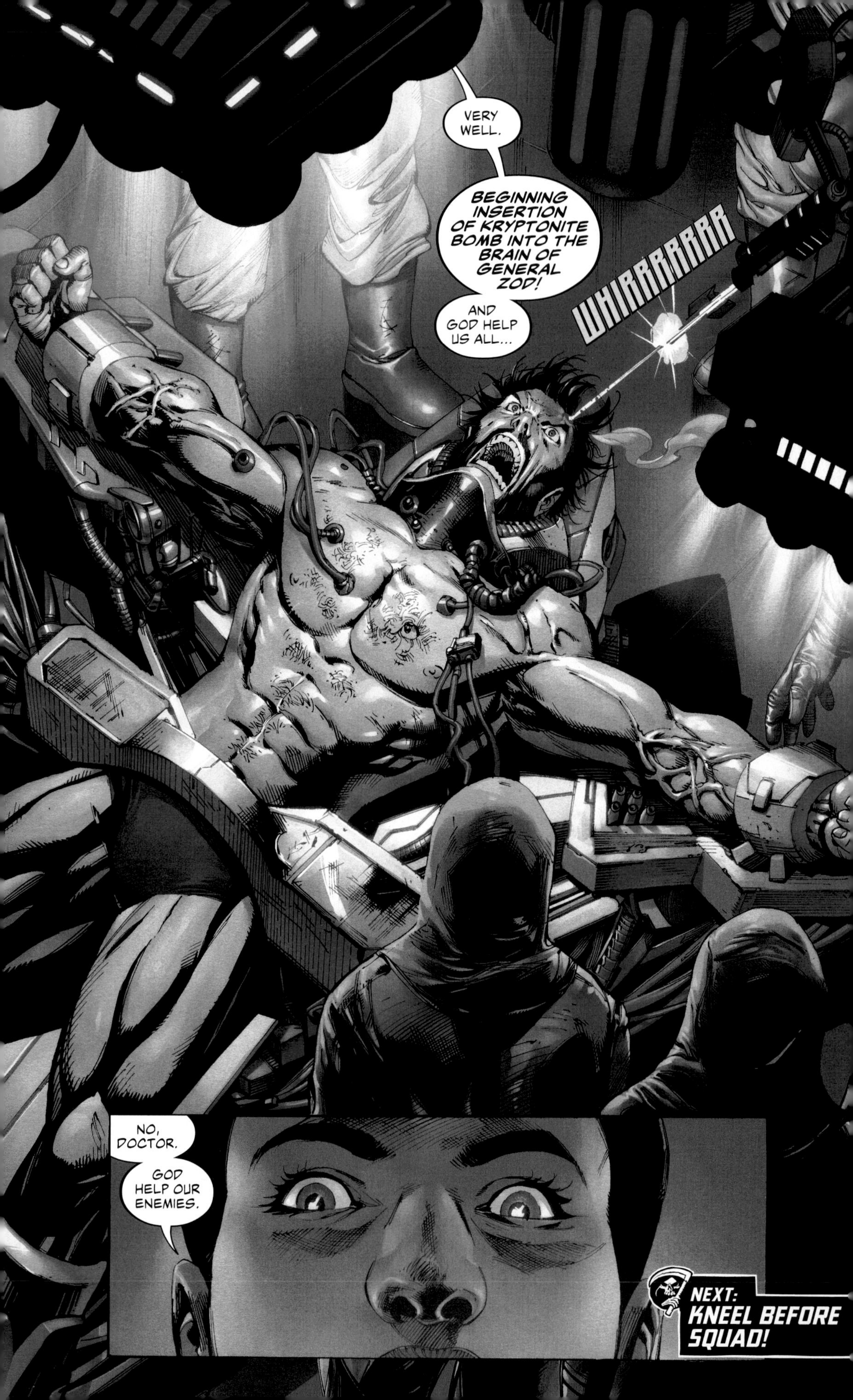
VERY WELL.
BEGINNING INSERTION OF KRYPTONITE BOMB INTO THE BRAIN OF GENERAL ZOD!
AND GOD HELP US ALL...
WHIRRRRRRRR
NO, DOCTOR.
GOD HELP OUR ENEMIES.
NEXT: KNEEL BEFORE SQUAD!

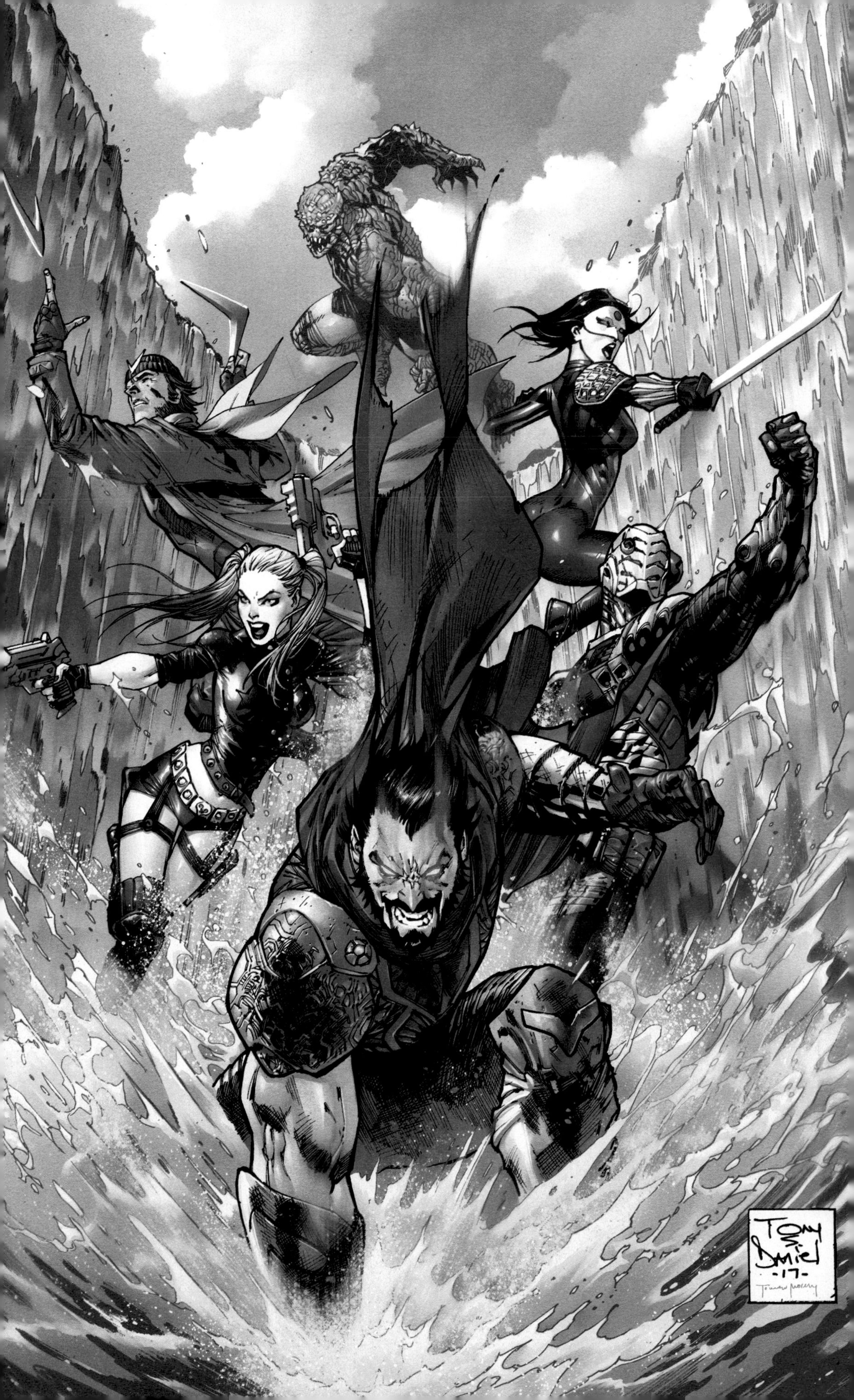
TONY S. DANIEL -17-

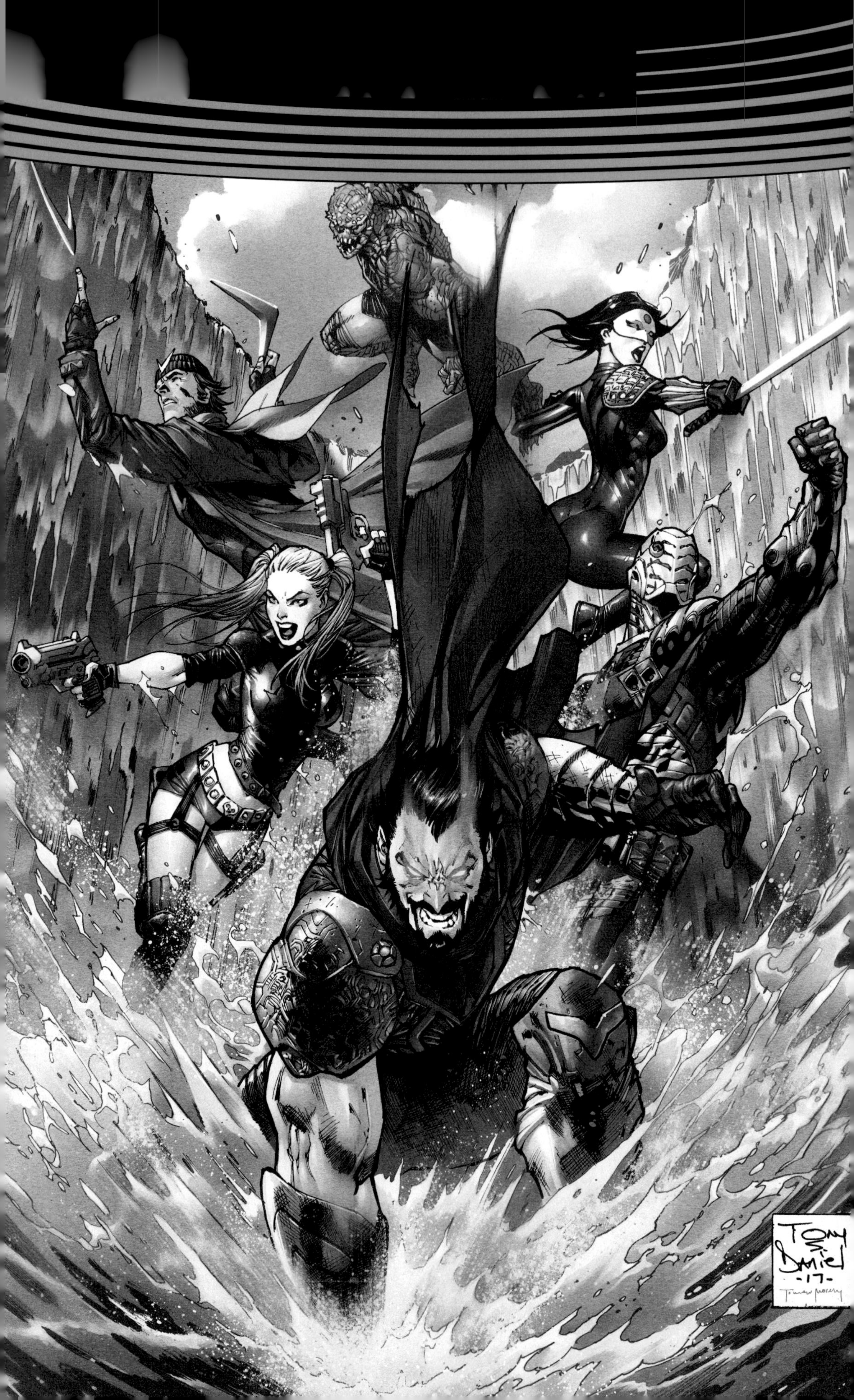
TONY S. DANIEL
-17-

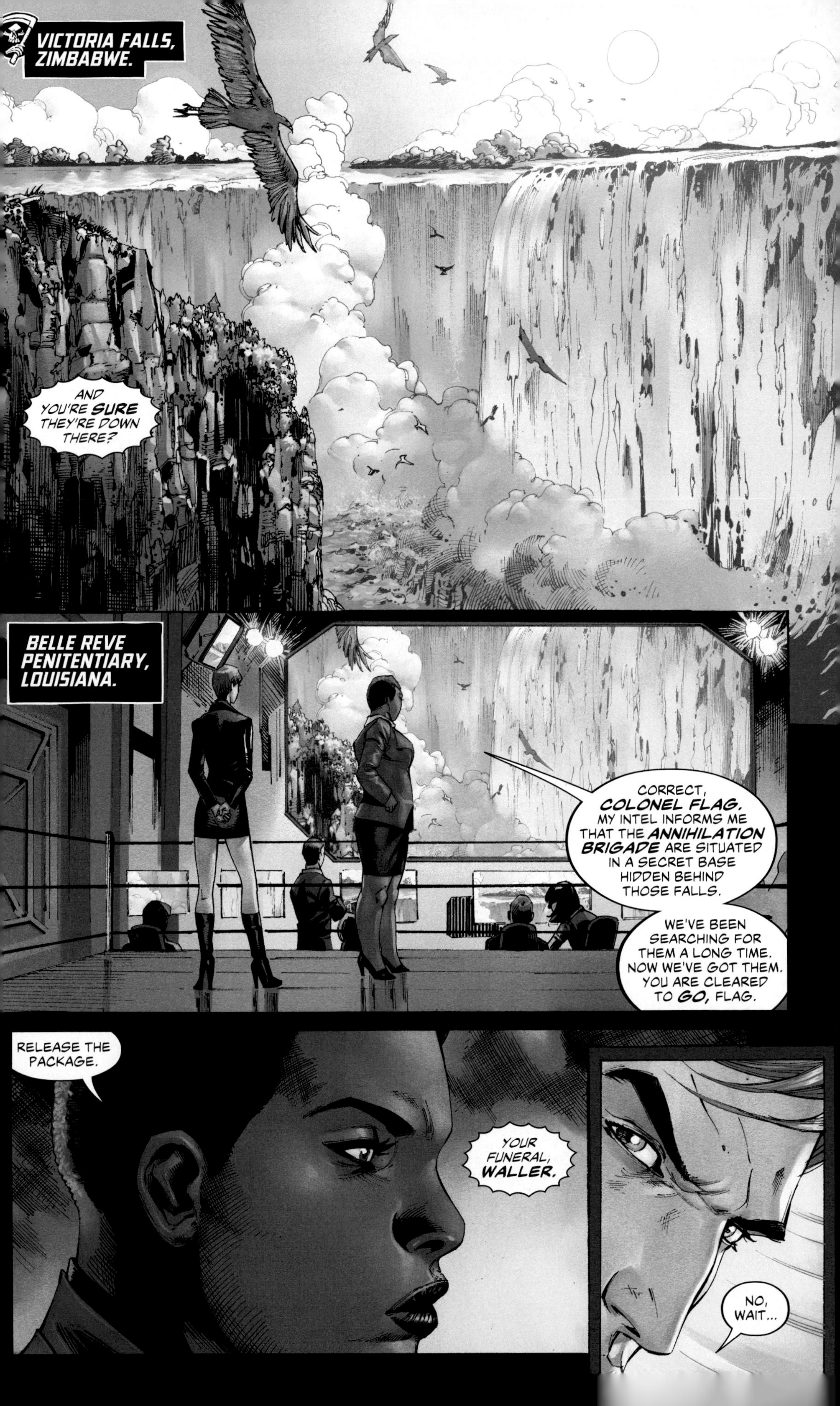
VICTORIA FALLS, ZIMBABWE.
AND YOU'RE SURE THEY'RE DOWN THERE?
BELLE REVE PENITENTIARY, LOUISIANA.
CORRECT, COLONEL FLAG. MY INTEL INFORMS ME THAT THE ANNIHILATION BRIGADE ARE SITUATED IN A SECRET BASE HIDDEN BEHIND THOSE FALLS.
WE'VE BEEN SEARCHING FOR THEM A LONG TIME. NOW WE'VE GOT THEM. YOU ARE CLEARED TO GO, FLAG.
RELEASE THE PACKAGE.
YOUR FUNERAL, WALLER.
NO, WAIT...

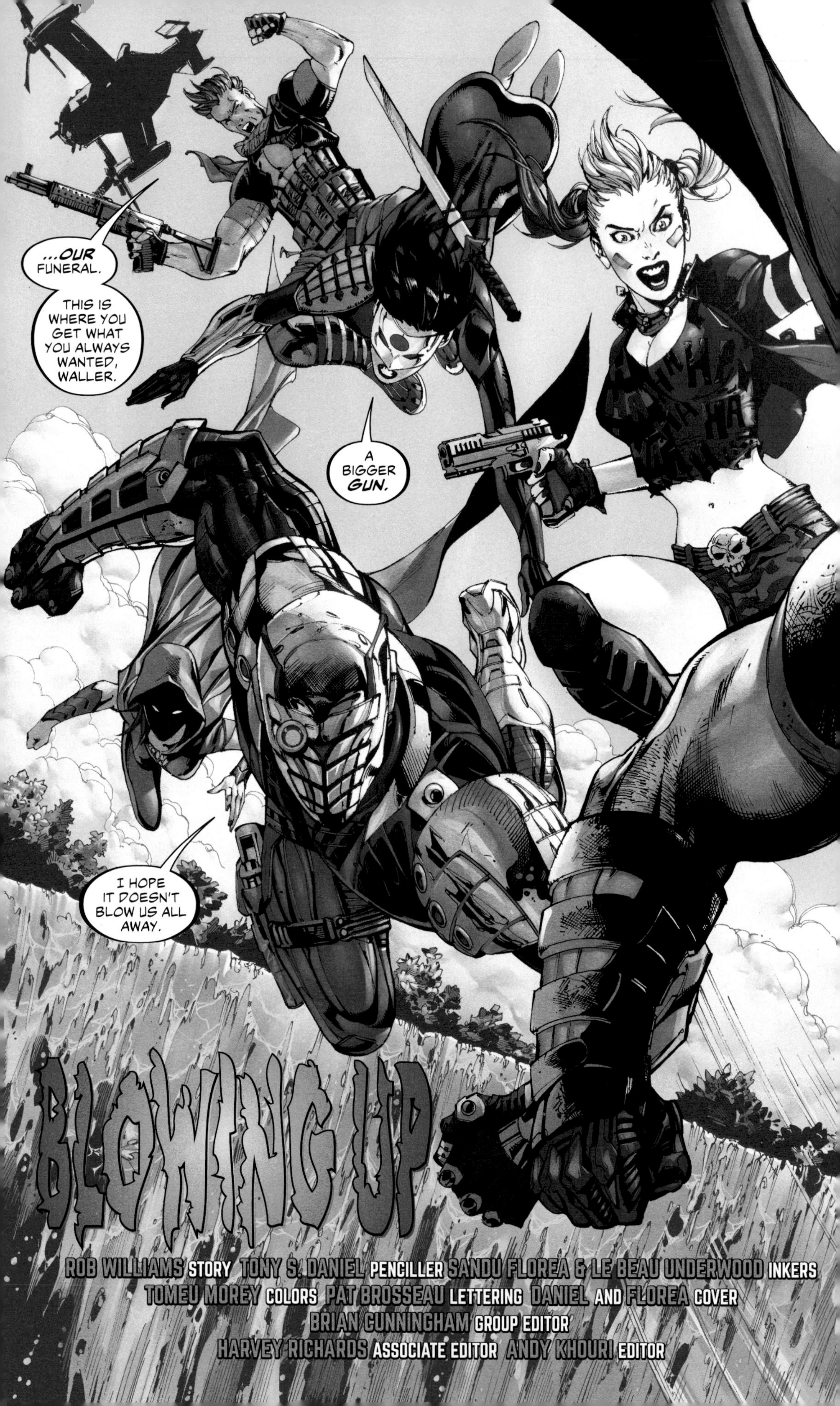

...OUR FUNERAL.
THIS IS WHERE YOU GET WHAT YOU ALWAYS WANTED, WALLER.
A BIGGER GUN.
I HOPE IT DOESN'T BLOW US ALL AWAY.
BLOWING UP
ROB WILLIAMS STORY TONY S. DANIEL PENCILLER SANDU FLOREA & LE BEAU UNDERWOOD INKERS
TOMEU MOREY COLORS PAT BROSSEAU LETTERING DANIEL AND FLOREA COVER
BRIAN CUNNINGHAM GROUP EDITOR
HARVEY RICHARDS ASSOCIATE EDITOR ANDY KHOURI EDITOR

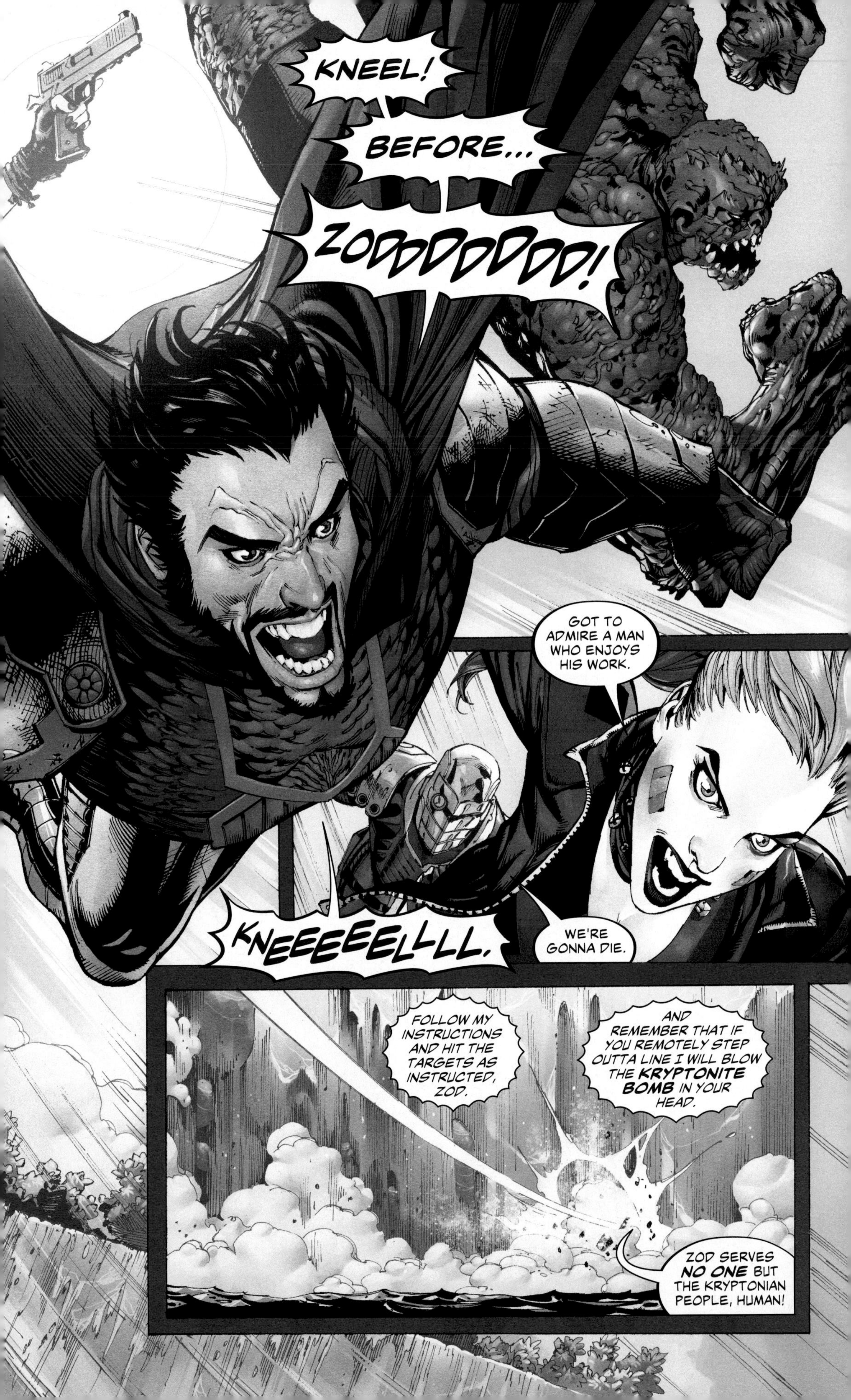
KNEEL!
BEFORE...
ZODDDDDDDD!
GOT TO ADMIRE A MAN WHO ENJOYS HIS WORK.
KNEEEEEELLLL.
WE'RE GONNA DIE.
FOLLOW MY INSTRUCTIONS AND HIT THE TARGETS AS INSTRUCTED, ZOD.
AND REMEMBER THAT IF YOU REMOTELY STEP OUTTA LINE I WILL BLOW THE KRYPTONITE BOMB IN YOUR HEAD.
ZOD SERVES NO ONE BUT THE KRYPTONIAN PEOPLE, HUMAN!

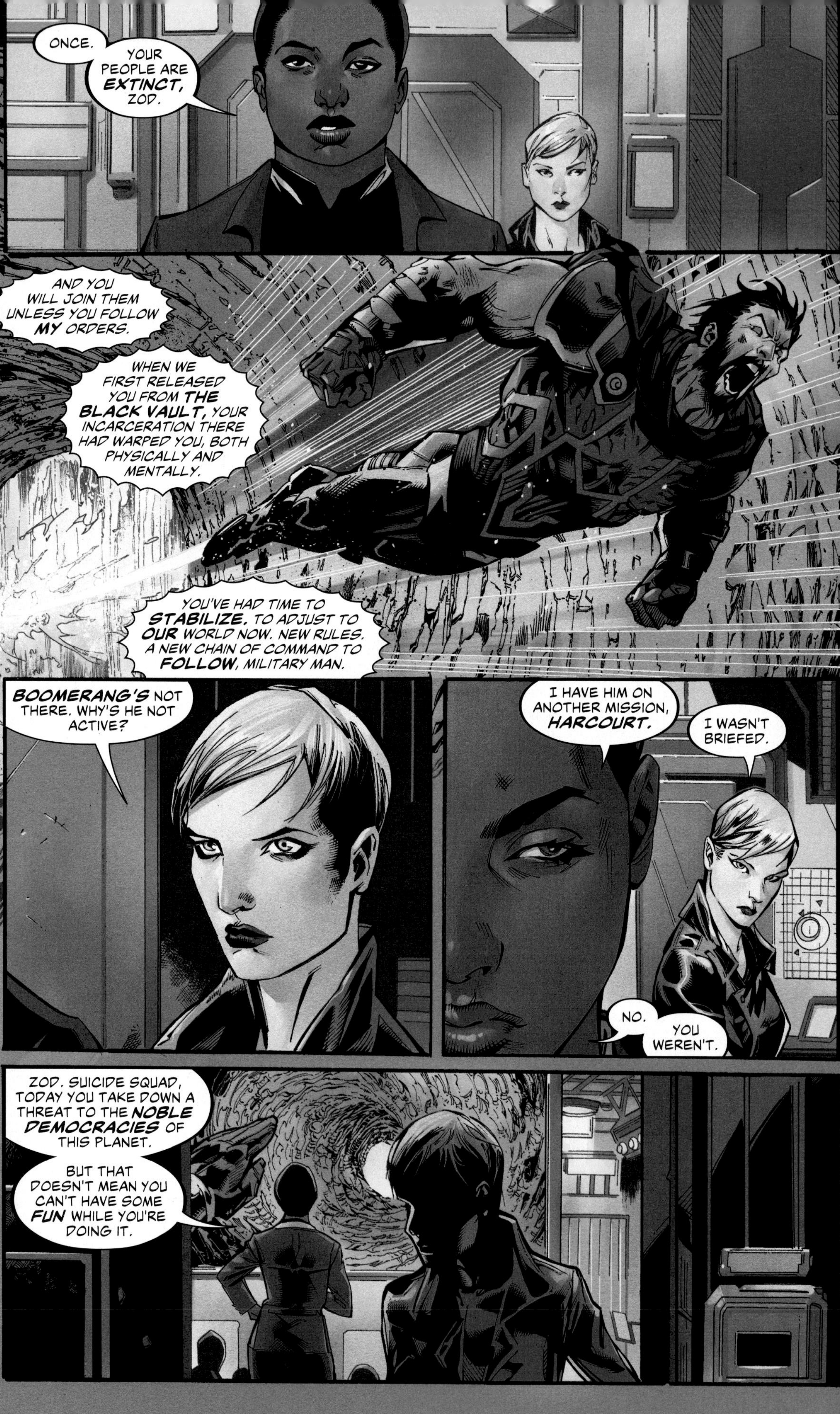
ONCE.
YOUR PEOPLE ARE EXTINCT, ZOD.
AND YOU WILL JOIN THEM UNLESS YOU FOLLOW MY ORDERS.
WHEN WE FIRST RELEASED YOU FROM THE BLACK VAULT, YOUR INCARCERATION THERE HAD WARPED YOU, BOTH PHYSICALLY AND MENTALLY.
YOU'VE HAD TIME TO STABILIZE. TO ADJUST TO OUR WORLD NOW. NEW RULES. A NEW CHAIN OF COMMAND TO FOLLOW, MILITARY MAN.
BOOMERANG'S NOT THERE. WHY'S HE NOT ACTIVE?
I HAVE HIM ON ANOTHER MISSION, HARCOURT.
I WASN'T BRIEFED.
NO.
YOU WEREN'T.
ZOD. SUICIDE SQUAD, TODAY YOU TAKE DOWN A THREAT TO THE NOBLE DEMOCRACIES OF THIS PLANET.
BUT THAT DOESN'T MEAN YOU CAN'T HAVE SOME FUN WHILE YOU'RE DOING IT.

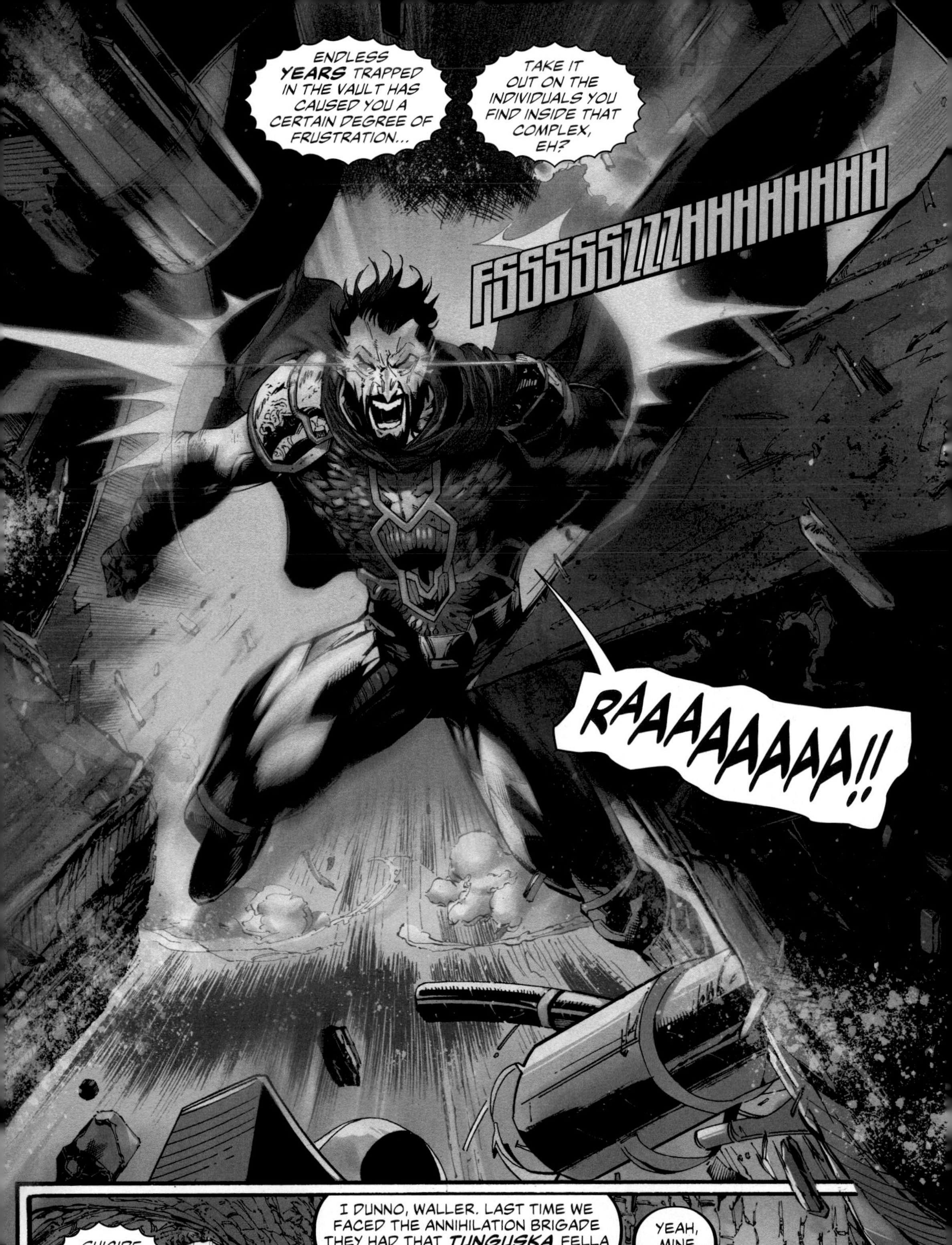
ENDLESS YEARS TRAPPED IN THE VAULT HAS CAUSED YOU A CERTAIN DEGREE OF FRUSTRATION...
TAKE IT OUT ON THE INDIVIDUALS YOU FIND INSIDE THAT COMPLEX, EH?
FSSSSSZZZHHHHHHHHH
RAAAAAAAA!!

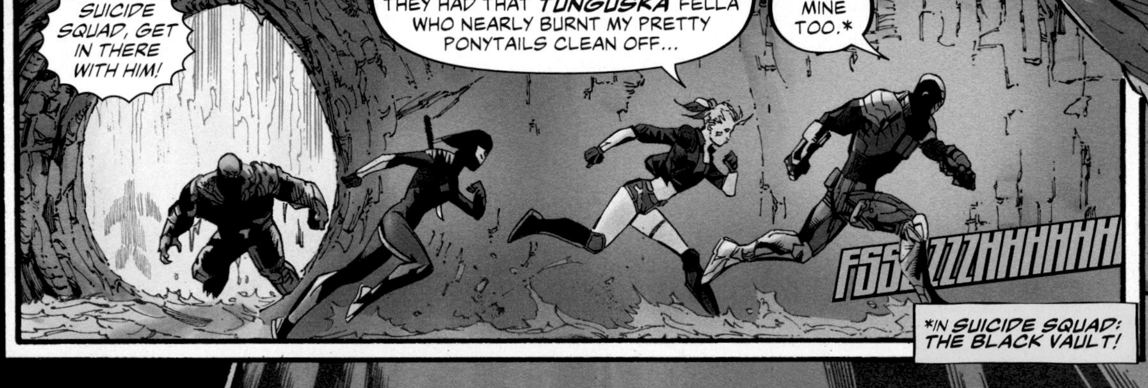
SUICIDE SQUAD, GET IN THERE WITH HIM!
I DUNNO, WALLER. LAST TIME WE FACED THE ANNIHILATION BRIGADE THEY HAD THAT TUNGUSKA FELLA WHO NEARLY BURNT MY PRETTY PONYTAILS CLEAN OFF...
YEAH, MINE TOO.*
FSSZZZHHHHHH
*IN SUICIDE SQUAD: THE BLACK VAULT!

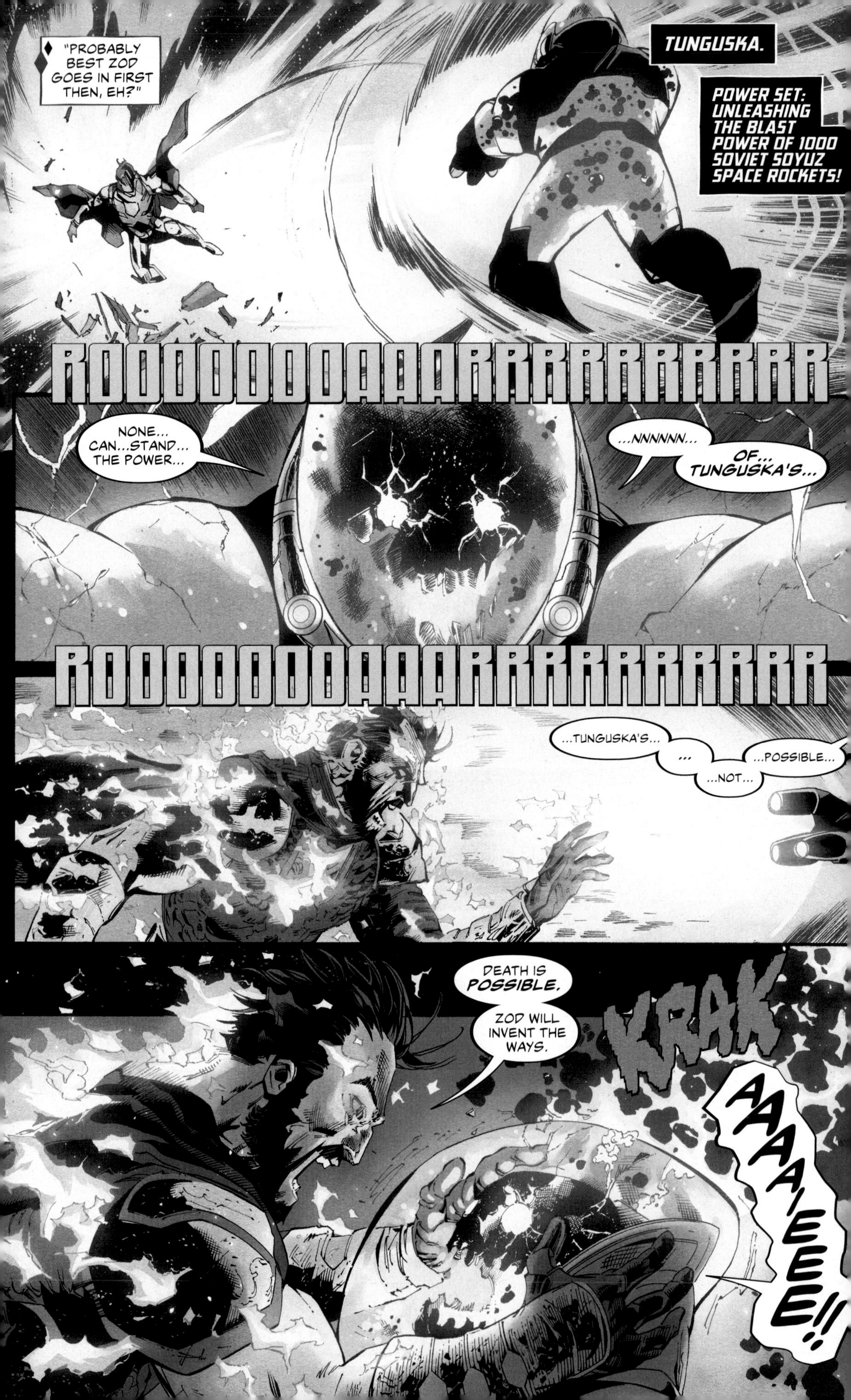

"PROBABLY BEST ZOD GOES IN FIRST THEN, EH?"
TUNGUSKA.
POWER SET: UNLEASHING THE BLAST POWER OF 1000 SOVIET SOYUZ SPACE ROCKETS!
ROOOOOOOAAARRRRRRRRRRR
NONE... CAN...STAND... THE POWER...
...NNNNNN...
OF... TUNGUSKA'S...
ROOOOOOOAAARRRRRRRRRRR
...TUNGUSKA'S...
...
...NOT...
...POSSIBLE...
DEATH IS POSSIBLE.
ZOD WILL INVENT THE WAYS.
KRAK
AAAAIEEEE!!

UNNGH!!

COSMONUT...

POWERSET: HEAD-BUTTING PEOPLE WITH HIS SOVIET HAMMERHEAD.

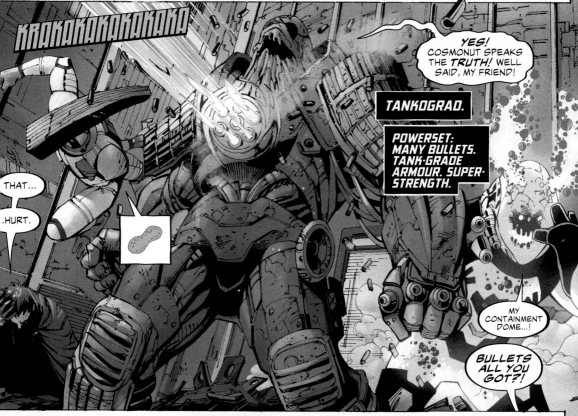

KRAKAKAKAKAKAKAKA

YES! COSMONUT SPEAKS THE *TRUTH!* WELL SAID, MY FRIEND!

TANKOGRAD.

POWERSET: MANY BULLETS. TANK-GRADE ARMOUR. SUPER-STRENGTH.

THAT......HURT.

MY CONTAINMENT DOME...!

BULLETS ALL YOU GOT?!

BULLETS WE CAN DO.

RAAAAAAA!!

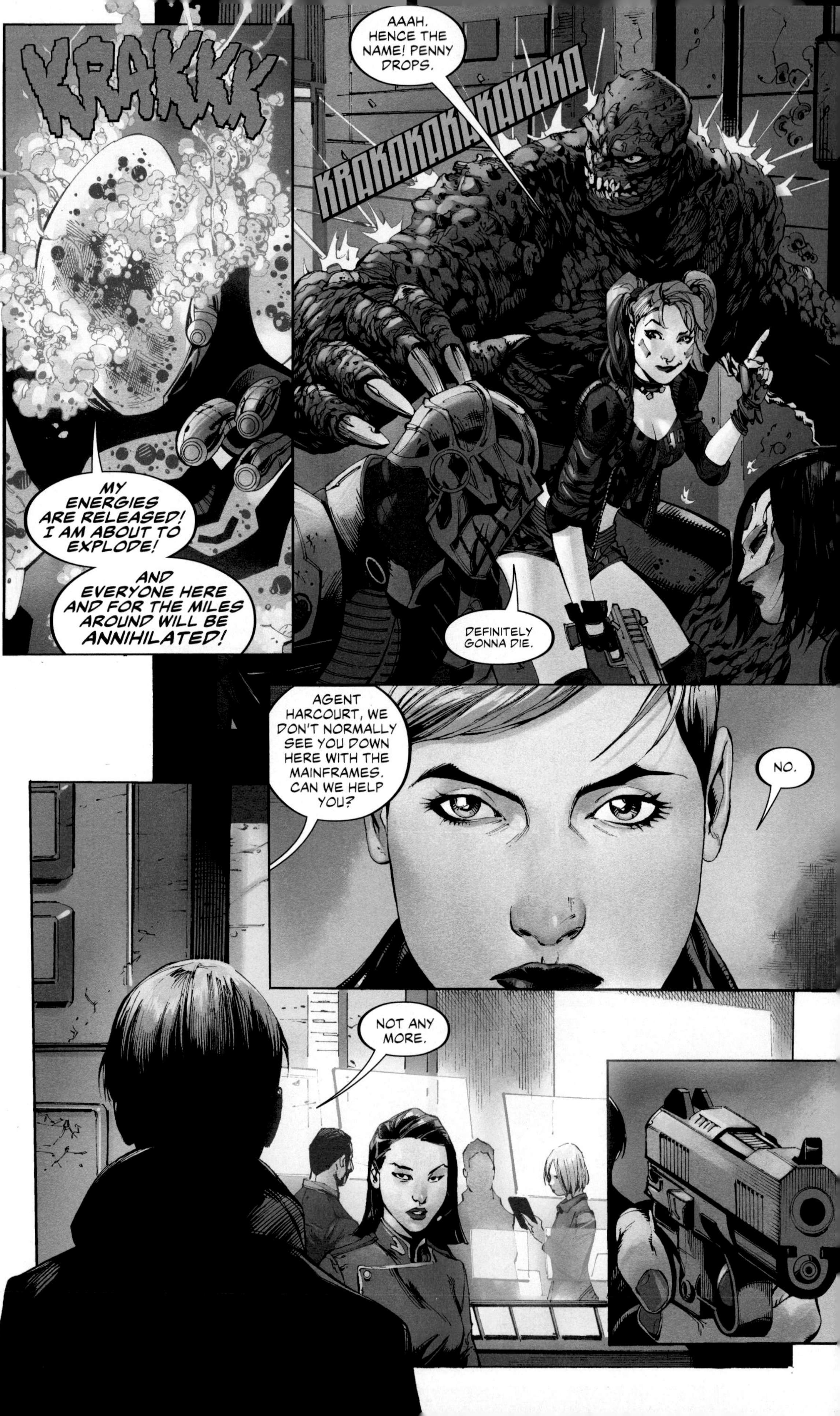
KRAKKK
MY ENERGIES ARE RELEASED! I AM ABOUT TO EXPLODE!
AND EVERYONE HERE AND FOR THE MILES AROUND WILL BE ANNIHILATED!
AAAH. HENCE THE NAME! PENNY DROPS.
KRAKAKAKAKAKAKA
DEFINITELY GONNA DIE.
AGENT HARCOURT, WE DON'T NORMALLY SEE YOU DOWN HERE WITH THE MAINFRAMES. CAN WE HELP YOU?
NO.
NOT ANY MORE.

BLAM

BLAM

BLAM

BLAM

EVEN IF THE BRIGADE SOMEHOW HOLDS TASK FORCE X AND RELEASES THE PRISONERS, WALLER KNOWS TOO MUCH. MY POSITION HERE IS NO LONGER VIABLE.

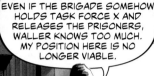

IF I CAN DOWNLOAD ZOD'S **KRYPTONITE BRAIN BOMB** FREQUENCIES, HE COULD BE A WEAPON FOR **OUR CAUSE** INSTEAD.

I AM SENDING YOU THE ZOD FREQUENCIES, NOW. ENCRYPTED CHANNEL, OF COURSE.

WALLER WAS NEVER GOING TO LET THE BRAIN BOMBS BE ENOUGH. SHE SET A FAILSAFE EXPLOSIVE DEVICE BENEATH BELLE REVE. JUST IN CASE OF A FULL-SCALE SUICIDE SQUAD RIOT.

ACTIVATED. BELLE REVE WILL BE WIPED FROM THE EARTH.

AND THE PLANET WILL BE **BETTER** FOR IT.

DIREKTOR KARLA, I AM RECORDING THIS MESSAGE. IF IT GETS TO YOU, WE NEED TO GREATLY ACCELERATE OUR PLANS. **THE PEOPLE** MUST RISE AND IT HAS TO BE **NOW.**

BELLE REVE SELF-DESTRUCT PROTOCOLS ACCESSED

SELF-DESTRUCT COUNTDOWN 02:59

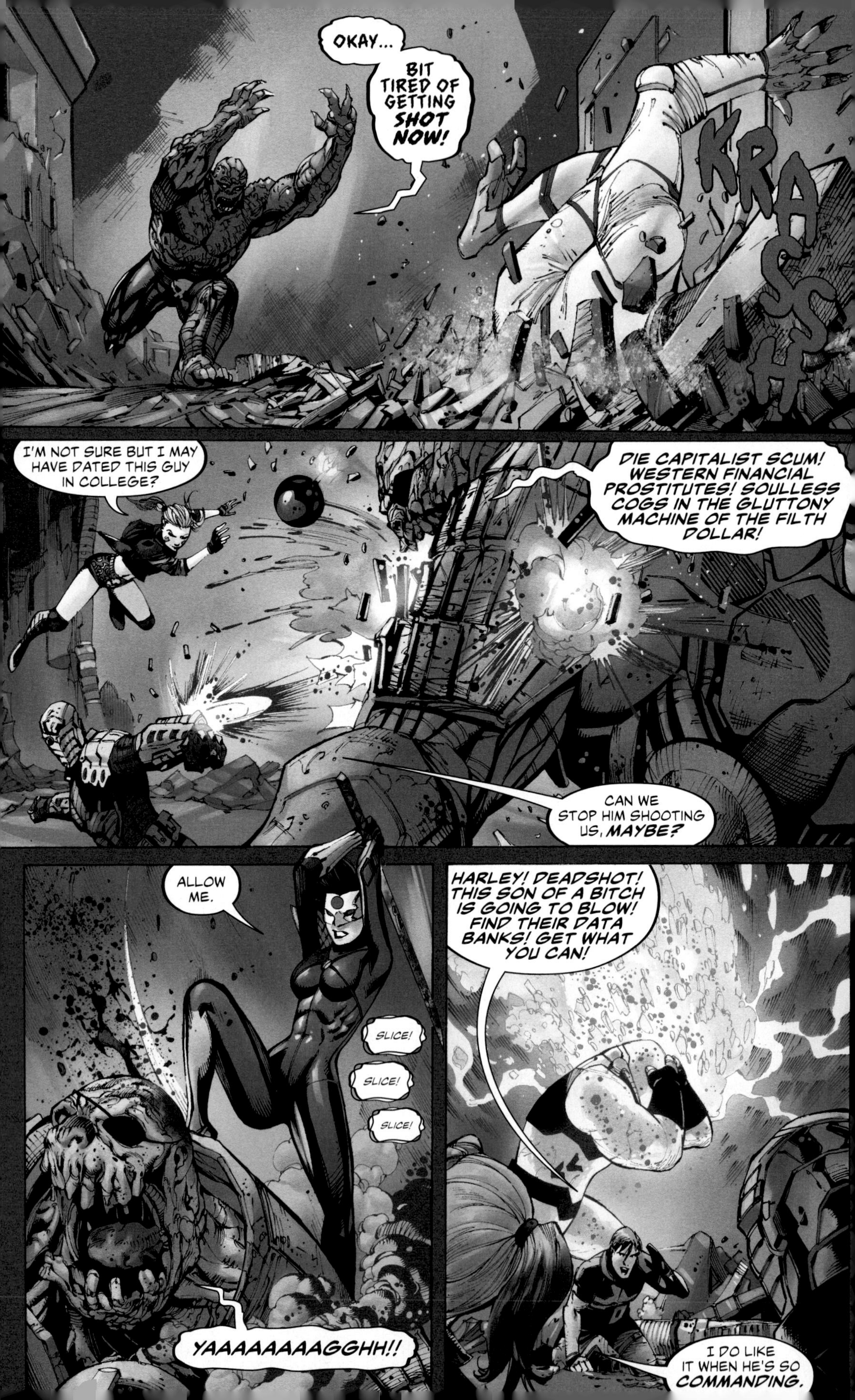
OKAY...
BIT TIRED OF GETTING SHOT NOW!
KRASSH
I'M NOT SURE BUT I MAY HAVE DATED THIS GUY IN COLLEGE?
DIE CAPITALIST SCUM! WESTERN FINANCIAL PROSTITUTES! SOULLESS COGS IN THE GLUTTONY MACHINE OF THE FILTH DOLLAR!
CAN WE STOP HIM SHOOTING US, MAYBE?
ALLOW ME.
SLICE!
SLICE!
SLICE!
YAAAAAAAAGGHH!!
HARLEY! DEADSHOT! THIS SON OF A BITCH IS GOING TO BLOW! FIND THEIR DATA BANKS! GET WHAT YOU CAN!
I DO LIKE IT WHEN HE'S SO COMMANDING.

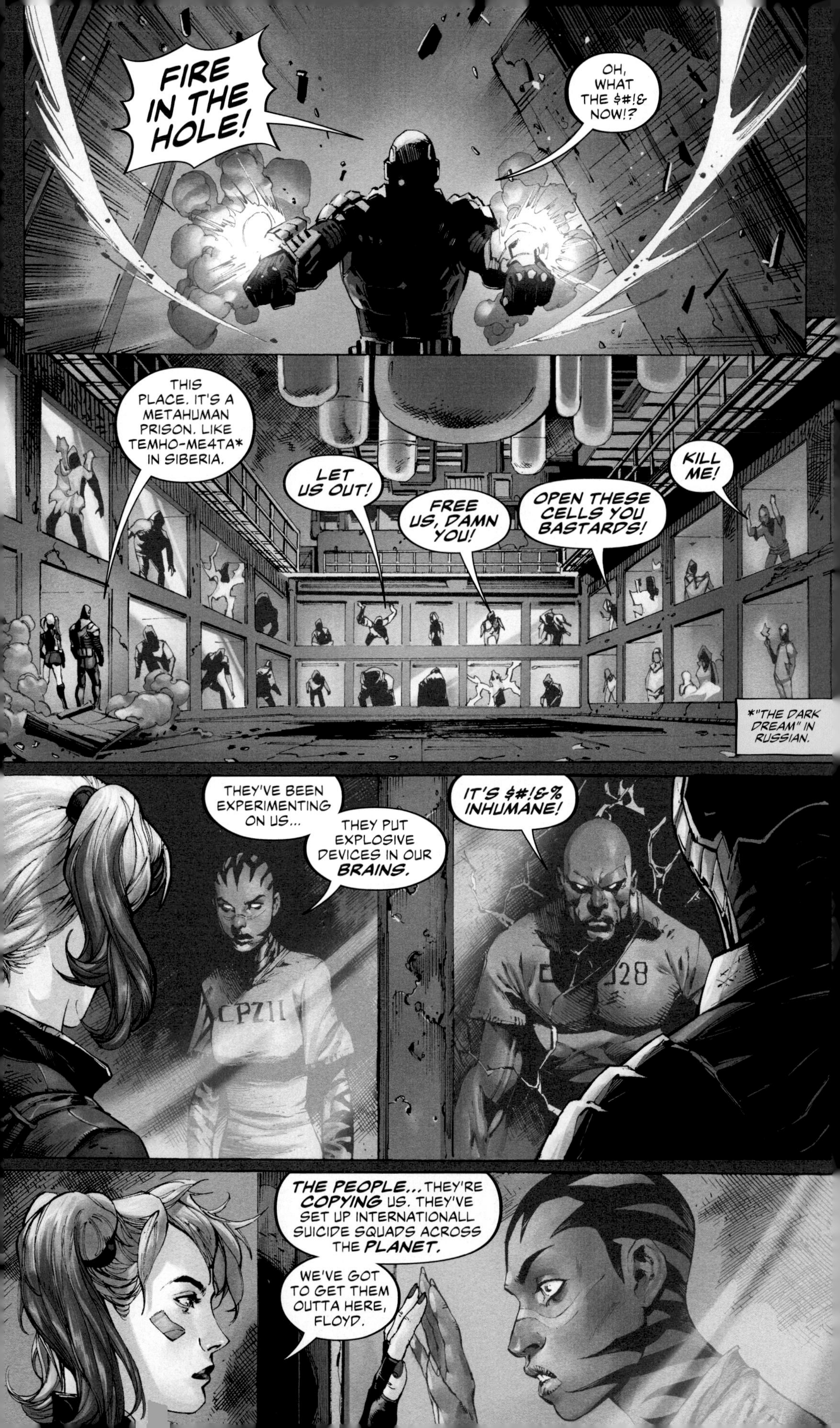
FIRE IN THE HOLE!
OH, WHAT THE $#!& NOW!?
THIS PLACE. IT'S A METAHUMAN PRISON. LIKE TEMHO-ME4TA* IN SIBERIA.
LET US OUT!
FREE US, DAMN YOU!
OPEN THESE CELLS YOU BASTARDS!
KILL ME!
*"THE DARK DREAM" IN RUSSIAN.
THEY'VE BEEN EXPERIMENTING ON US...
THEY PUT EXPLOSIVE DEVICES IN OUR BRAINS.
IT'S $#!&% INHUMANE!
CPZ11
THE PEOPLE... THEY'RE COPYING US. THEY'VE SET UP INTERNATIONAL SUICIDE SQUADS ACROSS THE PLANET.
WE'VE GOT TO GET THEM OUTTA HERE, FLOYD.

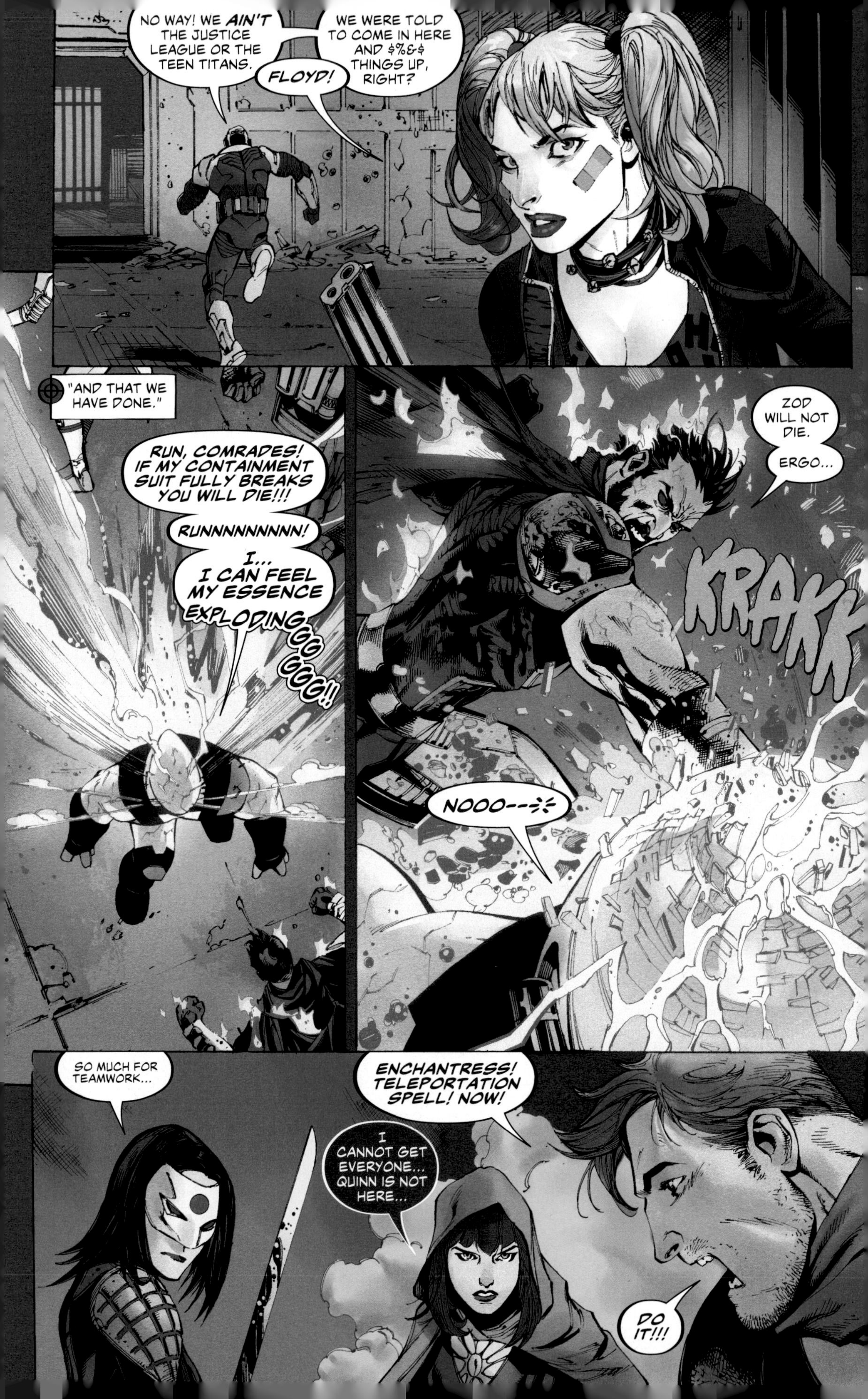
NO WAY! WE AIN'T THE JUSTICE LEAGUE OR THE TEEN TITANS.
WE WERE TOLD TO COME IN HERE AND $%&$ THINGS UP, RIGHT?
FLOYD!
"AND THAT WE HAVE DONE."
RUN, COMRADES! IF MY CONTAINMENT SUIT FULLY BREAKS YOU WILL DIE!!!
RUNNNNNNNNN!
I... I CAN FEEL MY ESSENCE EXPLODINGGG GGG!!
ZOD WILL NOT DIE.
ERGO...
KRAKK
NOOO--
SO MUCH FOR TEAMWORK...
ENCHANTRESS! TELEPORTATION SPELL! NOW!
I CANNOT GET EVERYONE... QUINN IS NOT HERE...
DO IT!!!

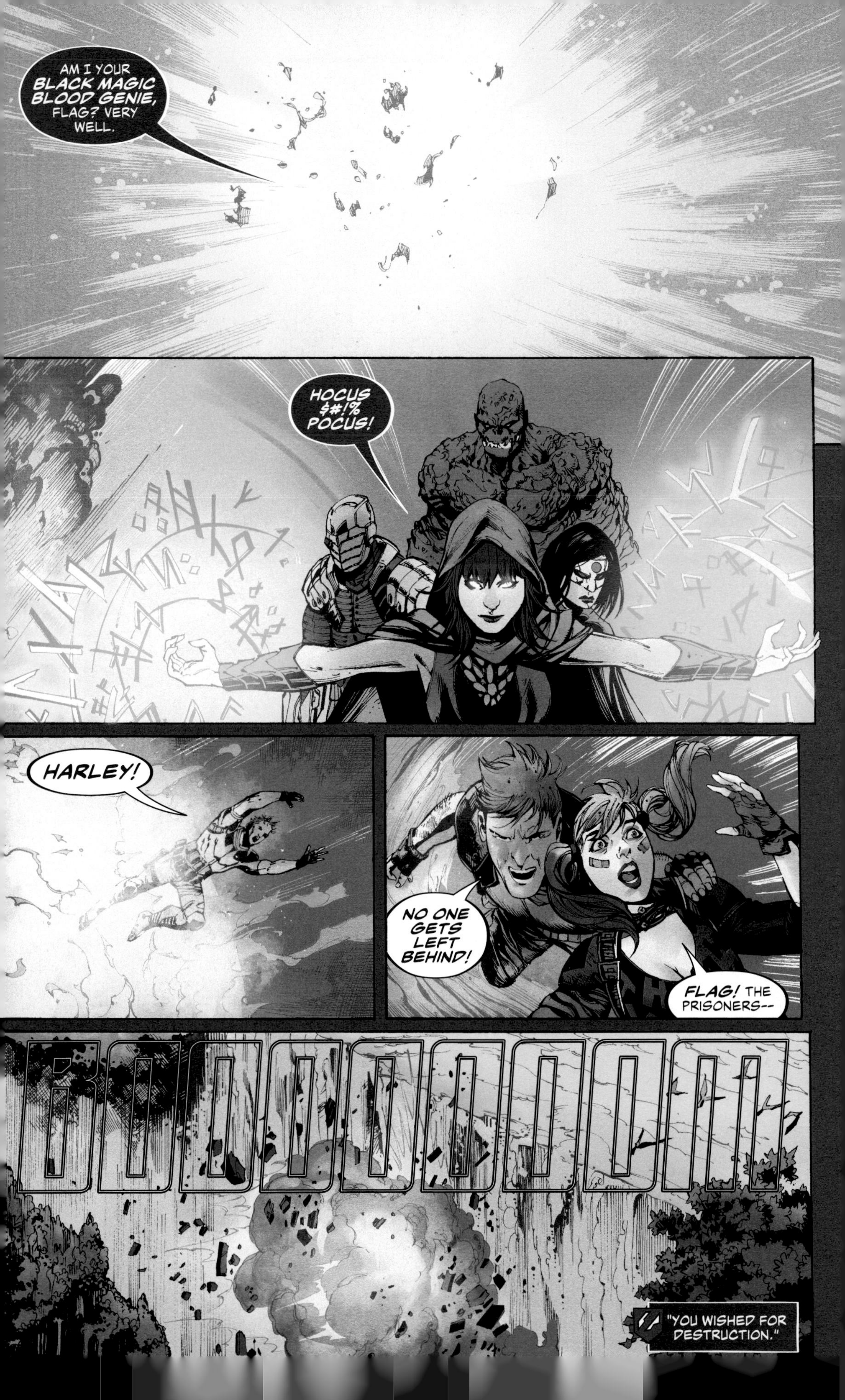
AM I YOUR BLACK MAGIC BLOOD GENIE, FLAG? VERY WELL.
HOCUS $#!% POCUS!
HARLEY!
NO ONE GETS LEFT BEHIND!
FLAG! THE PRISONERS--
BOOOOOOOOM
"YOU WISHED FOR DESTRUCTION."

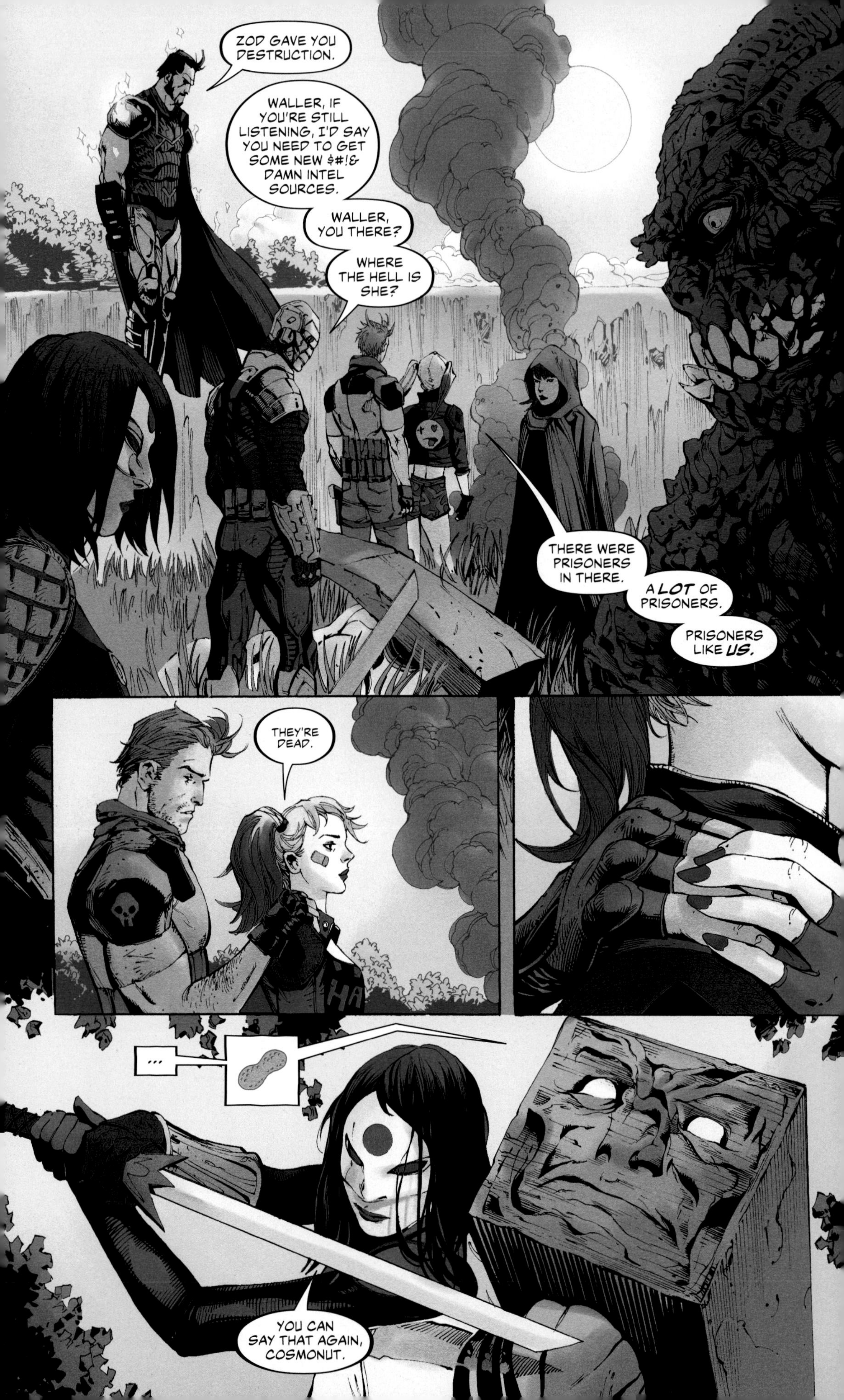
ZOD GAVE YOU DESTRUCTION.
WALLER, IF YOU'RE STILL LISTENING, I'D SAY YOU NEED TO GET SOME NEW $#!& DAMN INTEL SOURCES.
WALLER, YOU THERE?
WHERE THE HELL IS SHE?
THERE WERE PRISONERS IN THERE.
A LOT OF PRISONERS.
PRISONERS LIKE US.
THEY'RE DEAD.
...
YOU CAN SAY THAT AGAIN, COSMONUT.

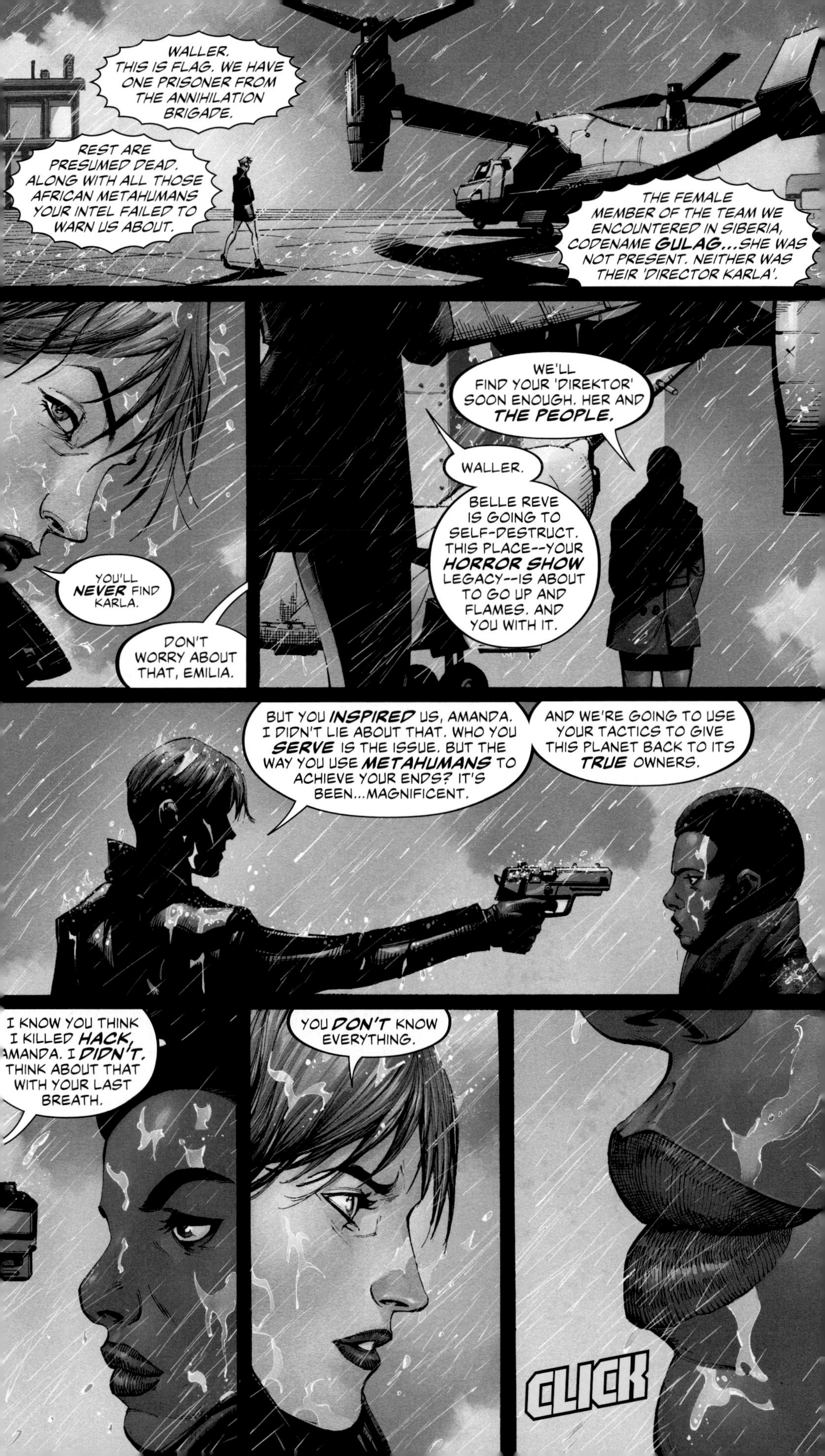
WALLER. THIS IS FLAG. WE HAVE ONE PRISONER FROM THE ANNIHILATION BRIGADE.
REST ARE PRESUMED DEAD. ALONG WITH ALL THOSE AFRICAN METAHUMANS YOUR INTEL FAILED TO WARN US ABOUT.
THE FEMALE MEMBER OF THE TEAM WE ENCOUNTERED IN SIBERIA, CODENAME GULAG... SHE WAS NOT PRESENT. NEITHER WAS THEIR 'DIRECTOR KARLA'.
YOU'LL NEVER FIND KARLA.
DON'T WORRY ABOUT THAT, EMILIA.
WE'LL FIND YOUR 'DIREKTOR' SOON ENOUGH. HER AND THE PEOPLE.
WALLER.
BELLE REVE IS GOING TO SELF-DESTRUCT. THIS PLACE--YOUR HORROR SHOW LEGACY--IS ABOUT TO GO UP AND FLAMES. AND YOU WITH IT.
BUT YOU INSPIRED US, AMANDA. I DIDN'T LIE ABOUT THAT. WHO YOU SERVE IS THE ISSUE. BUT THE WAY YOU USE METAHUMANS TO ACHIEVE YOUR ENDS? IT'S BEEN...MAGNIFICENT.
AND WE'RE GOING TO USE YOUR TACTICS TO GIVE THIS PLANET BACK TO ITS TRUE OWNERS.
I KNOW YOU THINK I KILLED HACK, AMANDA. I DIDN'T. THINK ABOUT THAT WITH YOUR LAST BREATH.
YOU DON'T KNOW EVERYTHING.
CLICK

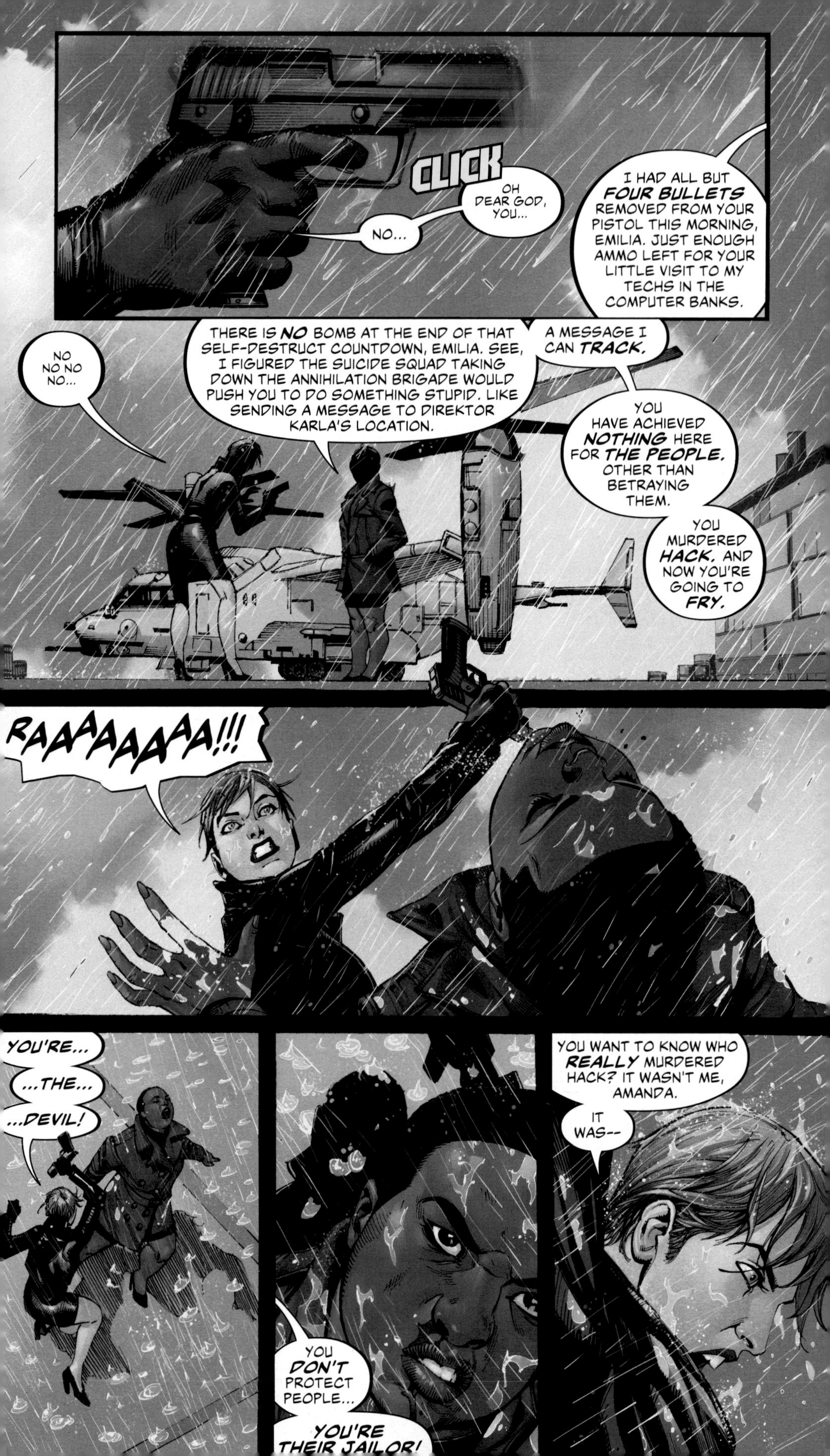
CLICK
OH DEAR GOD, YOU...
NO...
I HAD ALL BUT FOUR BULLETS REMOVED FROM YOUR PISTOL THIS MORNING, EMILIA. JUST ENOUGH AMMO LEFT FOR YOUR LITTLE VISIT TO MY TECHS IN THE COMPUTER BANKS.
NO NO NO NO...
THERE IS NO BOMB AT THE END OF THAT SELF-DESTRUCT COUNTDOWN, EMILIA. SEE, I FIGURED THE SUICIDE SQUAD TAKING DOWN THE ANNIHILATION BRIGADE WOULD PUSH YOU TO DO SOMETHING STUPID. LIKE SENDING A MESSAGE TO DIREKTOR KARLA'S LOCATION.
A MESSAGE I CAN TRACK.
YOU HAVE ACHIEVED NOTHING HERE FOR THE PEOPLE. OTHER THAN BETRAYING THEM.
YOU MURDERED HACK. AND NOW YOU'RE GOING TO FRY.
RAAAAAAAA!!!
YOU'RE...
...THE...
...DEVIL!
YOU DON'T PROTECT PEOPLE...
YOU'RE THEIR JAILOR!
YOU WANT TO KNOW WHO REALLY MURDERED HACK? IT WASN'T ME, AMANDA.
IT WAS--

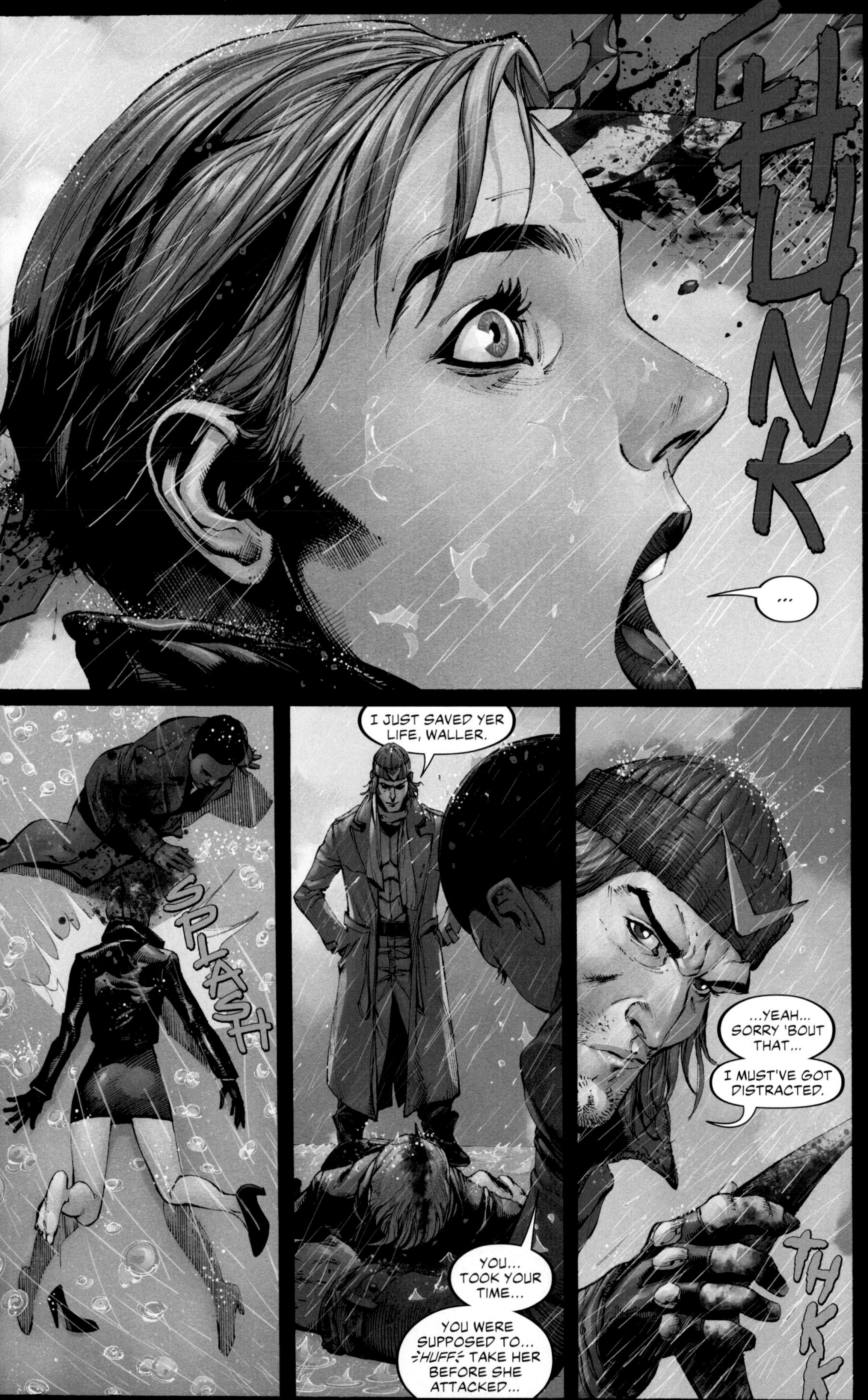
THUNK
...
SPLASH
I JUST SAVED YER LIFE, WALLER.
YOU... TOOK YOUR TIME...
YOU WERE SUPPOSED TO... HUFF TAKE HER BEFORE SHE ATTACKED...
...YEAH... SORRY 'BOUT THAT...
I MUST'VE GOT DISTRACTED.
THKK

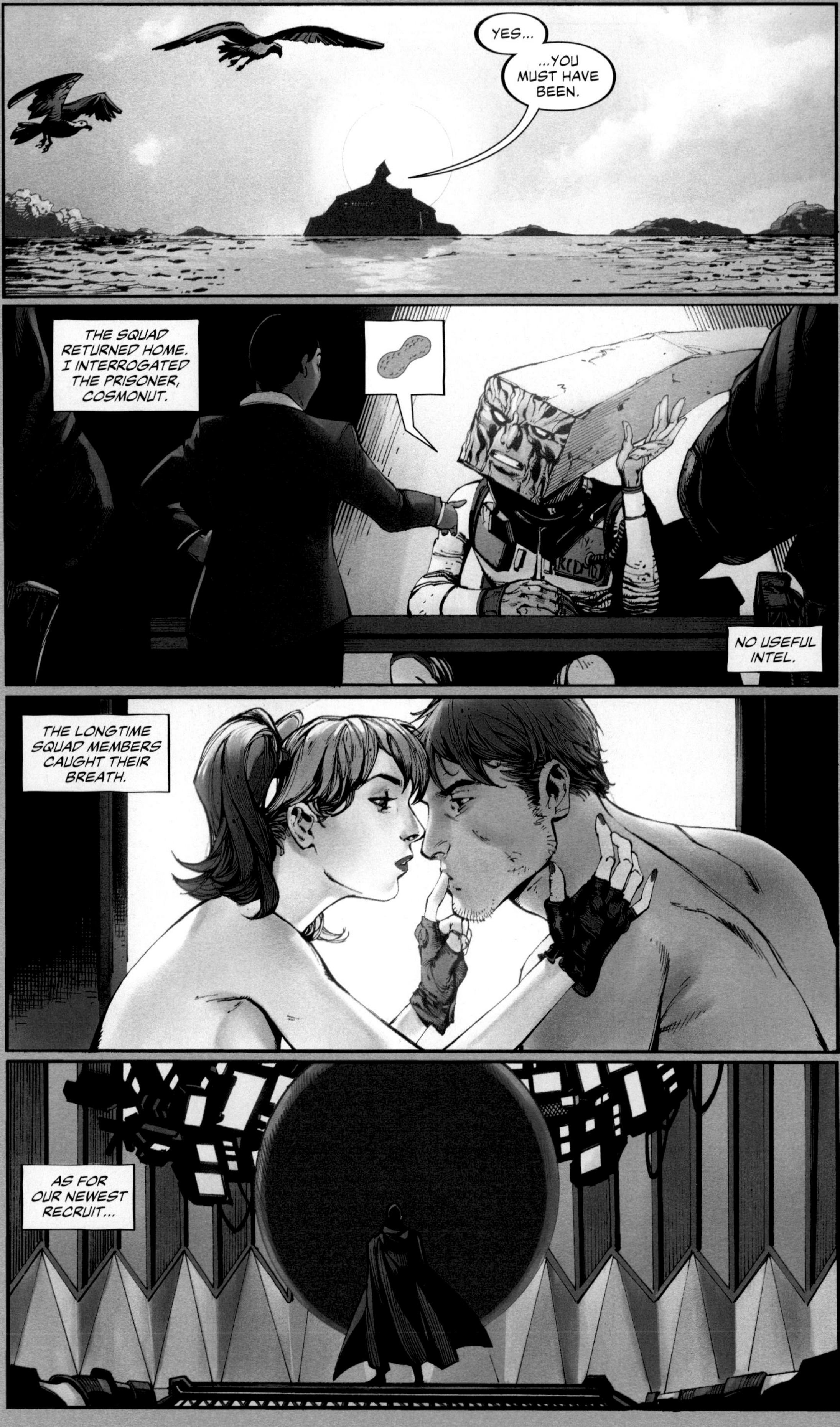
YES...
...YOU MUST HAVE BEEN.
THE SQUAD RETURNED HOME. I INTERROGATED THE PRISONER, COSMONUT.
NO USEFUL INTEL.
THE LONGTIME SQUAD MEMBERS CAUGHT THEIR BREATH.
AS FOR OUR NEWEST RECRUIT...

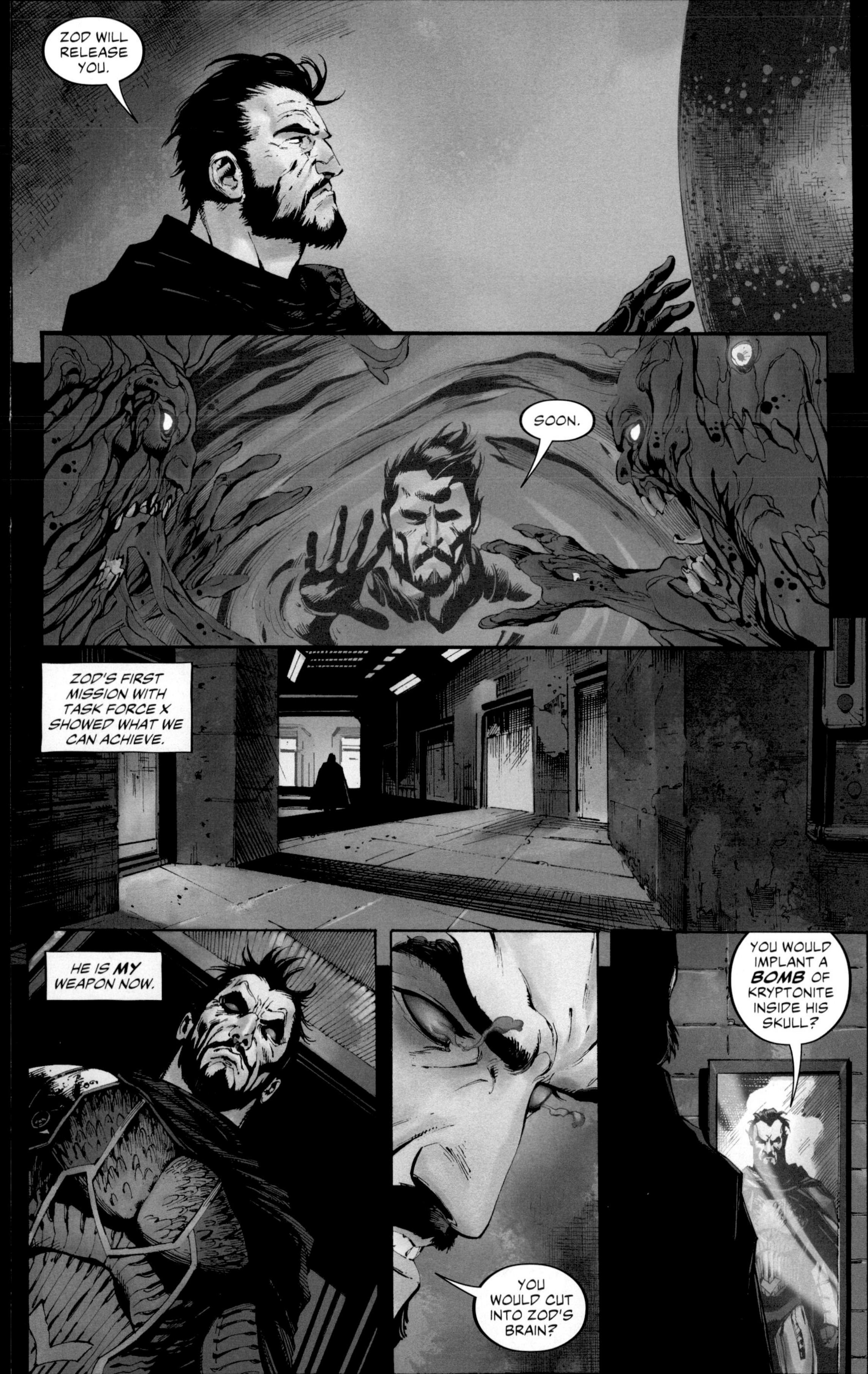
ZOD WILL RELEASE YOU.
SOON.
ZOD'S FIRST MISSION WITH TASK FORCE X SHOWED WHAT WE CAN ACHIEVE.
HE IS MY WEAPON NOW.
YOU WOULD IMPLANT A BOMB OF KRYPTONITE INSIDE HIS SKULL?
YOU WOULD CUT INTO ZOD'S BRAIN?

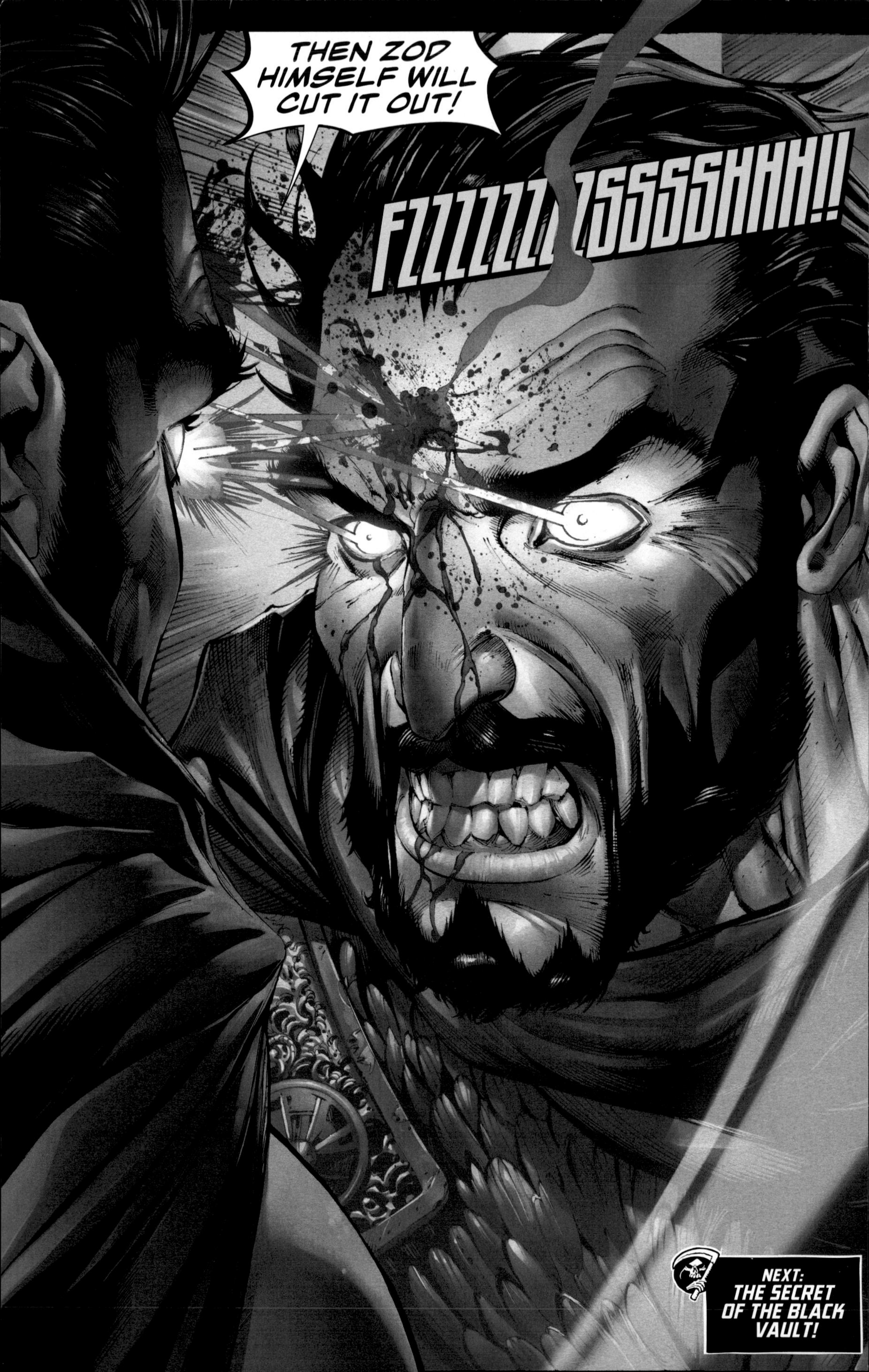
THEN ZOD HIMSELF WILL CUT IT OUT!
FZZZZZZZSSSSSSHHH!!
NEXT: THE SECRET OF THE BLACK VAULT!

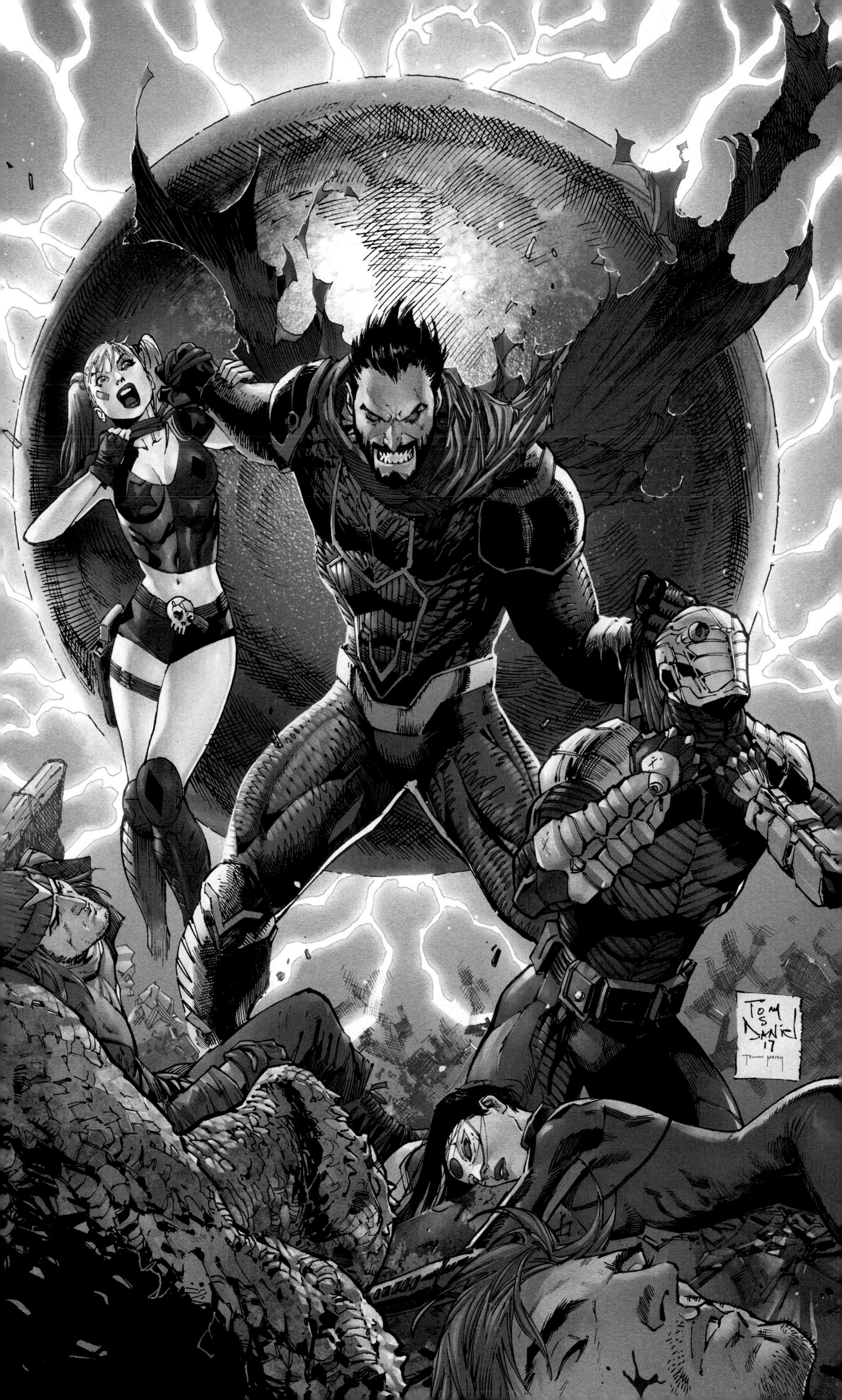
TOM S DANIEL 17

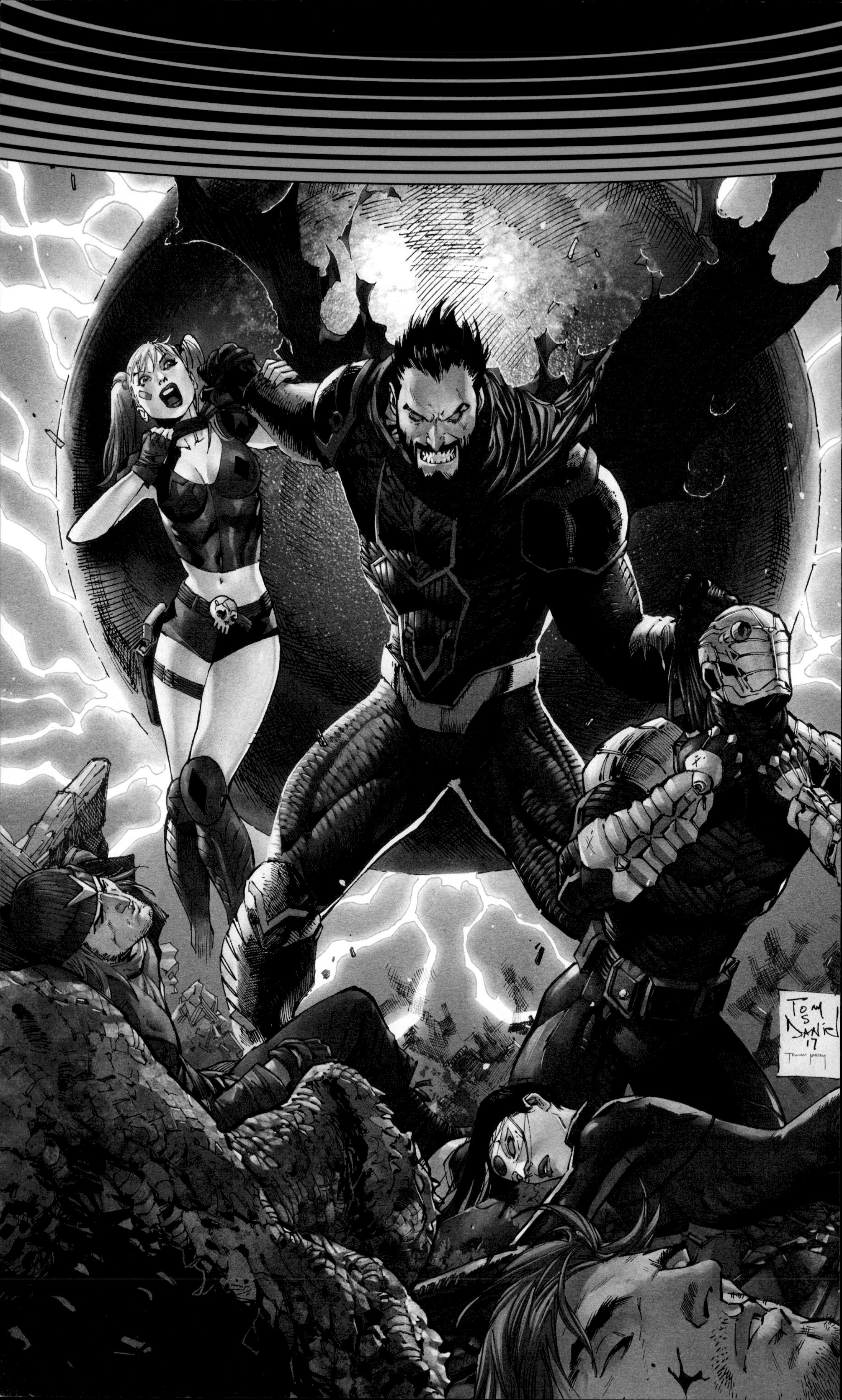

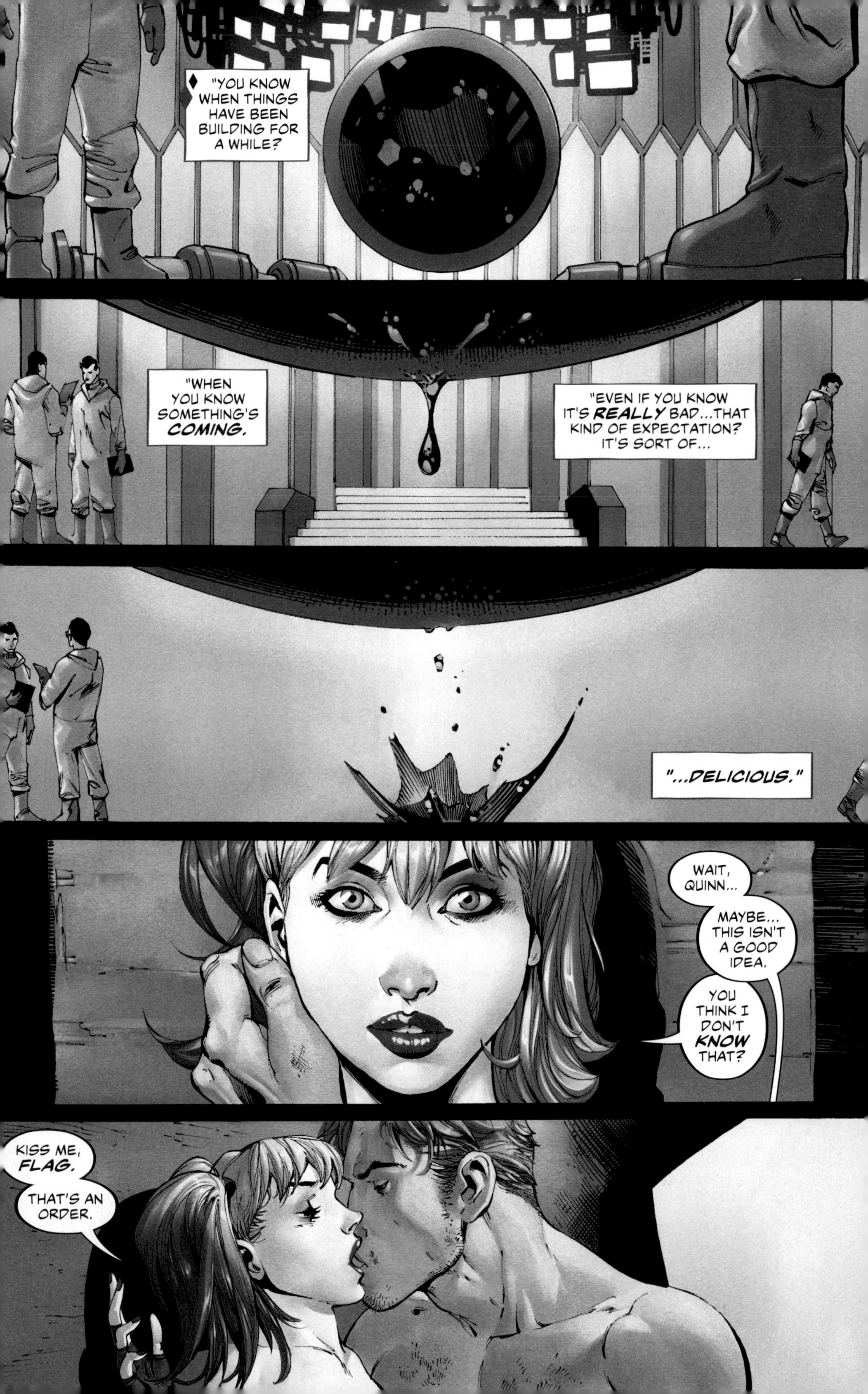
"YOU KNOW WHEN THINGS HAVE BEEN BUILDING FOR A WHILE?
"WHEN YOU KNOW SOMETHING'S COMING.
"EVEN IF YOU KNOW IT'S REALLY BAD...THAT KIND OF EXPECTATION? IT'S SORT OF...
"...DELICIOUS."
WAIT, QUINN...
MAYBE... THIS ISN'T A GOOD IDEA.
YOU THINK I DON'T KNOW THAT?
KISS ME, FLAG.
THAT'S AN ORDER.

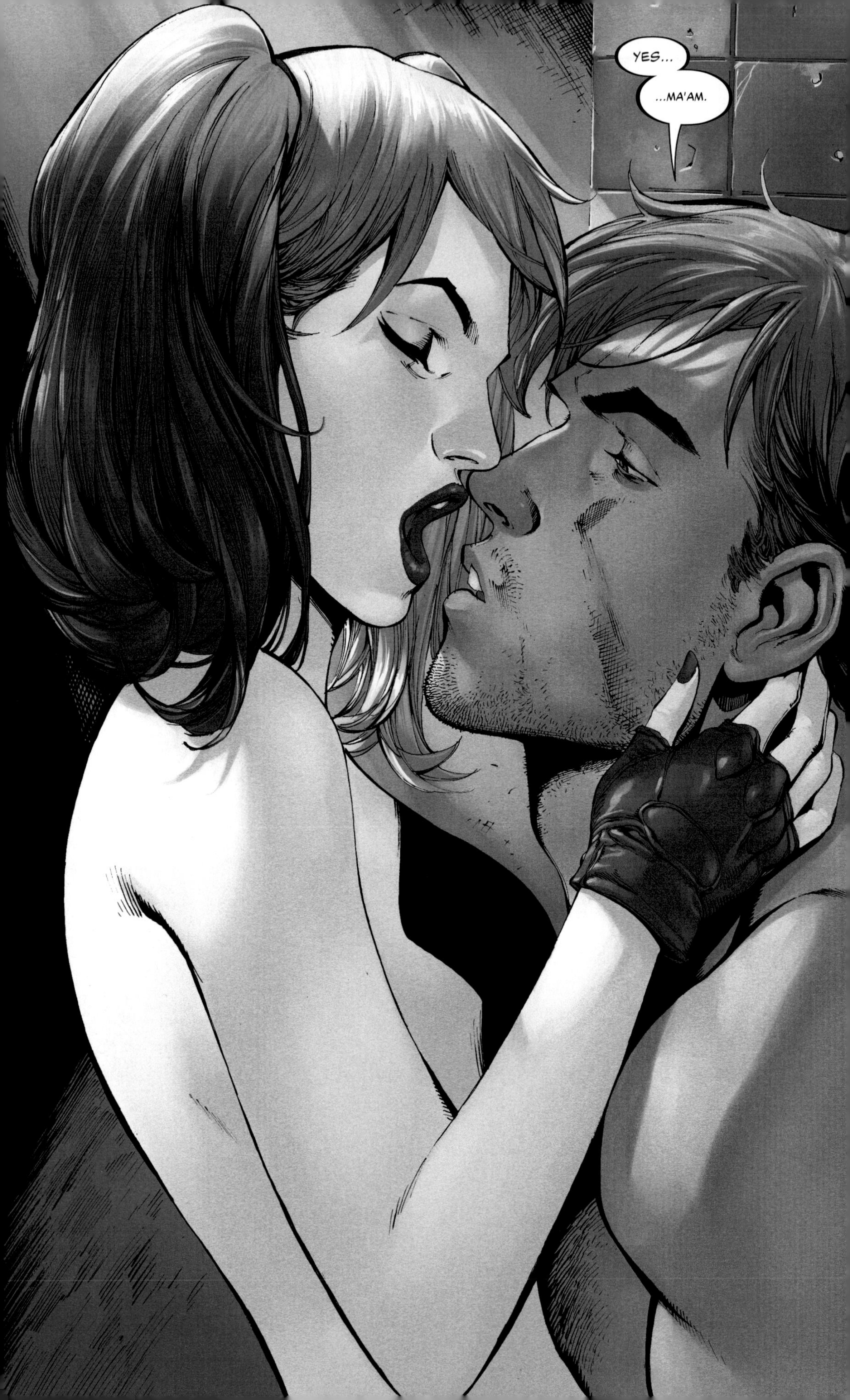
YES...
...MA'AM.

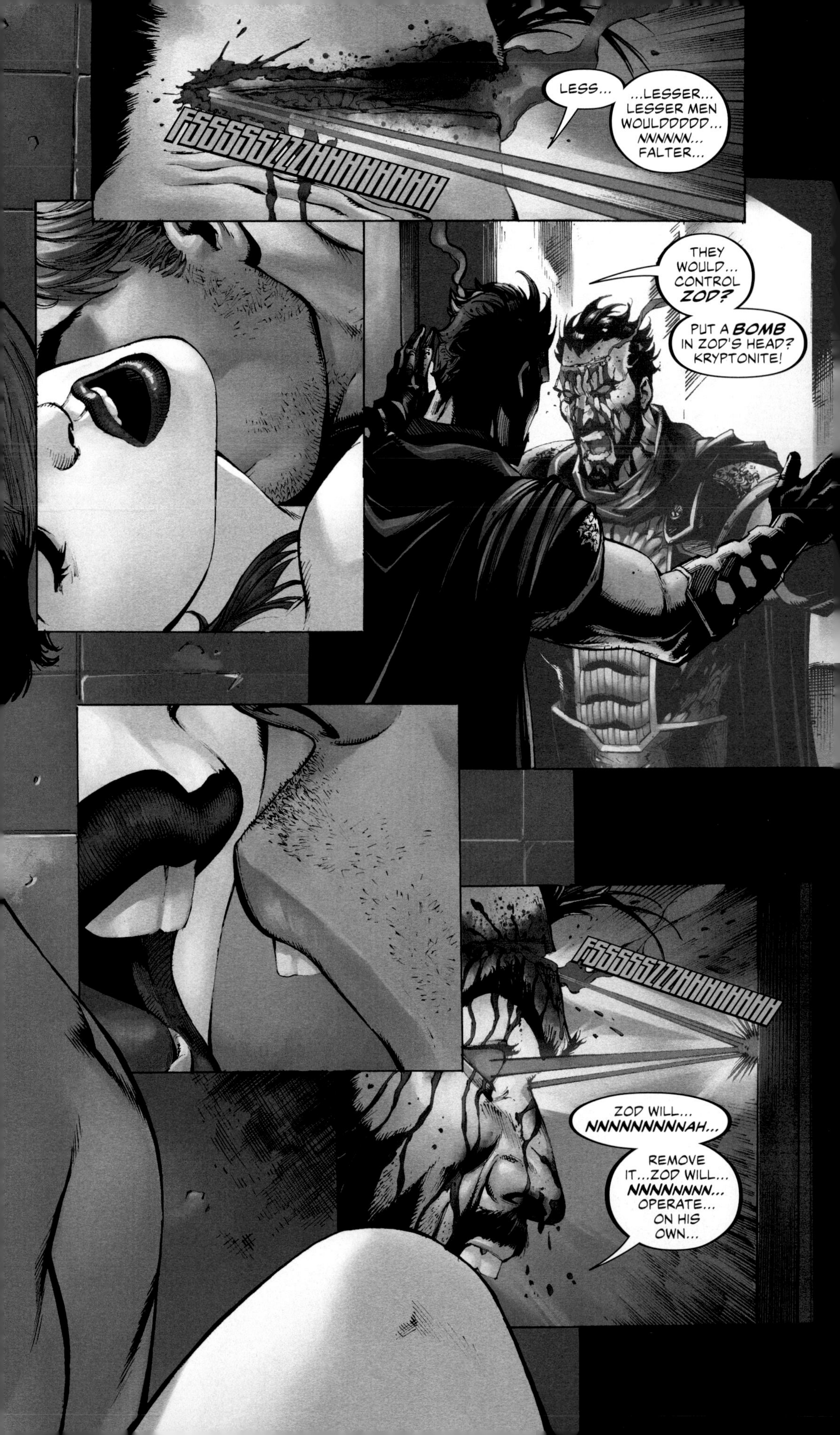
LESS...
...LESSER... LESSER MEN WOULDDDDD... NNNNNN... FALTER...
FSSSSSZZZHHHHHHHH
THEY WOULD... CONTROL ZOD?
PUT A BOMB IN ZOD'S HEAD? KRYPTONITE!
FSSSSSZZZHHHHHHHH
ZOD WILL... NNNNNNNNAH...
REMOVE IT...ZOD WILL... NNNNNNN... OPERATE... ON HIS OWN...

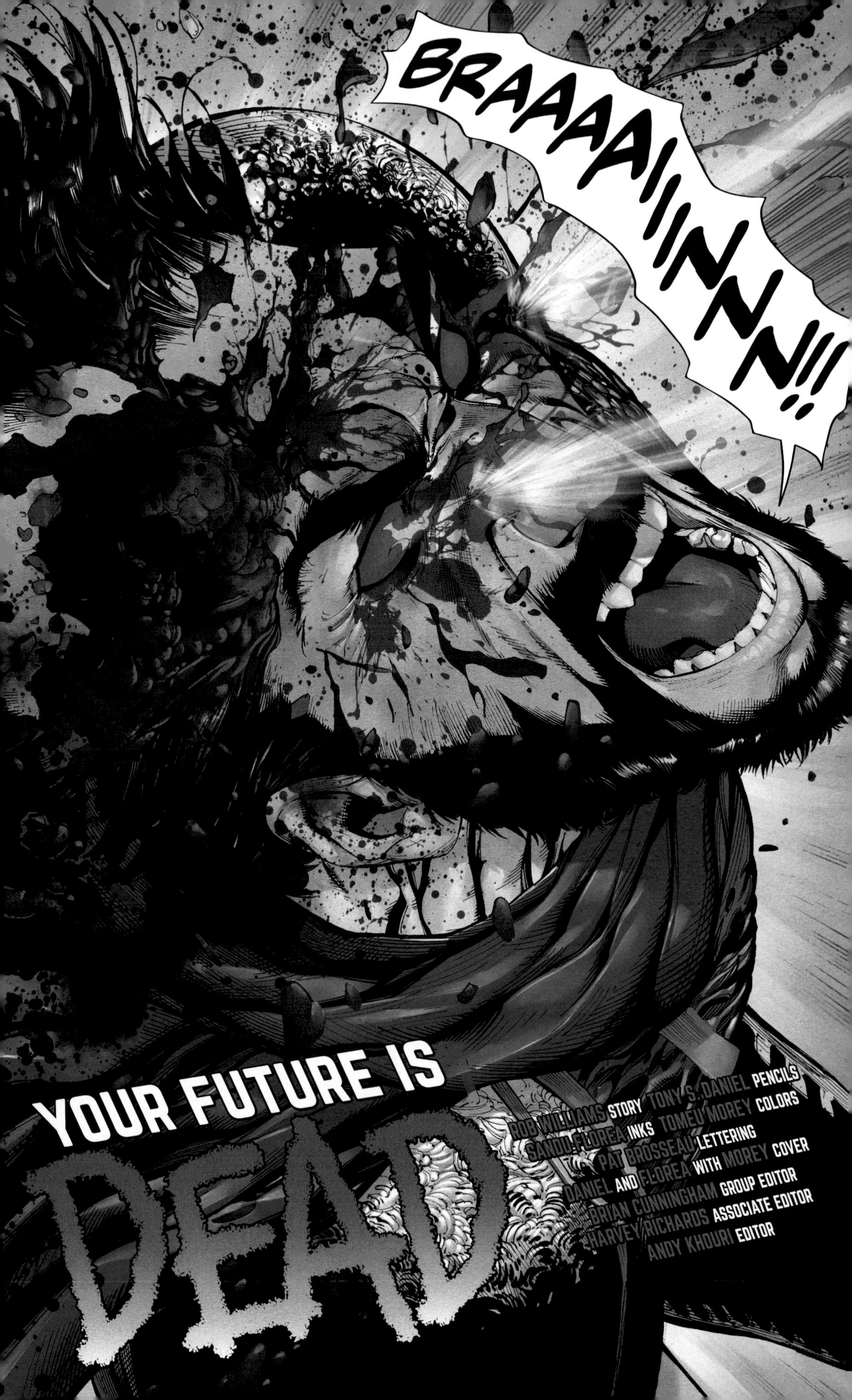
BRAAAAIIINNN!!
YOUR FUTURE IS
DEAD
ROB WILLIAMS STORY TONY S. DANIEL PENCILS
SANDU FLOREA INKS TOMEU MOREY COLORS
PAT BROSSEAU LETTERING
DANIEL AND FLOREA WITH MOREY COVER
BRIAN CUNNINGHAM GROUP EDITOR
HARVEY RICHARDS ASSOCIATE EDITOR
ANDY KHOURI EDITOR

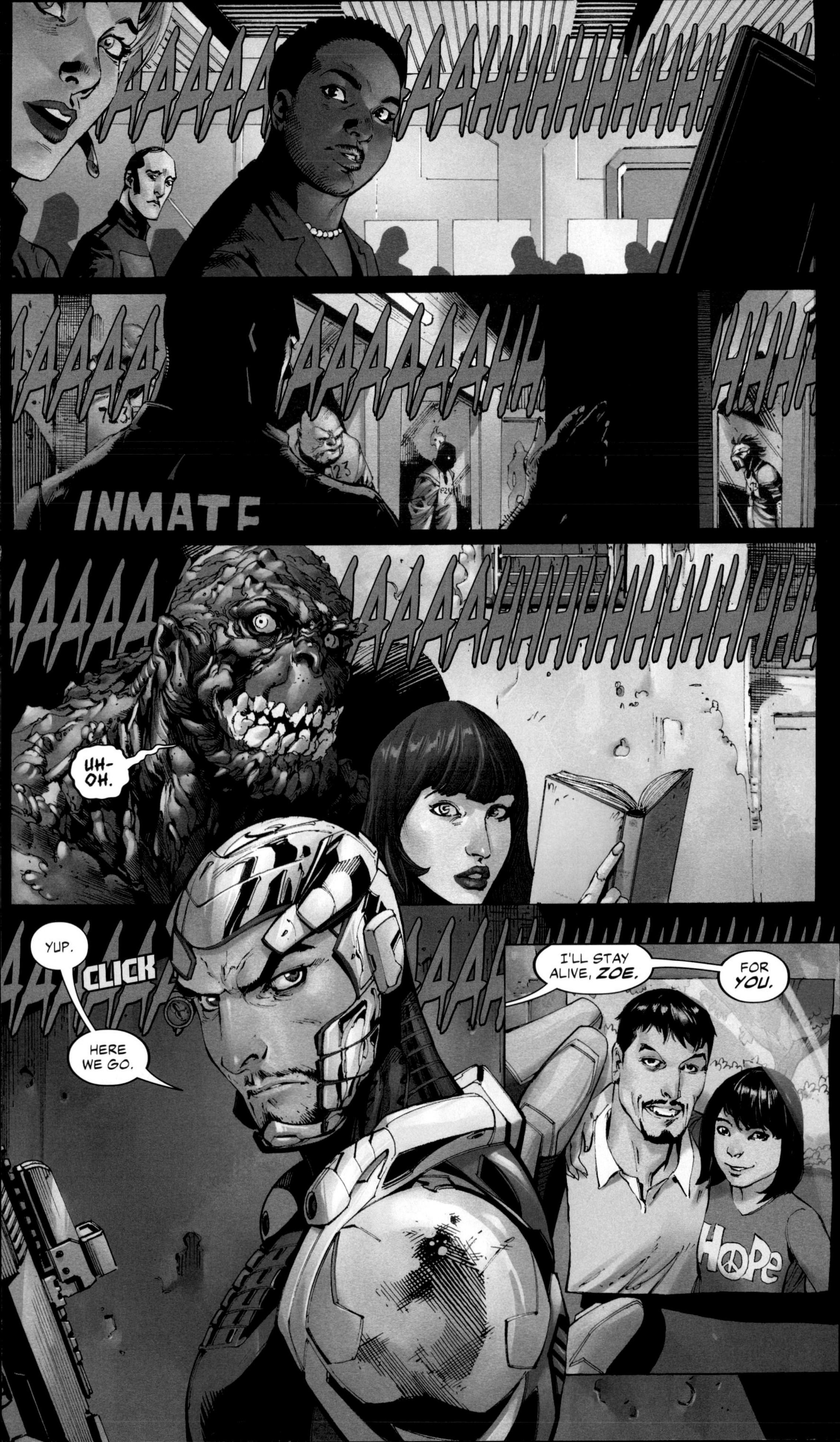
AAAAAAAAAAAAHHHHHHHHHHHHH
AAAAAAAAAAAAAHHHHHH
INMATE
AAAAAAAAAAAAAHHHHHHHHHHHHHHH
UH-OH.
AAAAAAAAAAAAAAA
YUP.
CLICK
HERE WE GO.
I'LL STAY ALIVE, ZOE.
FOR YOU.
HOPE

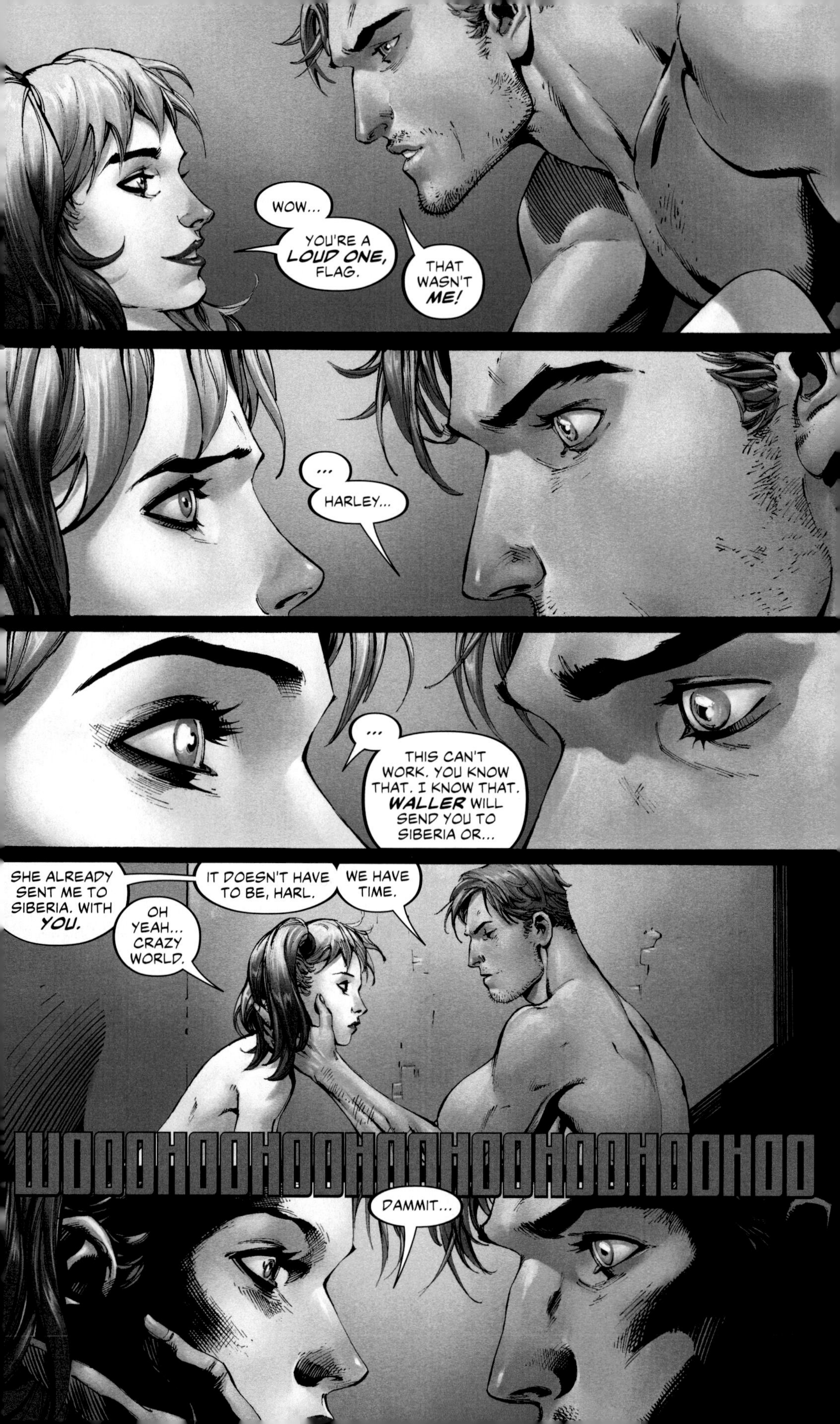
WOW...
YOU'RE A LOUD ONE, FLAG.
THAT WASN'T ME!
...
HARLEY...
...
THIS CAN'T WORK. YOU KNOW THAT. I KNOW THAT. WALLER WILL SEND YOU TO SIBERIA OR...
SHE ALREADY SENT ME TO SIBERIA. WITH YOU.
OH YEAH... CRAZY WORLD.
IT DOESN'T HAVE TO BE, HARL.
WE HAVE TIME.
WOOOHOOHOOHOOHOOHOOHOOHOO
DAMMIT...

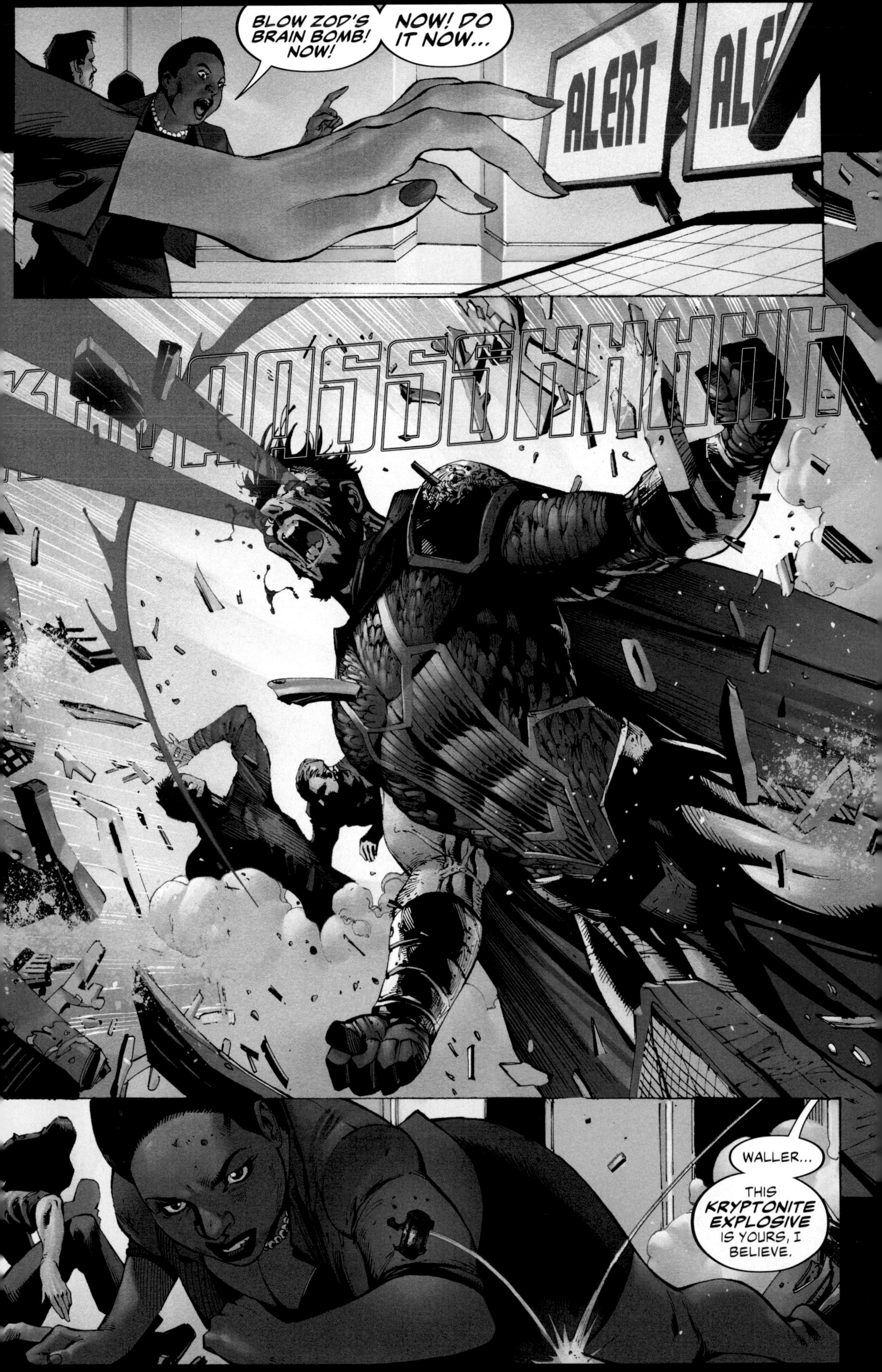
BLOW ZOD'S BRAIN BOMB! NOW!
NOW! DO IT NOW...
ALERT
WALLER...
THIS **KRYPTONITE EXPLOSIVE** IS YOURS, I BELIEVE.

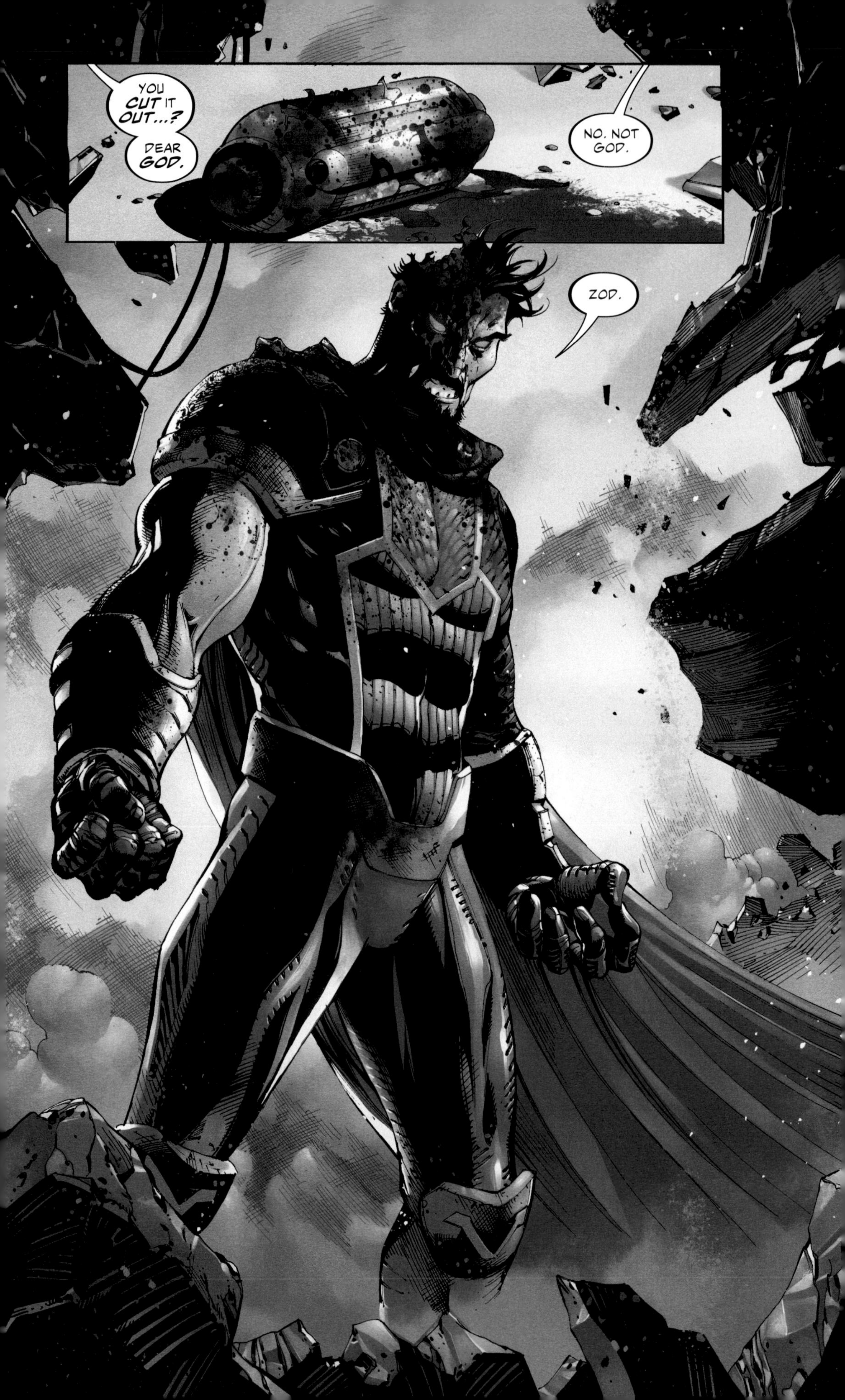
YOU CUT IT OUT...?
DEAR GOD.
NO. NOT GOD.
ZOD.

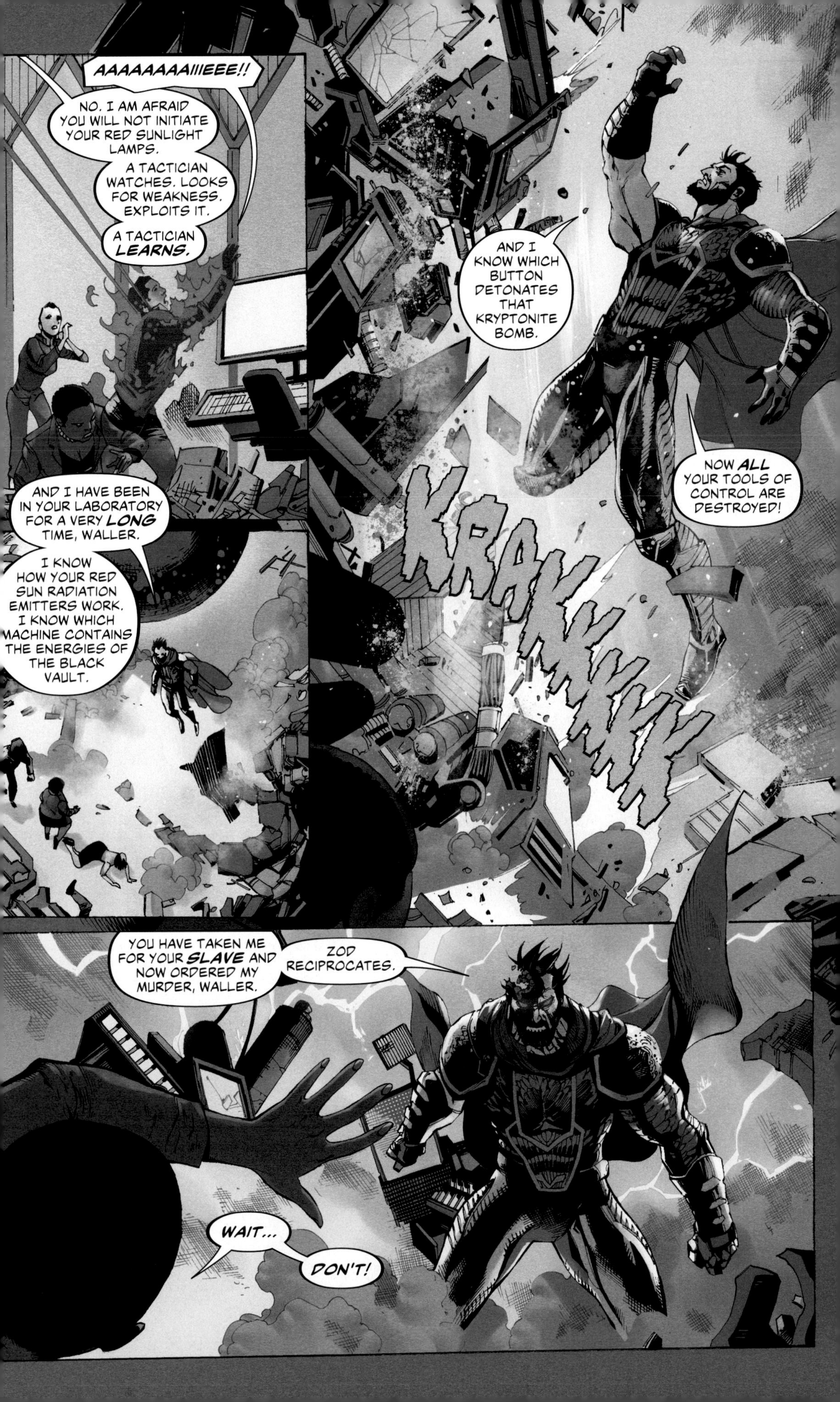
AAAAAAAAIIIEEE!!
NO. I AM AFRAID YOU WILL NOT INITIATE YOUR RED SUNLIGHT LAMPS.
A TACTICIAN WATCHES. LOOKS FOR WEAKNESS. EXPLOITS IT.
A TACTICIAN LEARNS.
AND I HAVE BEEN IN YOUR LABORATORY FOR A VERY LONG TIME, WALLER.
I KNOW HOW YOUR RED SUN RADIATION EMITTERS WORK. I KNOW WHICH MACHINE CONTAINS THE ENERGIES OF THE BLACK VAULT.
AND I KNOW WHICH BUTTON DETONATES THAT KRYPTONITE BOMB.
KRAKKKKKK
NOW ALL YOUR TOOLS OF CONTROL ARE DESTROYED!
YOU HAVE TAKEN ME FOR YOUR SLAVE AND NOW ORDERED MY MURDER, WALLER.
ZOD RECIPROCATES.
WAIT...
DON'T!

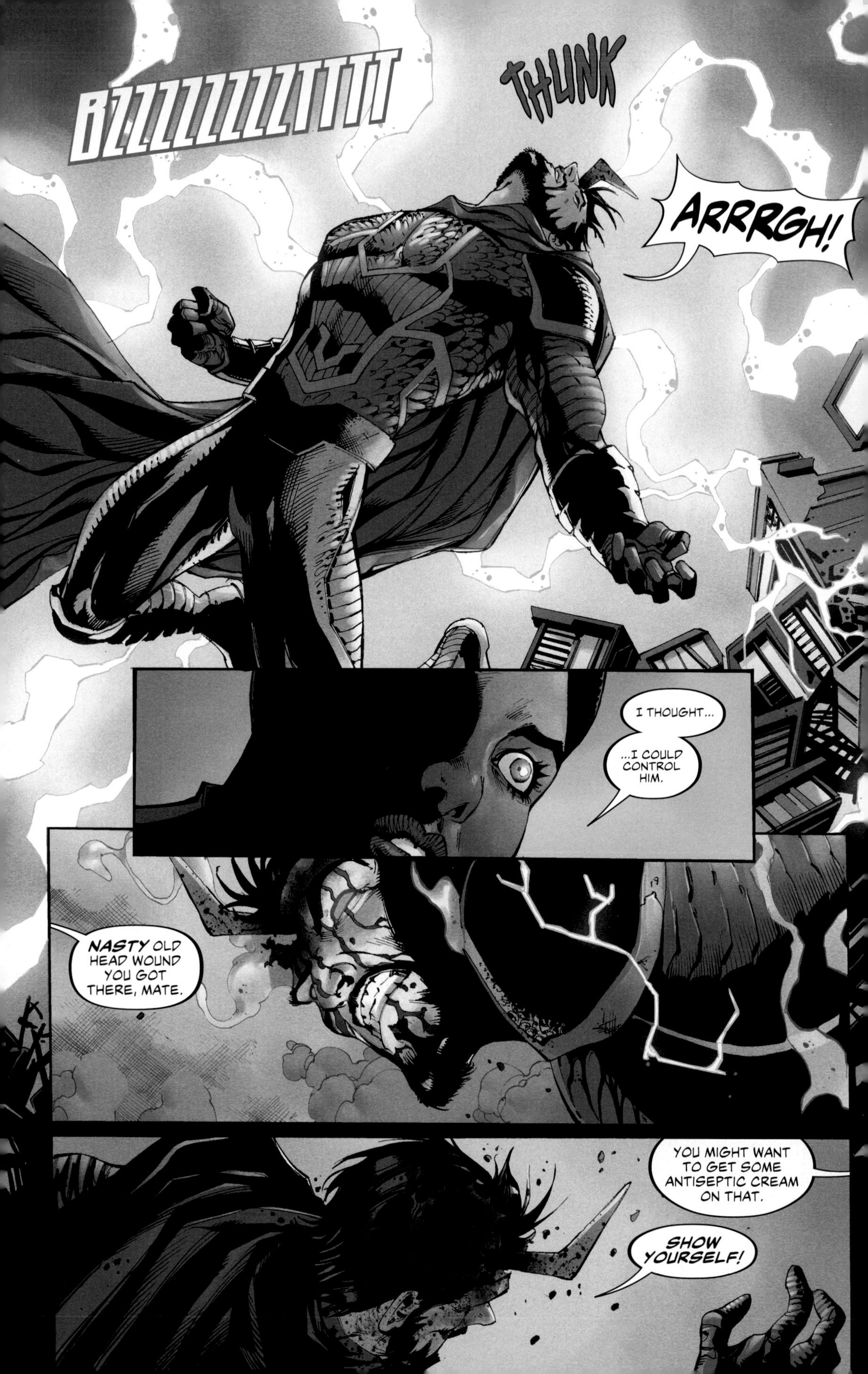
BZZZZZZZZZTTTTT
THUNK
ARRRGH!
I THOUGHT...
...I COULD CONTROL HIM.
NASTY OLD HEAD WOUND YOU GOT THERE, MATE.
YOU MIGHT WANT TO GET SOME ANTISEPTIC CREAM ON THAT.
SHOW YOURSELF!

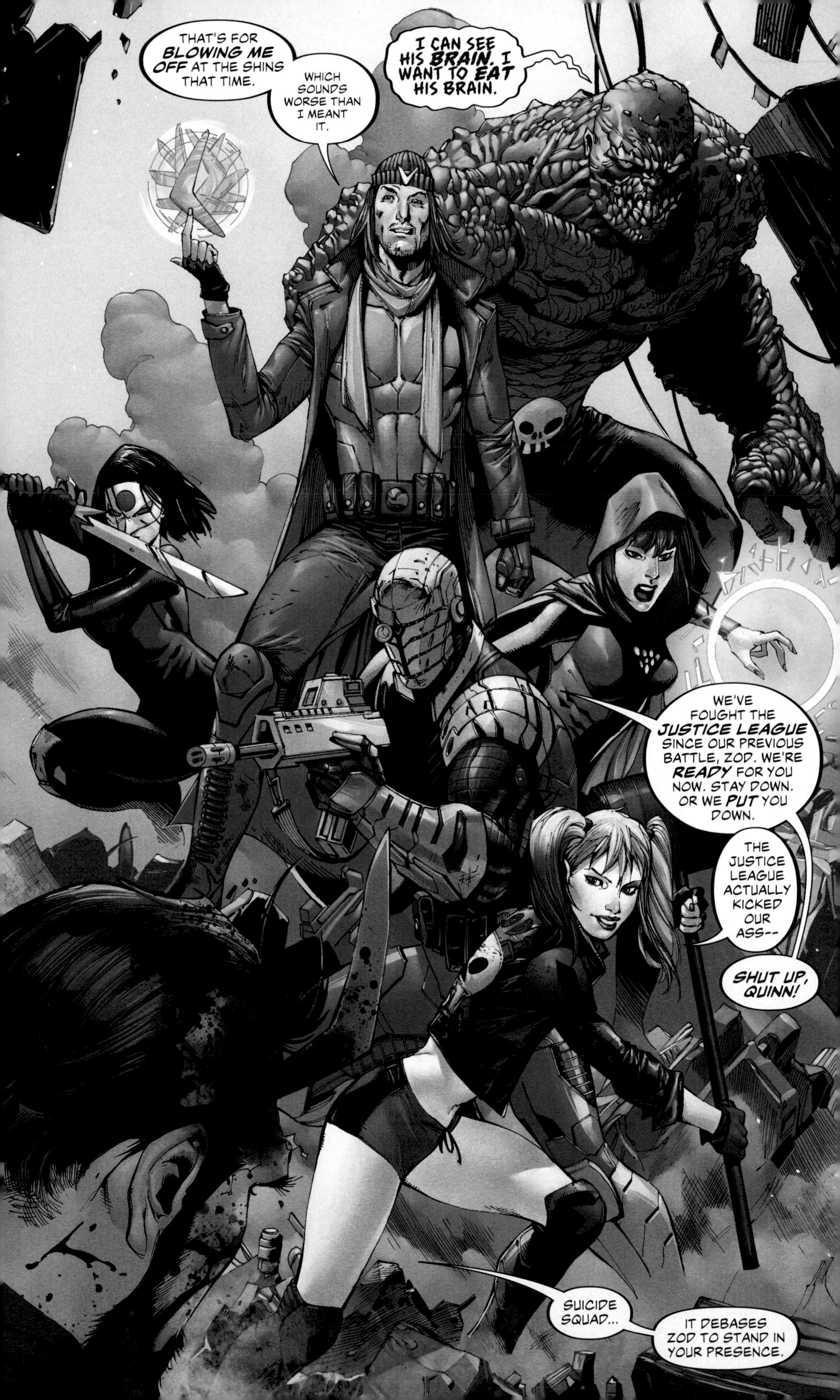

THAT'S FOR BLOWING ME OFF AT THE SHINS THAT TIME.
WHICH SOUNDS WORSE THAN I MEANT IT.
I CAN SEE HIS BRAIN. I WANT TO EAT HIS BRAIN.
WE'VE FOUGHT THE JUSTICE LEAGUE SINCE OUR PREVIOUS BATTLE, ZOD. WE'RE READY FOR YOU NOW. STAY DOWN. OR WE PUT YOU DOWN.
THE JUSTICE LEAGUE ACTUALLY KICKED OUR ASS--
SHUT UP, QUINN!
SUICIDE SQUAD...
IT DEBASES ZOD TO STAND IN YOUR PRESENCE.

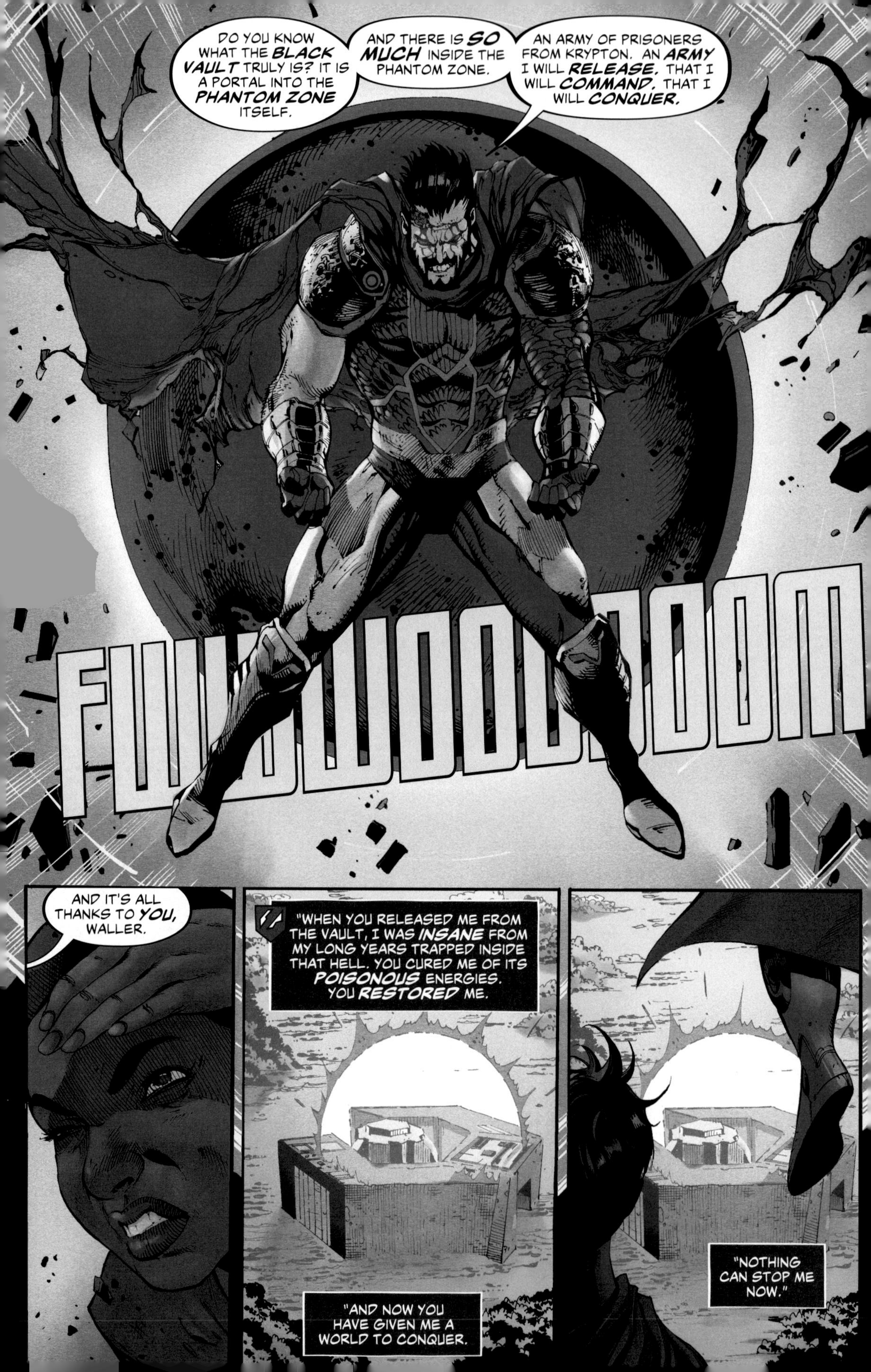
DO YOU KNOW WHAT THE BLACK VAULT TRULY IS? IT IS A PORTAL INTO THE PHANTOM ZONE ITSELF.
AND THERE IS SO MUCH INSIDE THE PHANTOM ZONE.
AN ARMY OF PRISONERS FROM KRYPTON. AN ARMY I WILL RELEASE. THAT I WILL COMMAND. THAT I WILL CONQUER.
AND IT'S ALL THANKS TO YOU, WALLER.
"WHEN YOU RELEASED ME FROM THE VAULT, I WAS INSANE FROM MY LONG YEARS TRAPPED INSIDE THAT HELL. YOU CURED ME OF ITS POISONOUS ENERGIES. YOU RESTORED ME.
"AND NOW YOU HAVE GIVEN ME A WORLD TO CONQUER.
"NOTHING CAN STOP ME NOW."

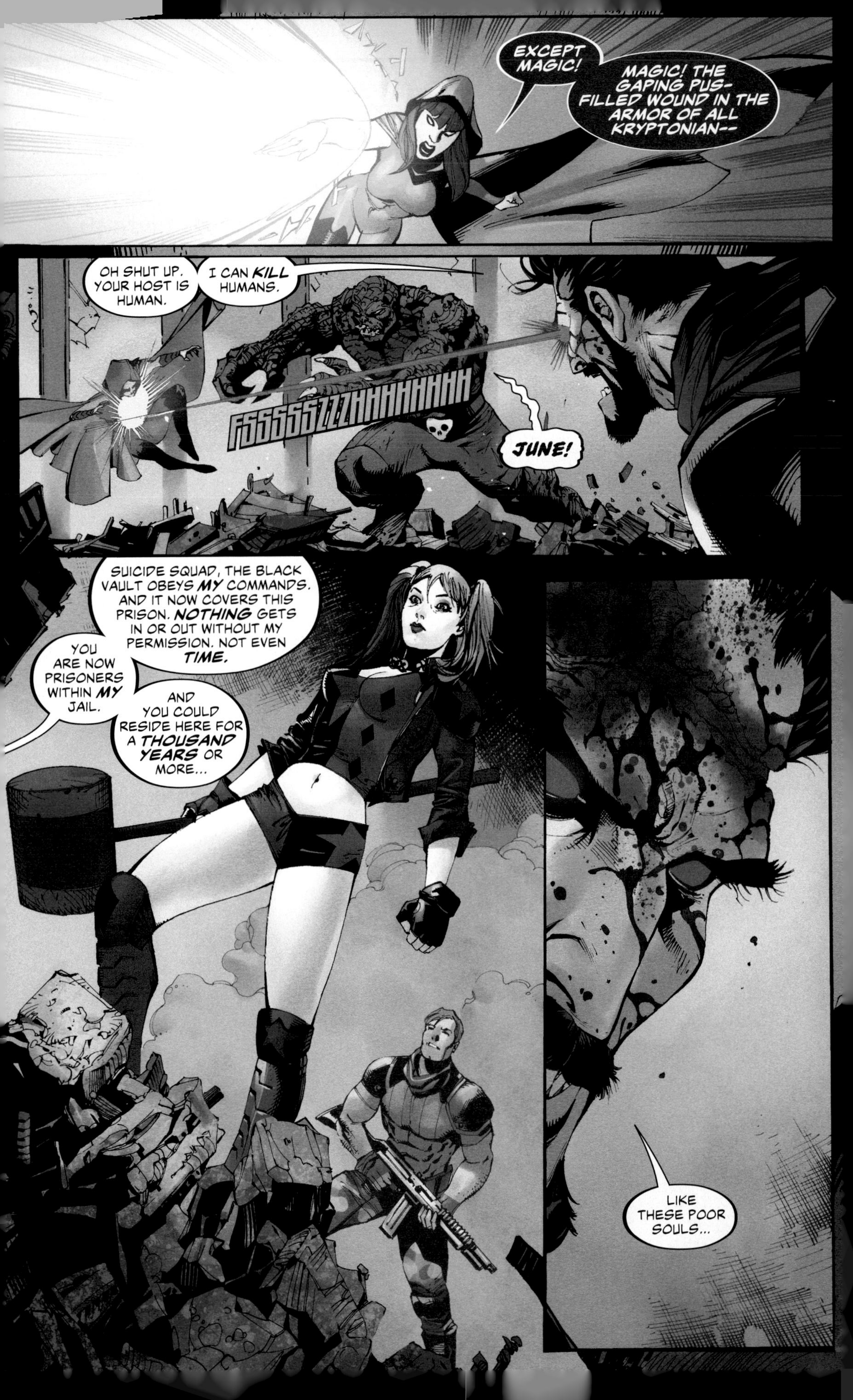
EXCEPT MAGIC!
MAGIC! THE GAPING PUS-FILLED WOUND IN THE ARMOR OF ALL KRYPTONIAN--
OH SHUT UP. YOUR HOST IS HUMAN.
I CAN KILL HUMANS.
FSSSSSZZZHHHHHHHH
JUNE!
SUICIDE SQUAD, THE BLACK VAULT OBEYS MY COMMANDS. AND IT NOW COVERS THIS PRISON. NOTHING GETS IN OR OUT WITHOUT MY PERMISSION. NOT EVEN TIME.
YOU ARE NOW PRISONERS WITHIN MY JAIL.
AND YOU COULD RESIDE HERE FOR A THOUSAND YEARS OR MORE...
LIKE THESE POOR SOULS...

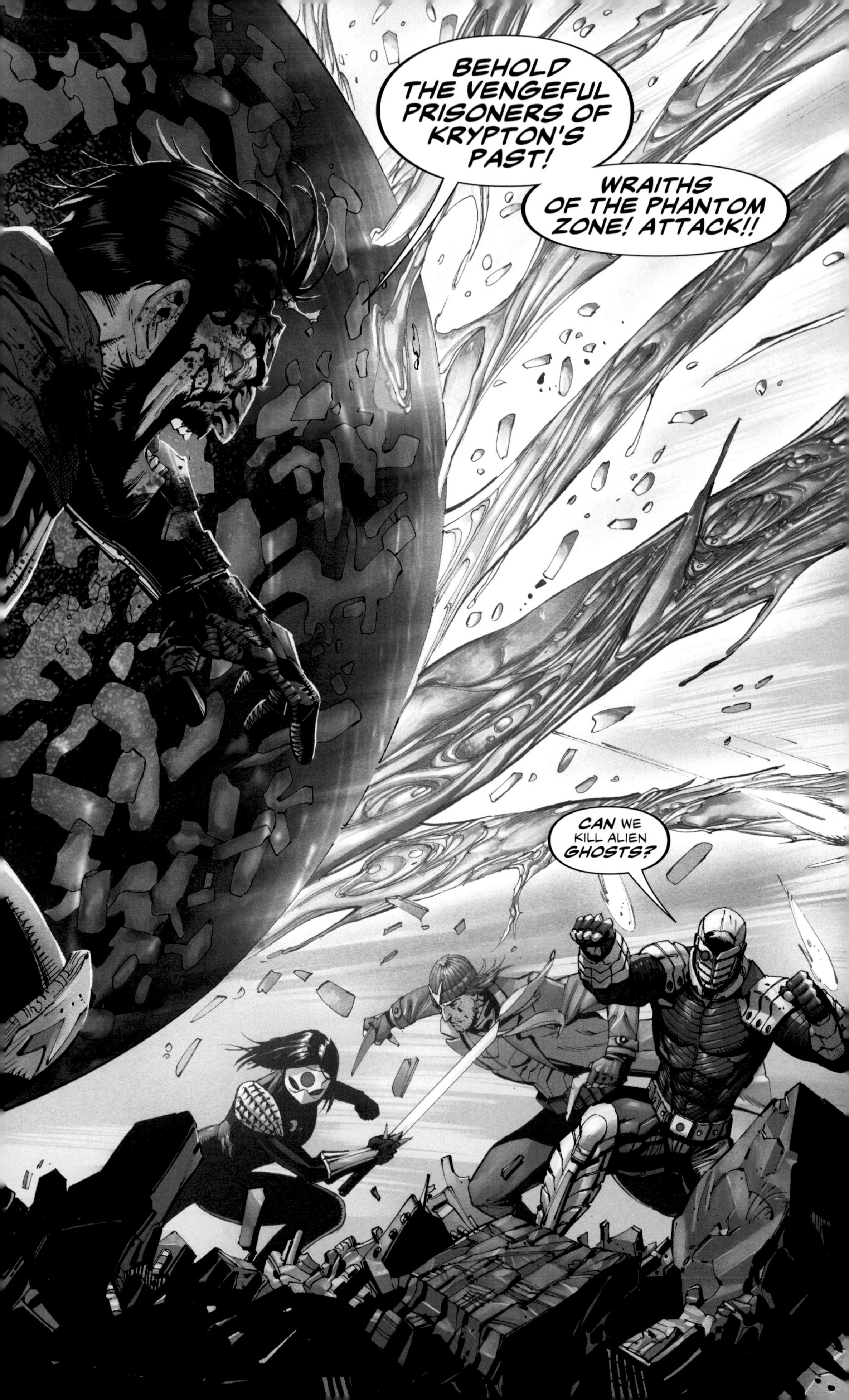
BEHOLD THE VENGEFUL PRISONERS OF KRYPTON'S PAST!
WRAITHS OF THE PHANTOM ZONE! ATTACK!!
CAN WE KILL ALIEN GHOSTS?

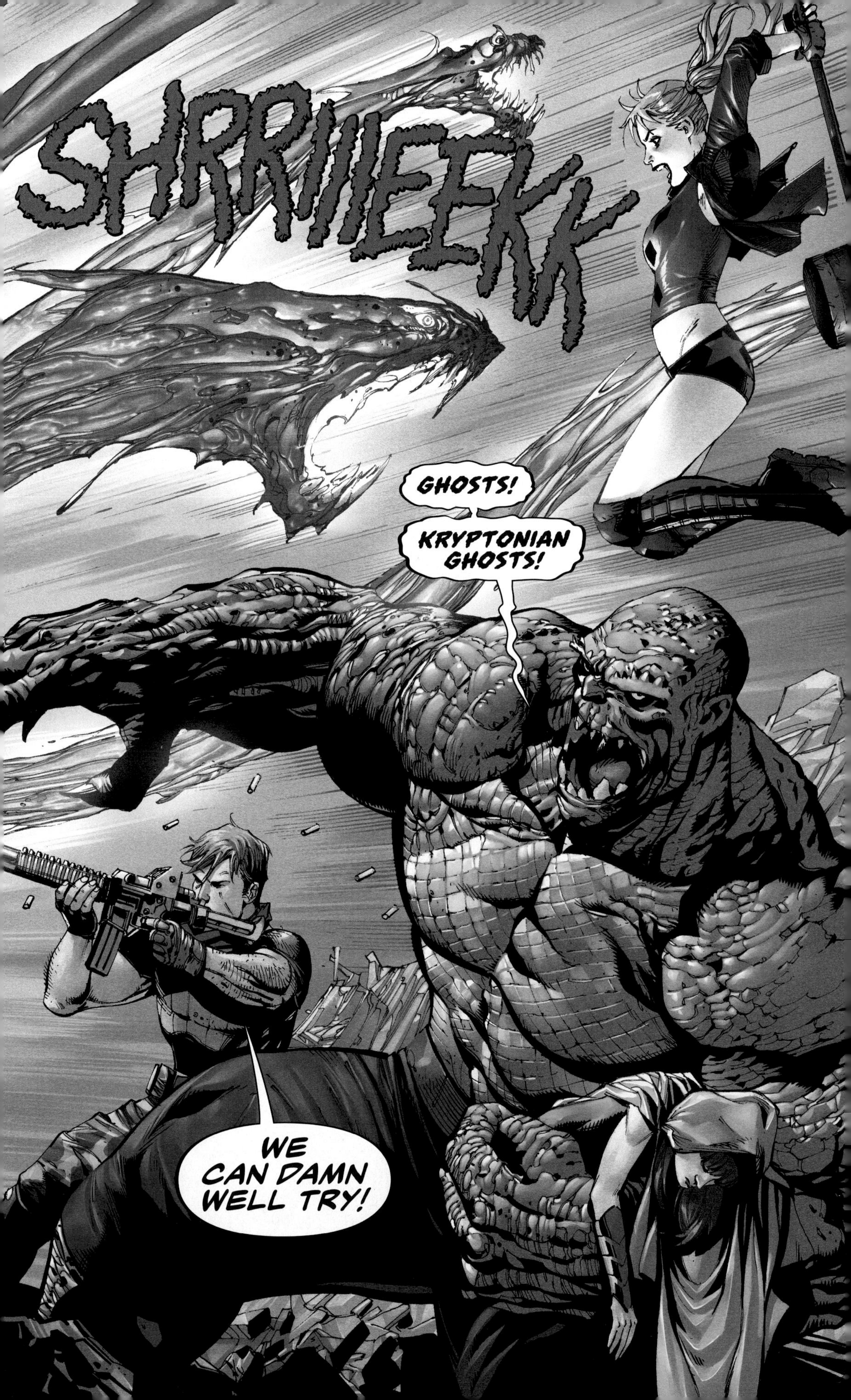
SHRRIIIEEKK
GHOSTS!
KRYPTONIAN GHOSTS!
WE CAN DAMN WELL TRY!

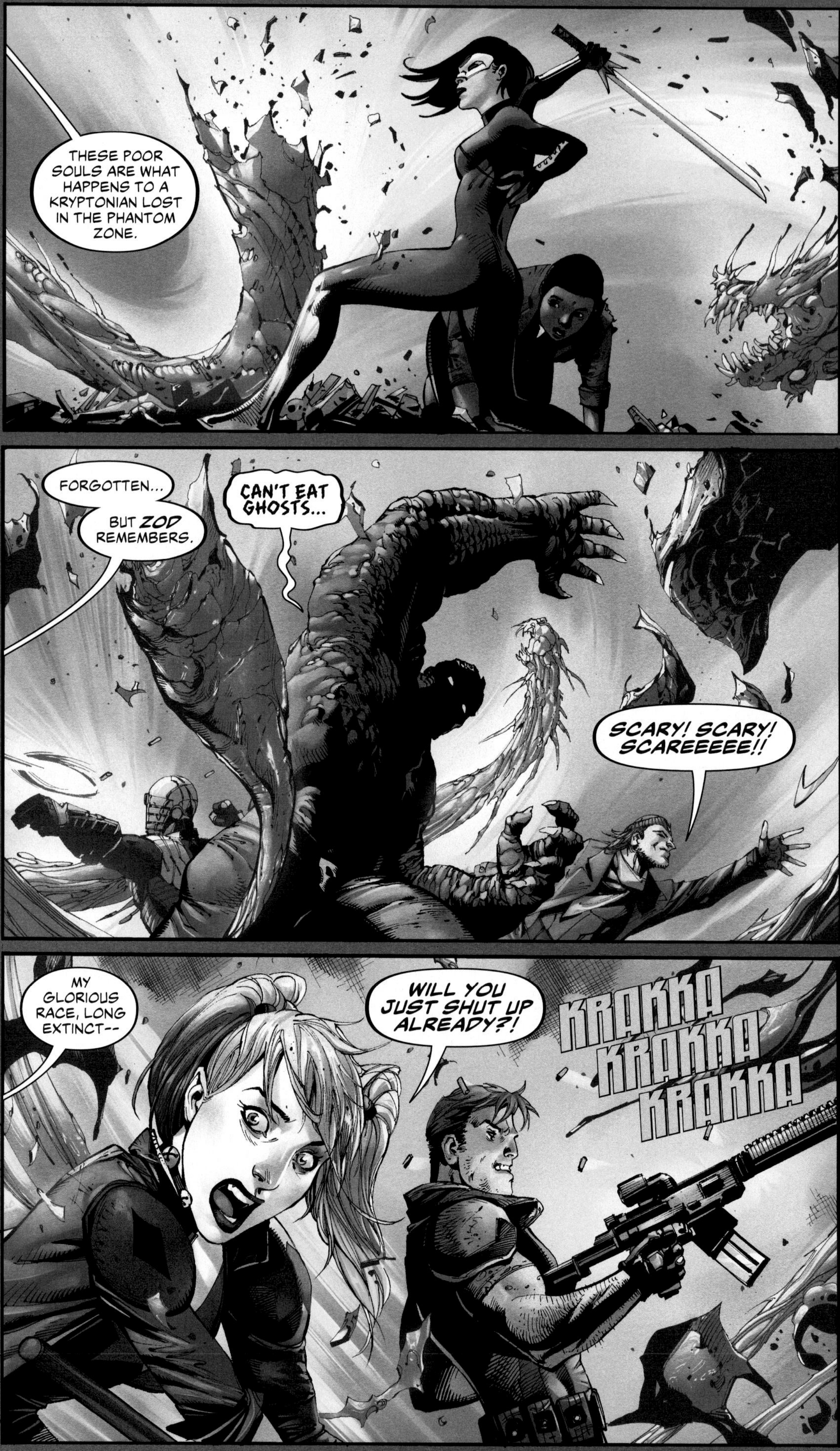
THESE POOR SOULS ARE WHAT HAPPENS TO A KRYPTONIAN LOST IN THE PHANTOM ZONE.
FORGOTTEN...
BUT ZOD REMEMBERS.
CAN'T EAT GHOSTS...
SCARY! SCARY! SCAREEEEE!!
MY GLORIOUS RACE, LONG EXTINCT--
WILL YOU JUST SHUT UP ALREADY?!
KRAKKA KRAKKA KRAKKA

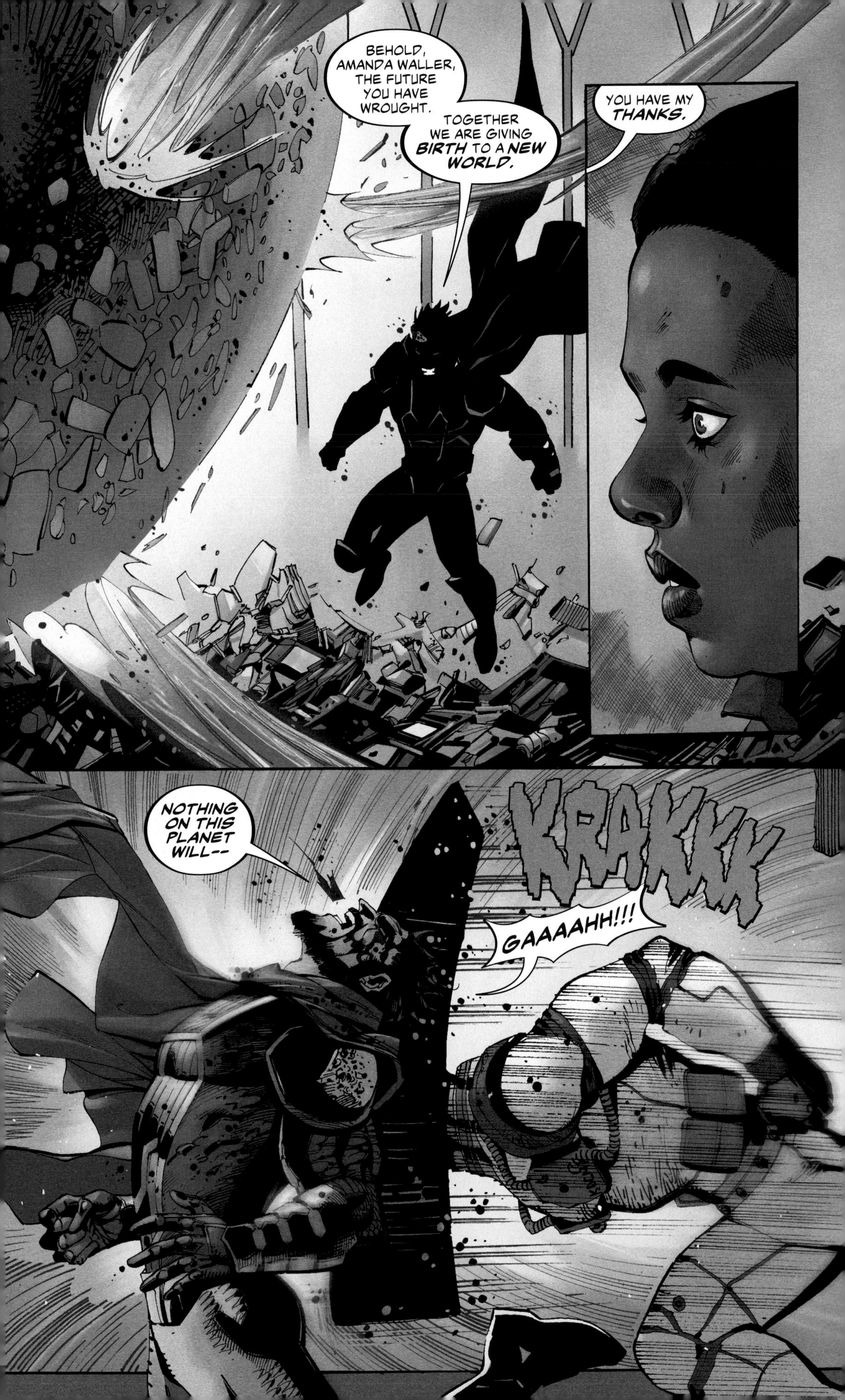
BEHOLD, AMANDA WALLER, THE FUTURE YOU HAVE WROUGHT.
TOGETHER WE ARE GIVING BIRTH TO A NEW WORLD.
YOU HAVE MY THANKS.
NOTHING ON THIS PLANET WILL--
KRAKKK
GAAAAHH!!!

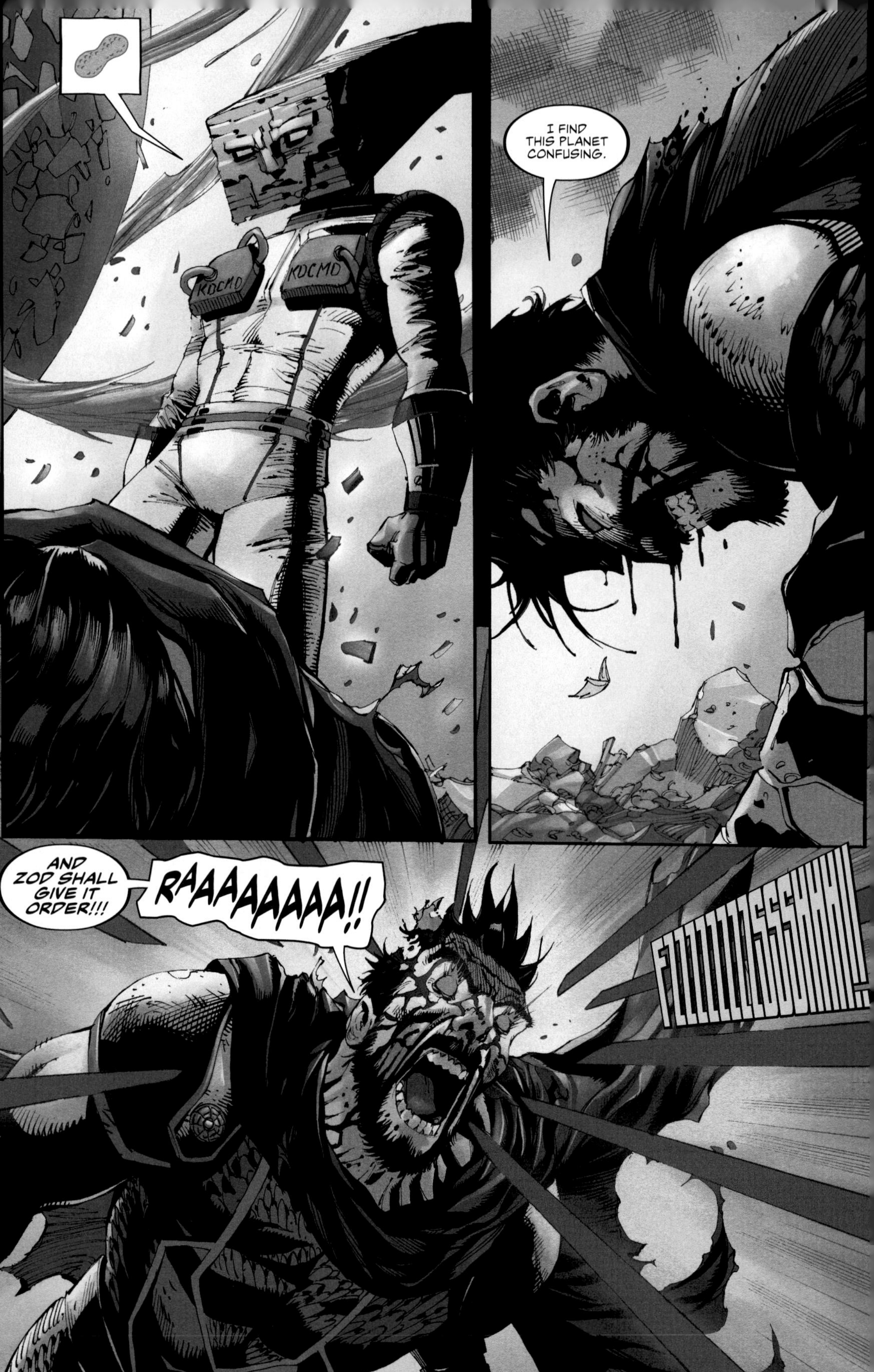
KDCMD
KDCMD
I FIND THIS PLANET CONFUSING.
AND ZOD SHALL GIVE IT ORDER!!!
RAAAAAAAAA!!
FZZZZZZZSSSHHH!!

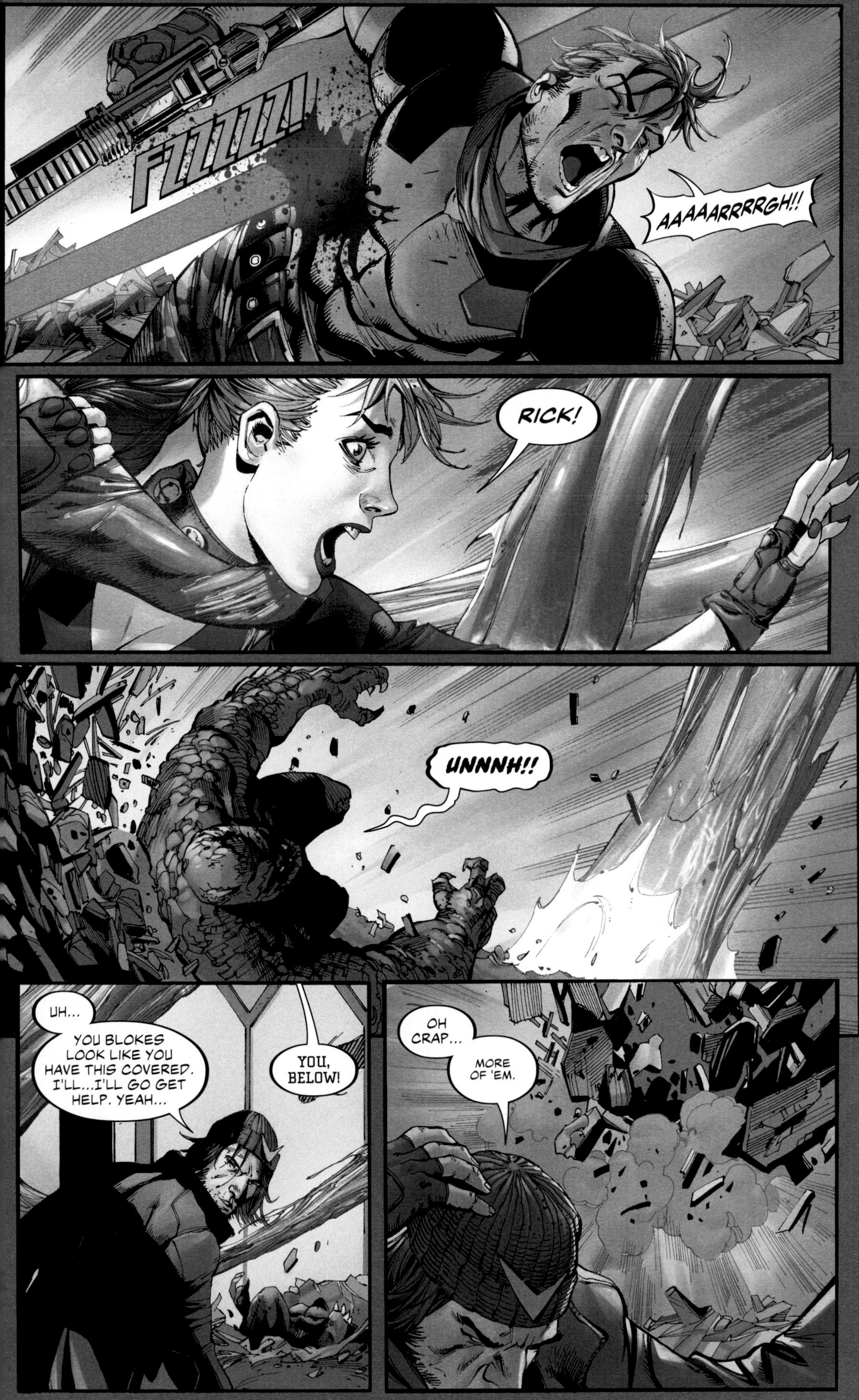
FZZZZZ!
AAAAARRRRGH!!
RICK!
UNNNH!!
UH...
YOU BLOKES LOOK LIKE YOU HAVE THIS COVERED. I'LL...I'LL GO GET HELP. YEAH...
YOU, BELOW!
OH CRAP...
MORE OF 'EM.

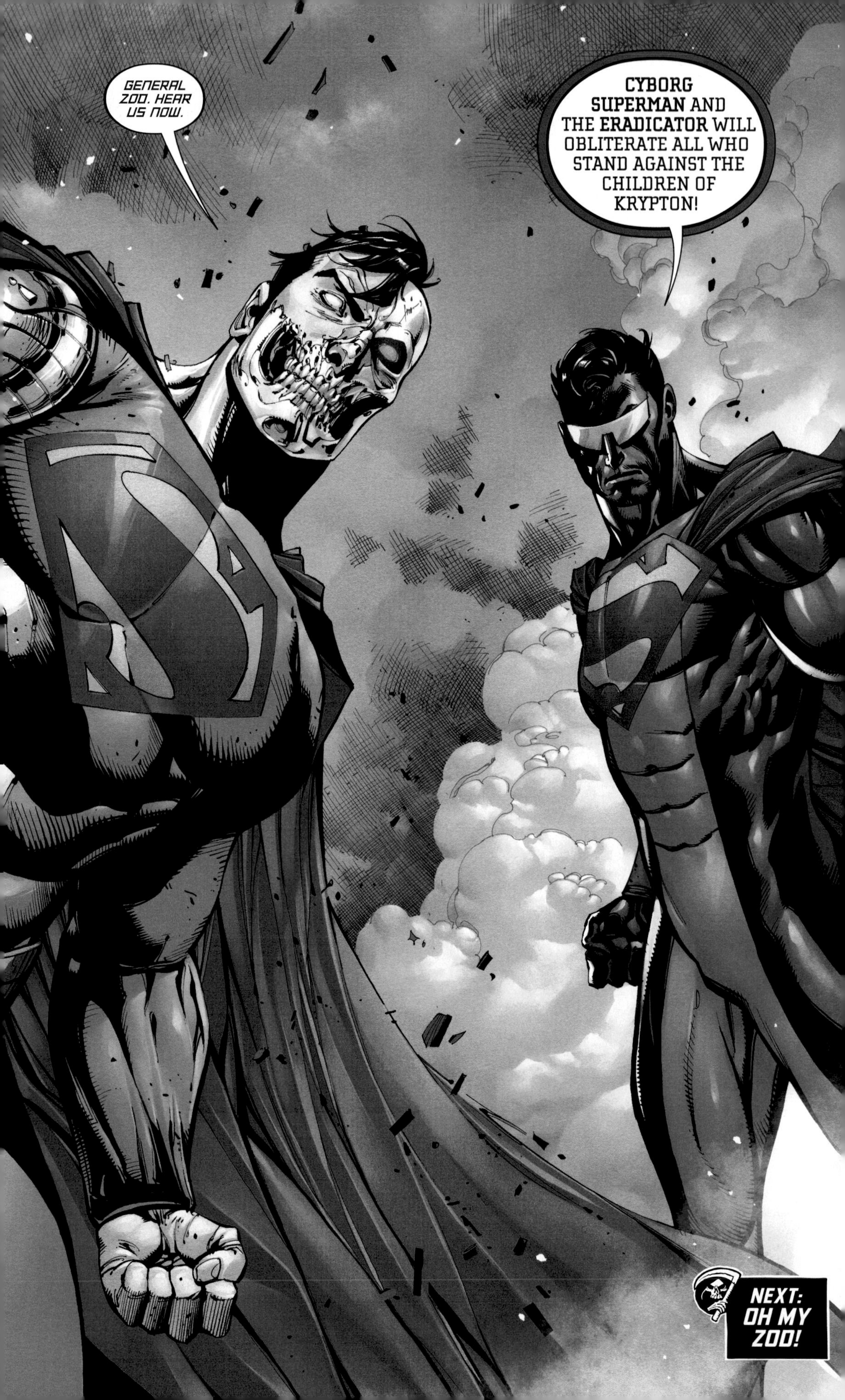
GENERAL ZOD. HEAR US NOW.
CYBORG SUPERMAN AND THE ERADICATOR WILL OBLITERATE ALL WHO STAND AGAINST THE CHILDREN OF KRYPTON!
NEXT: OH MY ZOD!

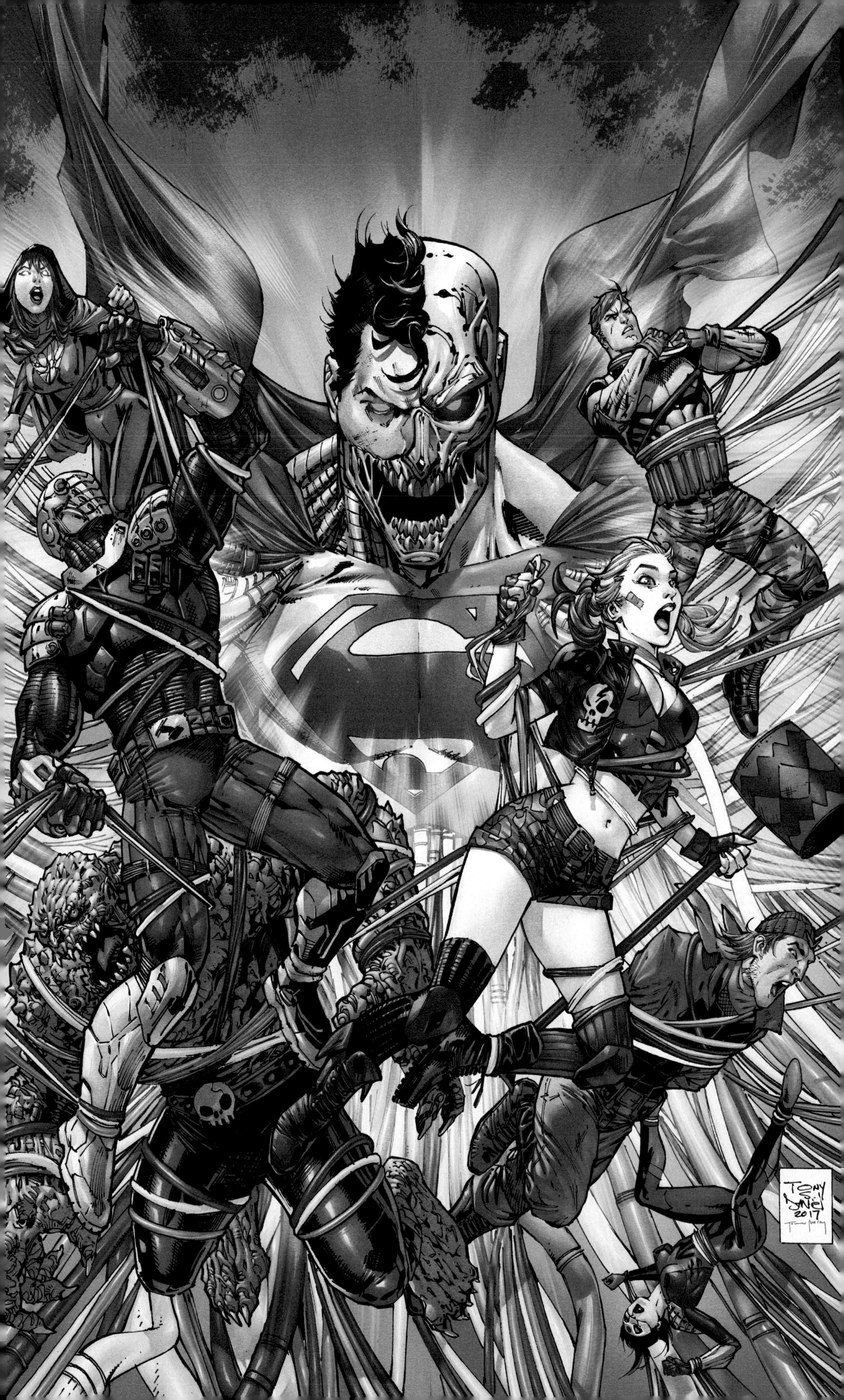
TONY S. DANIEL 2017

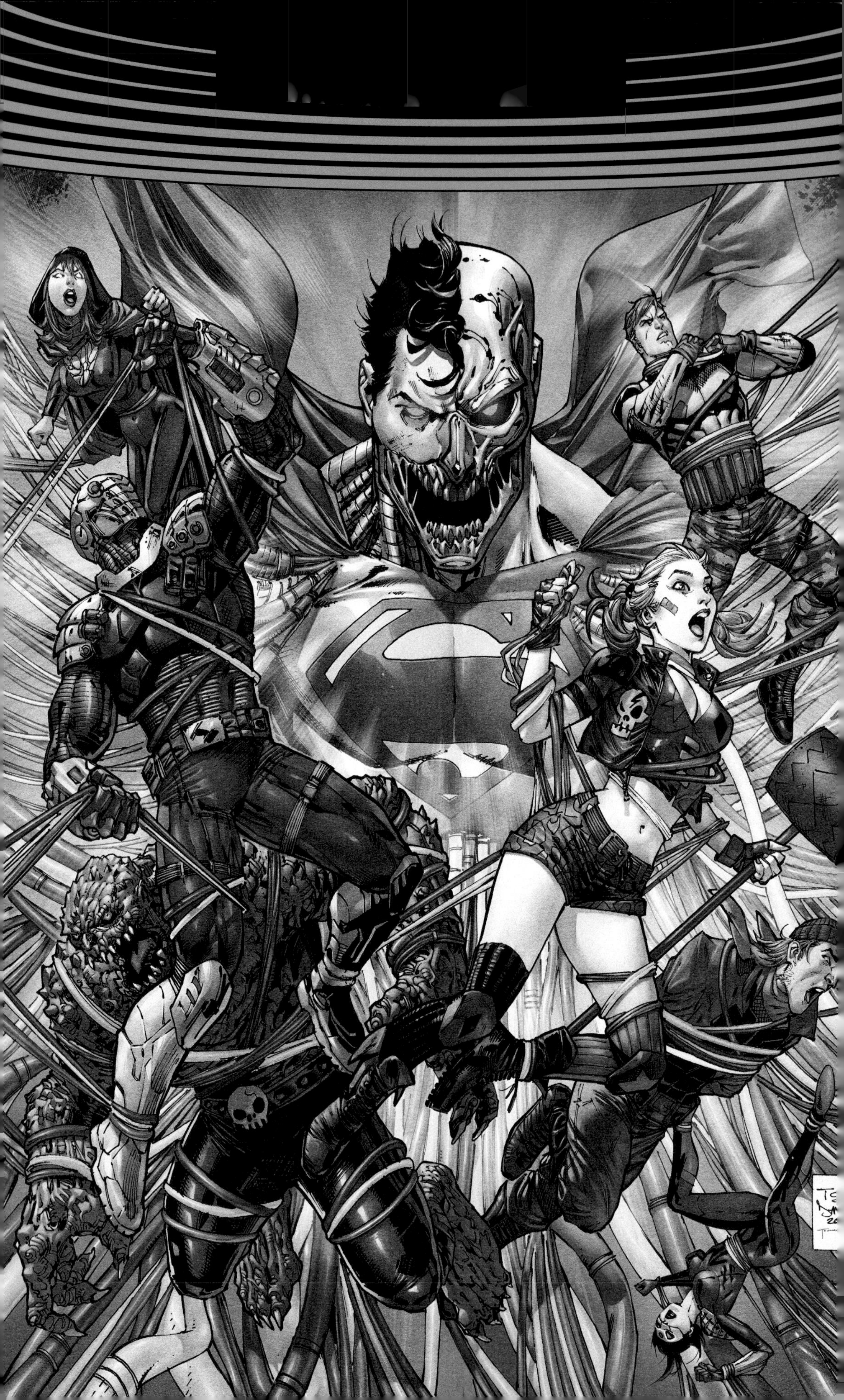

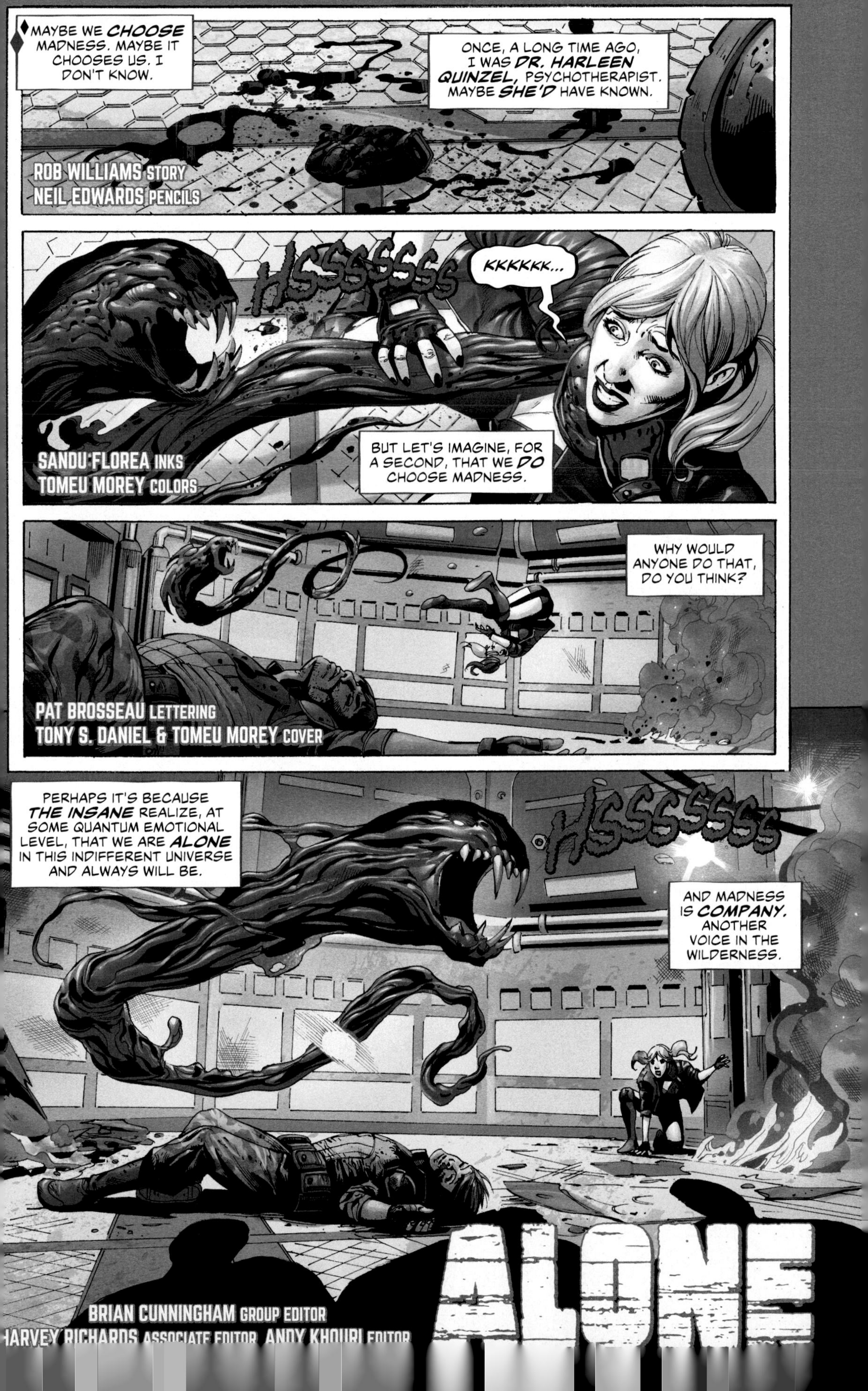
MAYBE WE CHOOSE MADNESS. MAYBE IT CHOOSES US. I DON'T KNOW.
ONCE, A LONG TIME AGO, I WAS DR. HARLEEN QUINZEL, PSYCHOTHERAPIST. MAYBE SHE'D HAVE KNOWN.
ROB WILLIAMS STORY
NEIL EDWARDS PENCILS
HSSSSSSS
KKKKKK...
SANDU FLOREA INKS
TOMEU MOREY COLORS
BUT LET'S IMAGINE, FOR A SECOND, THAT WE DO CHOOSE MADNESS.
WHY WOULD ANYONE DO THAT, DO YOU THINK?
PAT BROSSEAU LETTERING
TONY S. DANIEL & TOMEU MOREY COVER
PERHAPS IT'S BECAUSE THE INSANE REALIZE, AT SOME QUANTUM EMOTIONAL LEVEL, THAT WE ARE ALONE IN THIS INDIFFERENT UNIVERSE AND ALWAYS WILL BE.
HSSSSSSS
AND MADNESS IS COMPANY. ANOTHER VOICE IN THE WILDERNESS.
ALONE
BRIAN CUNNINGHAM GROUP EDITOR
HARVEY RICHARDS ASSOCIATE EDITOR ANDY KHOURI EDITOR

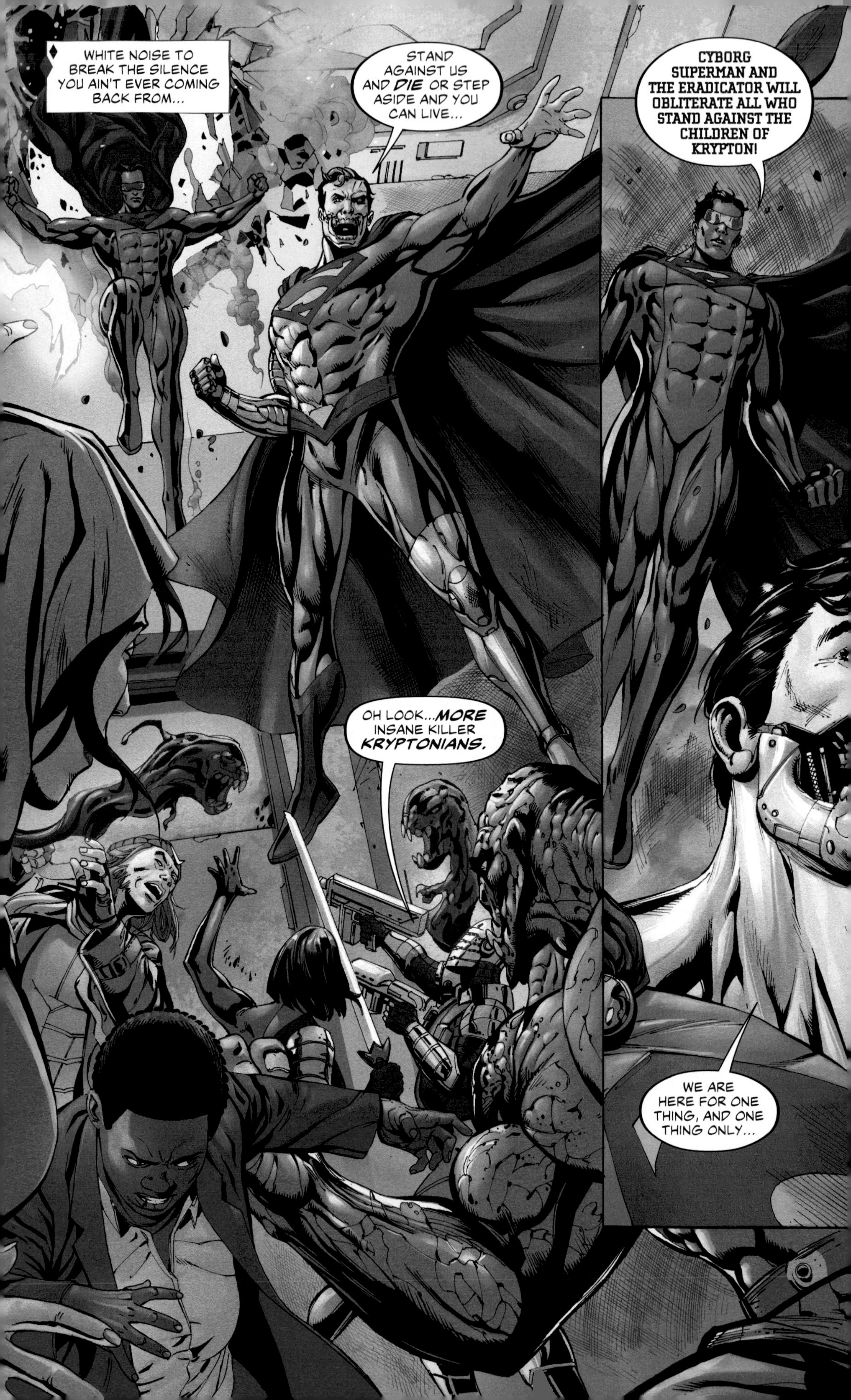
WHITE NOISE TO BREAK THE SILENCE YOU AIN'T EVER COMING BACK FROM...
STAND AGAINST US AND DIE OR STEP ASIDE AND YOU CAN LIVE...
CYBORG SUPERMAN AND THE ERADICATOR WILL OBLITERATE ALL WHO STAND AGAINST THE CHILDREN OF KRYPTON!
OH LOOK...MORE INSANE KILLER KRYPTONIANS.
WE ARE HERE FOR ONE THING, AND ONE THING ONLY...

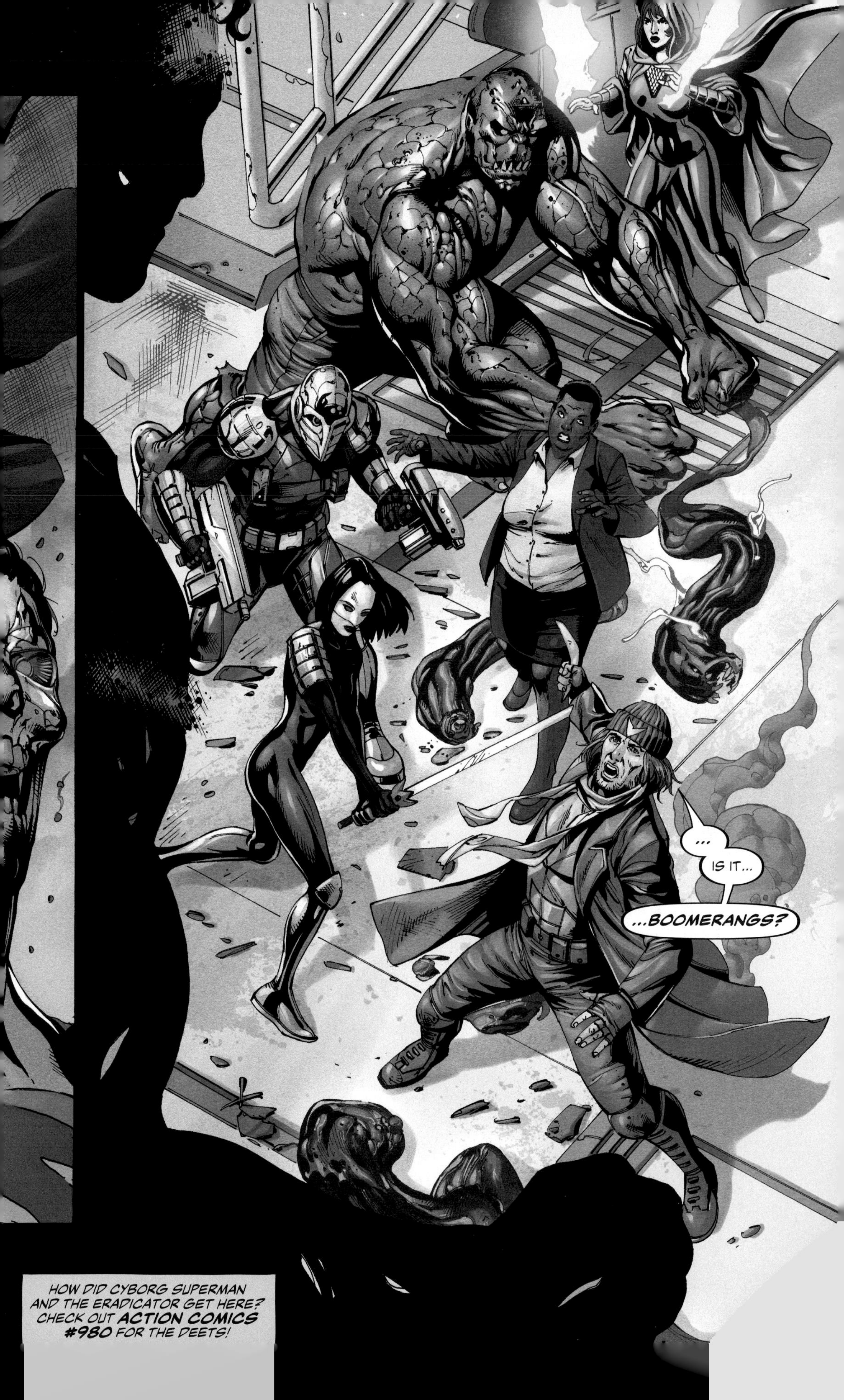
...
IS IT...
...BOOMERANGS?
HOW DID CYBORG SUPERMAN AND THE ERADICATOR GET HERE? CHECK OUT ACTION COMICS #980 FOR THE DEETS!

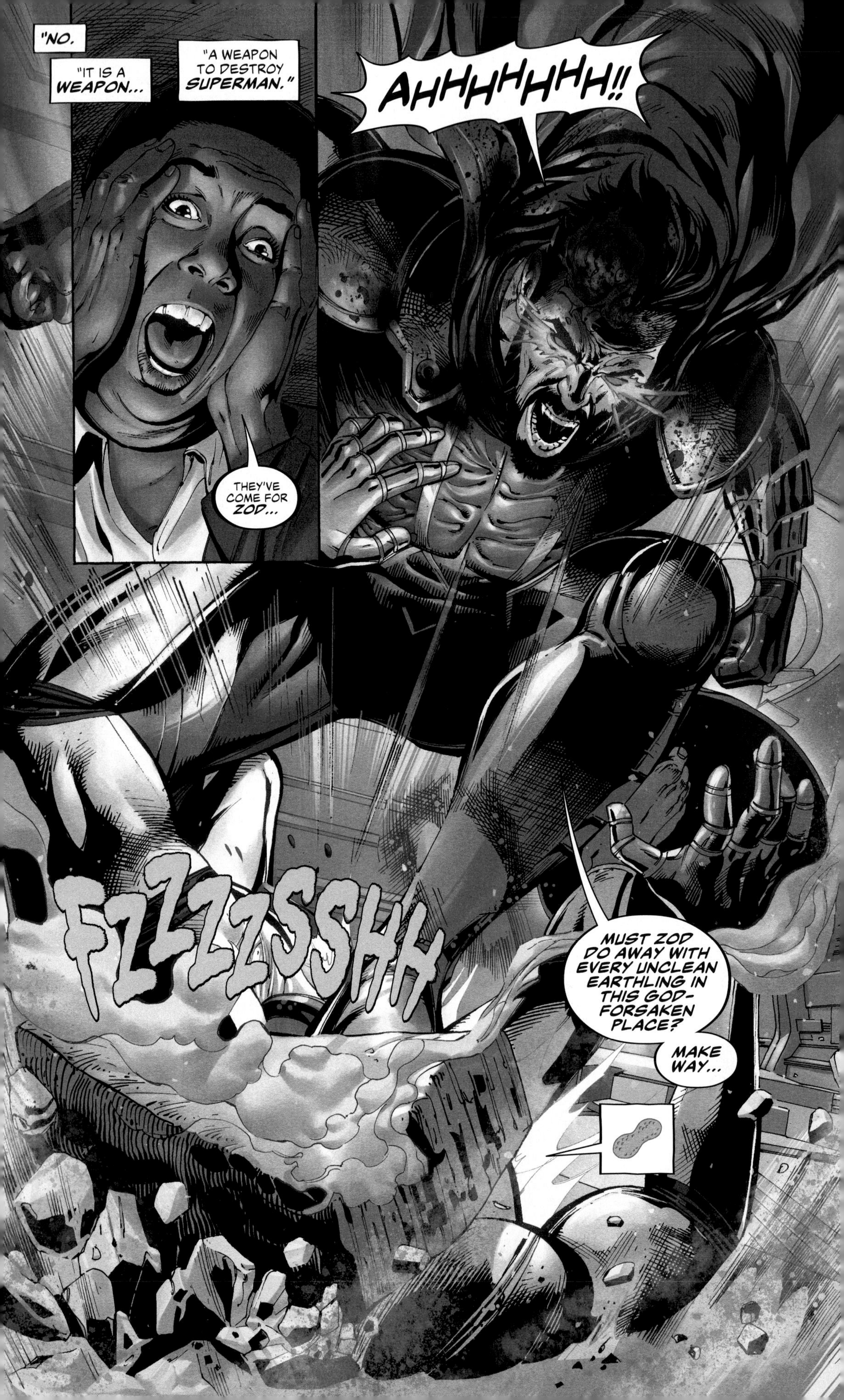
"NO.
"IT IS A WEAPON...
"A WEAPON TO DESTROY SUPERMAN."
AHHHHHHH!!
THEY'VE COME FOR ZOD...
FZZZZSSHH
MUST ZOD DO AWAY WITH EVERY UNCLEAN EARTHLING IN THIS GOD-FORSAKEN PLACE?
MAKE WAY...

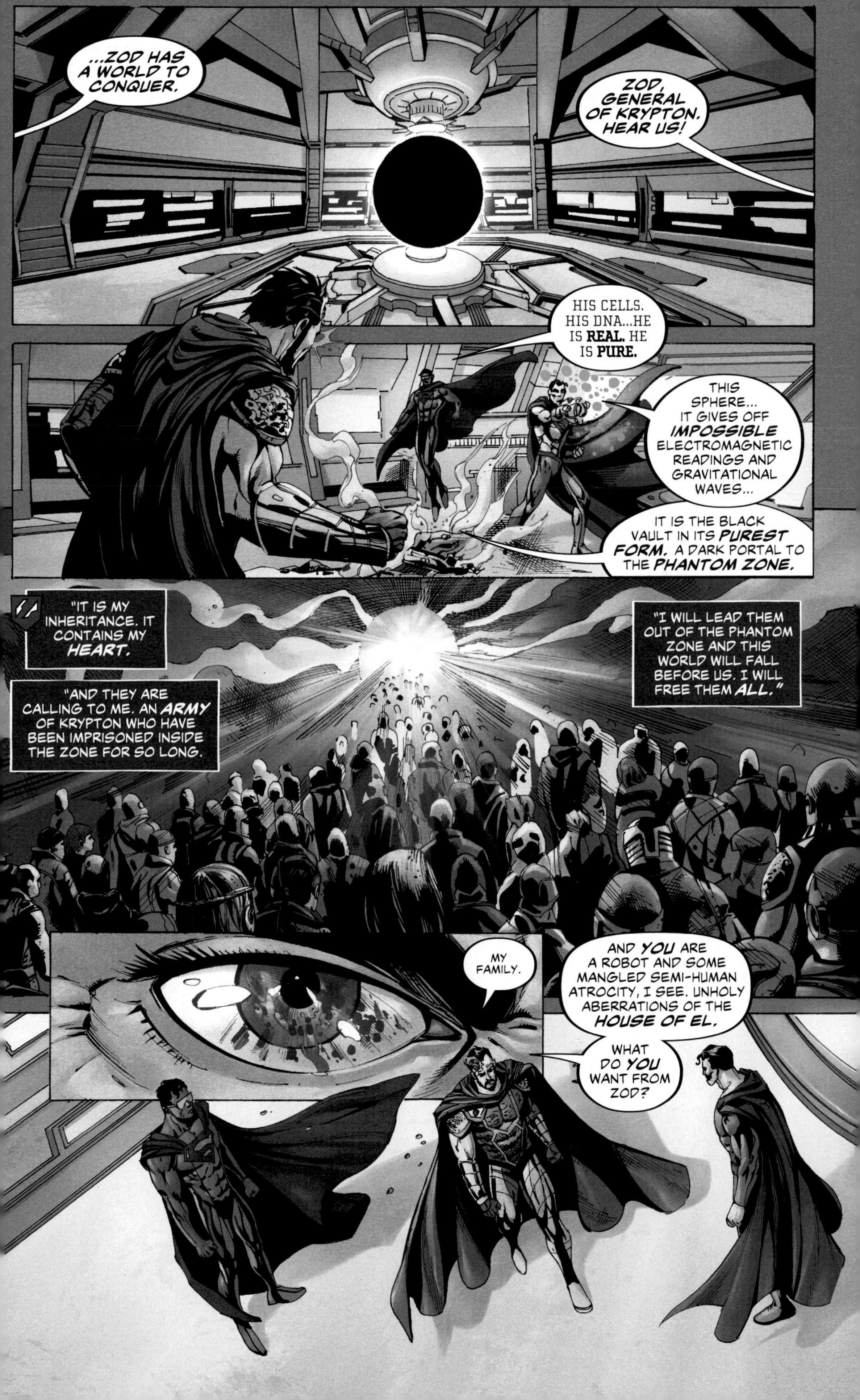
...ZOD HAS A WORLD TO CONQUER.
ZOD, GENERAL OF KRYPTON. HEAR US!
HIS CELLS. HIS DNA...HE IS REAL. HE IS PURE.
THIS SPHERE... IT GIVES OFF IMPOSSIBLE ELECTROMAGNETIC READINGS AND GRAVITATIONAL WAVES...
IT IS THE BLACK VAULT IN ITS PUREST FORM. A DARK PORTAL TO THE PHANTOM ZONE.
"IT IS MY INHERITANCE. IT CONTAINS MY HEART.
"AND THEY ARE CALLING TO ME. AN ARMY OF KRYPTON WHO HAVE BEEN IMPRISONED INSIDE THE ZONE FOR SO LONG.
"I WILL LEAD THEM OUT OF THE PHANTOM ZONE AND THIS WORLD WILL FALL BEFORE US. I WILL FREE THEM ALL."
MY FAMILY.
AND YOU ARE A ROBOT AND SOME MANGLED SEMI-HUMAN ATROCITY, I SEE. UNHOLY ABERRATIONS OF THE HOUSE OF EL.
WHAT DO YOU WANT FROM ZOD?

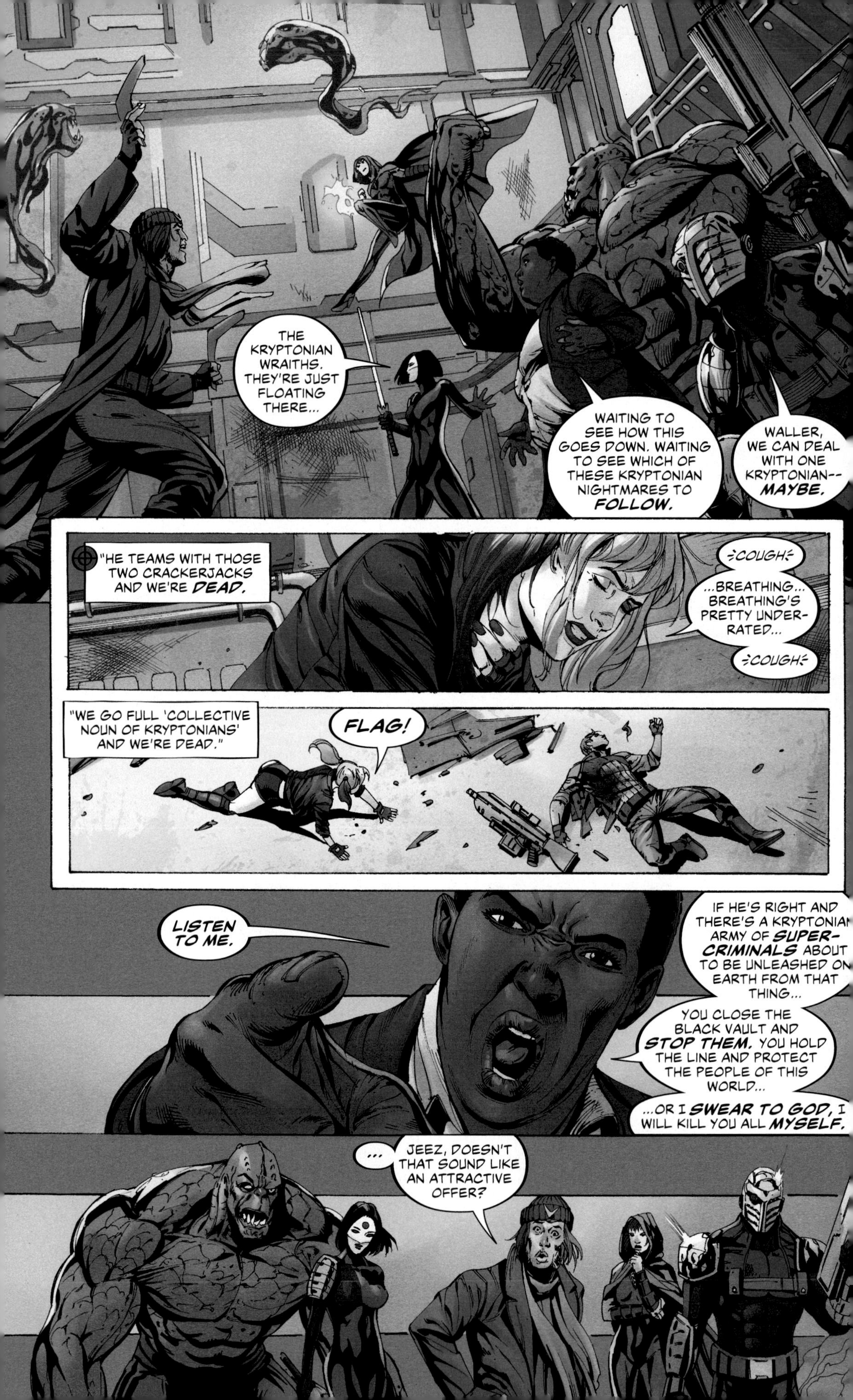
THE KRYPTONIAN WRAITHS. THEY'RE JUST FLOATING THERE...
WAITING TO SEE HOW THIS GOES DOWN. WAITING TO SEE WHICH OF THESE KRYPTONIAN NIGHTMARES TO FOLLOW.
WALLER, WE CAN DEAL WITH ONE KRYPTONIAN-- MAYBE.
"HE TEAMS WITH THOSE TWO CRACKERJACKS AND WE'RE DEAD.
COUGH
...BREATHING... BREATHING'S PRETTY UNDER-RATED...
COUGH
"WE GO FULL 'COLLECTIVE NOUN OF KRYPTONIANS' AND WE'RE DEAD."
FLAG!
LISTEN TO ME.
IF HE'S RIGHT AND THERE'S A KRYPTONIAN ARMY OF SUPER-CRIMINALS ABOUT TO BE UNLEASHED ON EARTH FROM THAT THING...
YOU CLOSE THE BLACK VAULT AND STOP THEM. YOU HOLD THE LINE AND PROTECT THE PEOPLE OF THIS WORLD...
...OR I SWEAR TO GOD, I WILL KILL YOU ALL MYSELF.
...
JEEZ, DOESN'T THAT SOUND LIKE AN ATTRACTIVE OFFER?

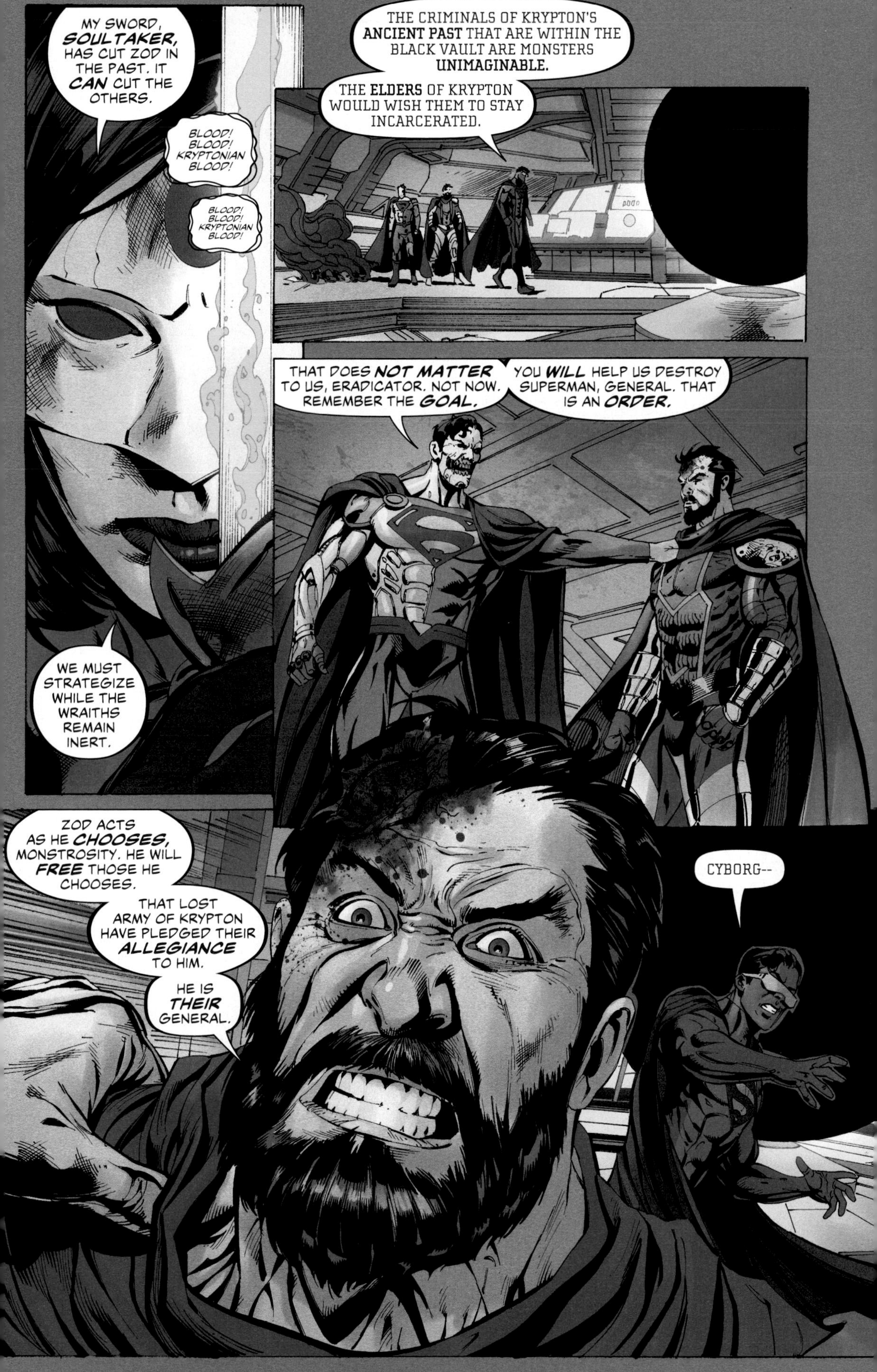
MY SWORD, SOULTAKER, HAS CUT ZOD IN THE PAST. IT CAN CUT THE OTHERS.
THE CRIMINALS OF KRYPTON'S ANCIENT PAST THAT ARE WITHIN THE BLACK VAULT ARE MONSTERS UNIMAGINABLE.
THE ELDERS OF KRYPTON WOULD WISH THEM TO STAY INCARCERATED.
BLOOD! BLOOD! KRYPTONIAN BLOOD!
BLOOD! BLOOD! KRYPTONIAN BLOOD!
THAT DOES NOT MATTER TO US, ERADICATOR. NOT NOW. REMEMBER THE GOAL.
YOU WILL HELP US DESTROY SUPERMAN, GENERAL. THAT IS AN ORDER.
WE MUST STRATEGIZE WHILE THE WRAITHS REMAIN INERT.
ZOD ACTS AS HE CHOOSES, MONSTROSITY. HE WILL FREE THOSE HE CHOOSES.
THAT LOST ARMY OF KRYPTON HAVE PLEDGED THEIR ALLEGIANCE TO HIM.
HE IS THEIR GENERAL.
CYBORG--

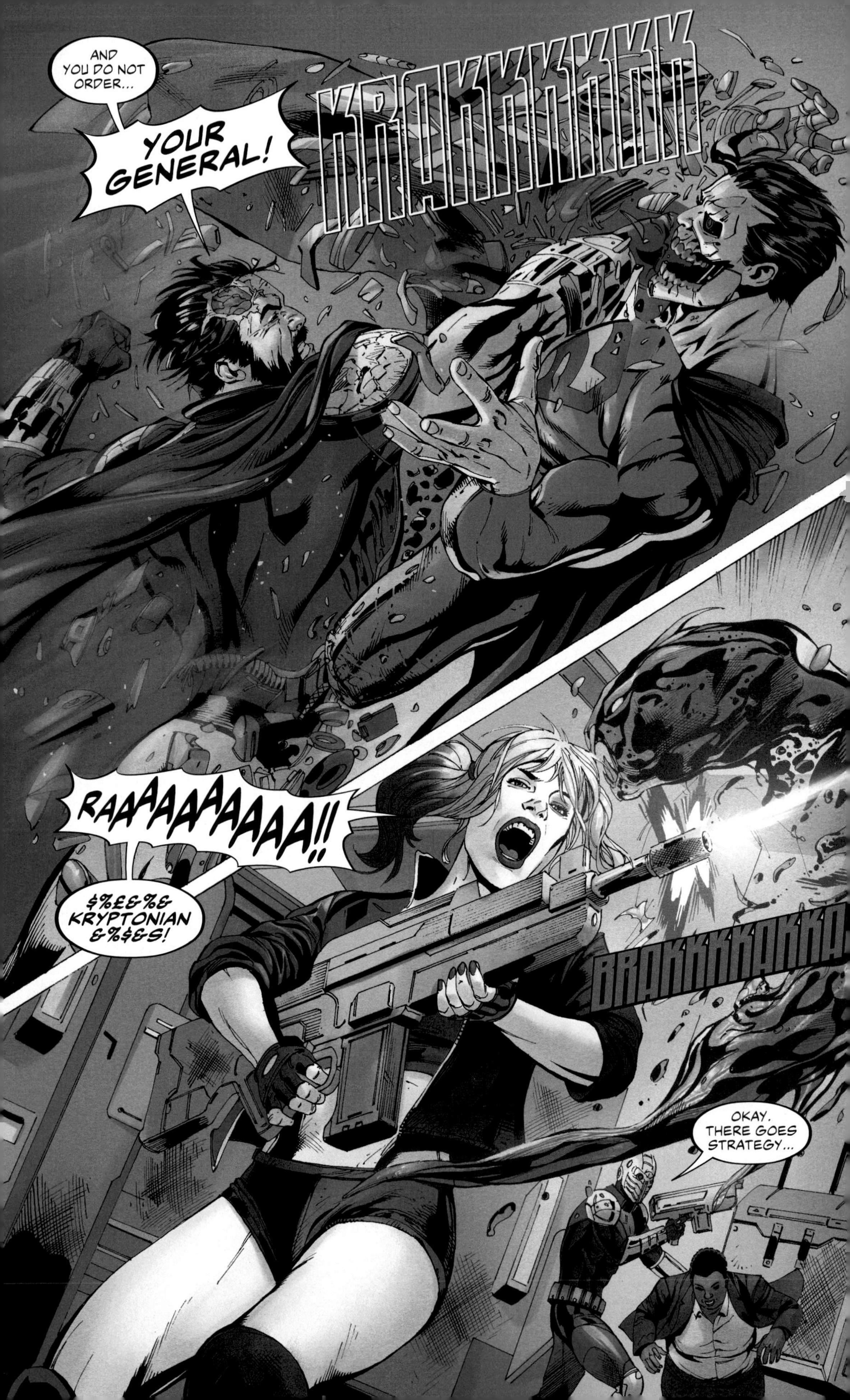
AND YOU DO NOT ORDER...
YOUR GENERAL!
KRAKKKKKKK
RAAAAAAAAAA!!
$%£&%& KRYPTONIAN &%$&S!
BRAKKKAKKA
OKAY. THERE GOES STRATEGY...

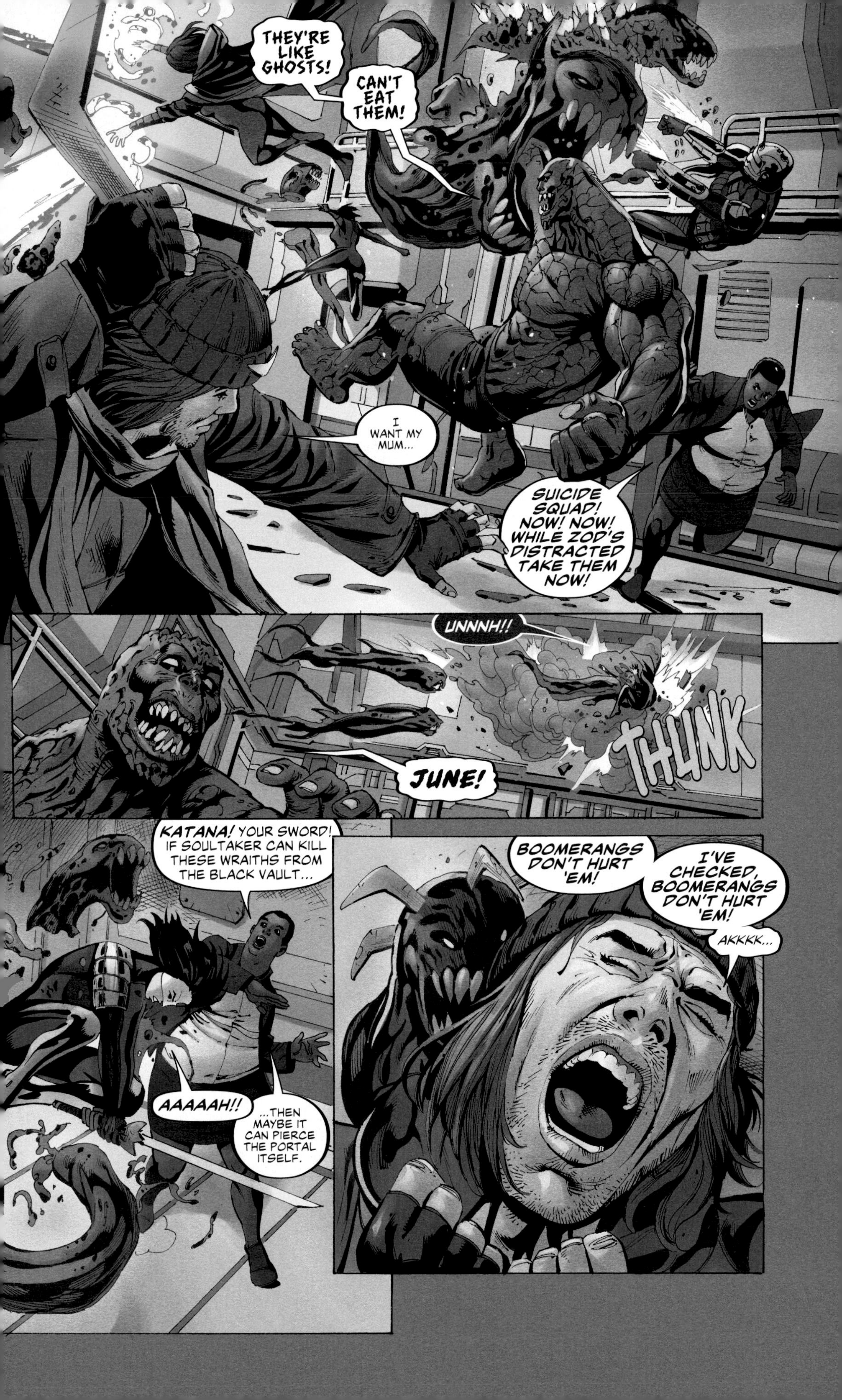
THEY'RE LIKE GHOSTS!
CAN'T EAT THEM!
I WANT MY MUM...
SUICIDE SQUAD! NOW! NOW! WHILE ZOD'S DISTRACTED TAKE THEM NOW!
UNNNH!!
JUNE!
THUNK
KATANA! YOUR SWORD! IF SOULTAKER CAN KILL THESE WRAITHS FROM THE BLACK VAULT...
AAAAAH!!
...THEN MAYBE IT CAN PIERCE THE PORTAL ITSELF.
BOOMERANGS DON'T HURT 'EM!
I'VE CHECKED, BOOMERANGS DON'T HURT 'EM!
AKKKK...

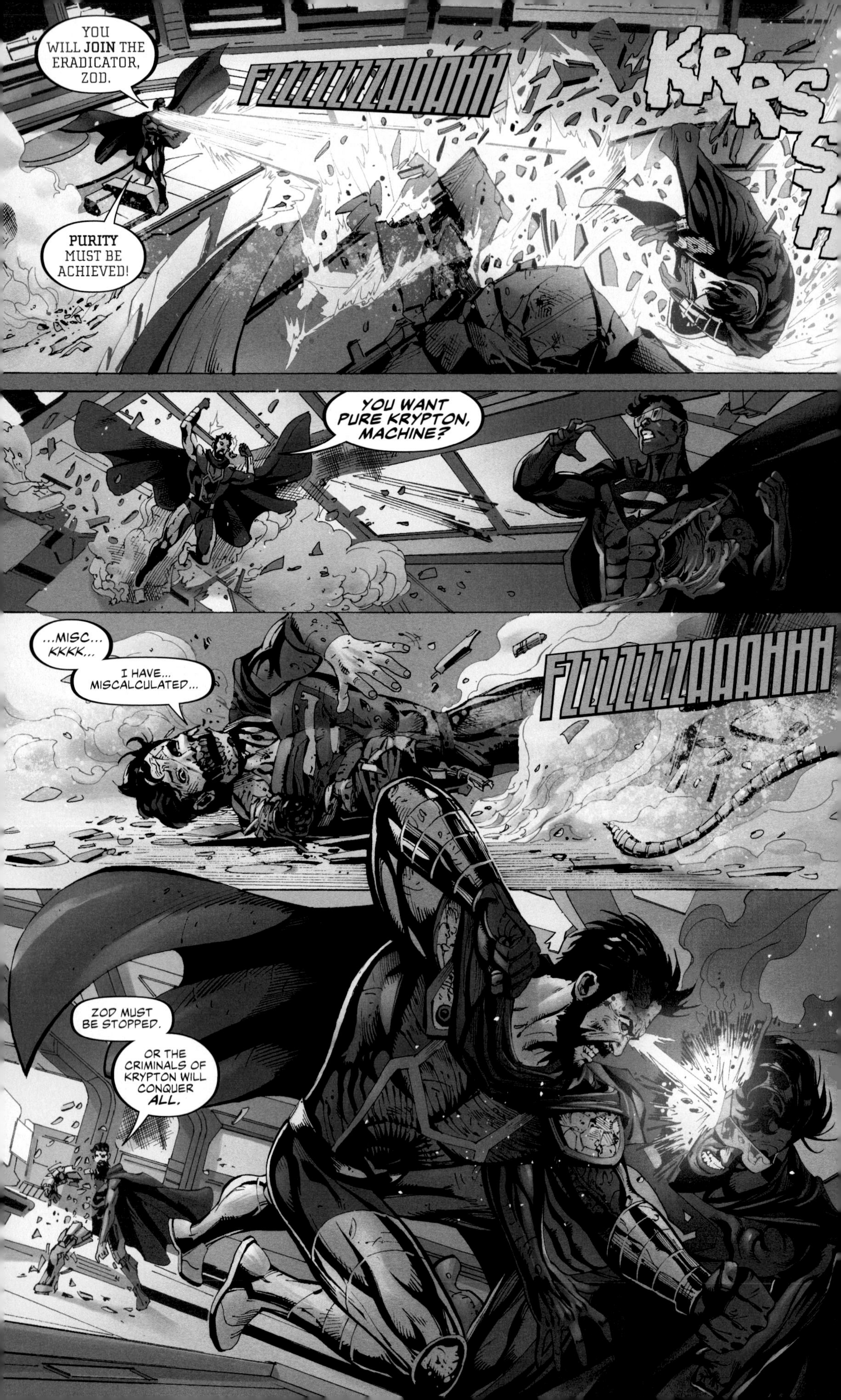
YOU WILL JOIN THE ERADICATOR, ZOD.
FZZZZZZZAAAAHH
KRRSSH
PURITY MUST BE ACHIEVED!
YOU WANT PURE KRYPTON, MACHINE?
...MISC... KKKK...
I HAVE... MISCALCULATED...
FZZZZZZZAAAAHHH
ZOD MUST BE STOPPED.
OR THE CRIMINALS OF KRYPTON WILL CONQUER ALL.

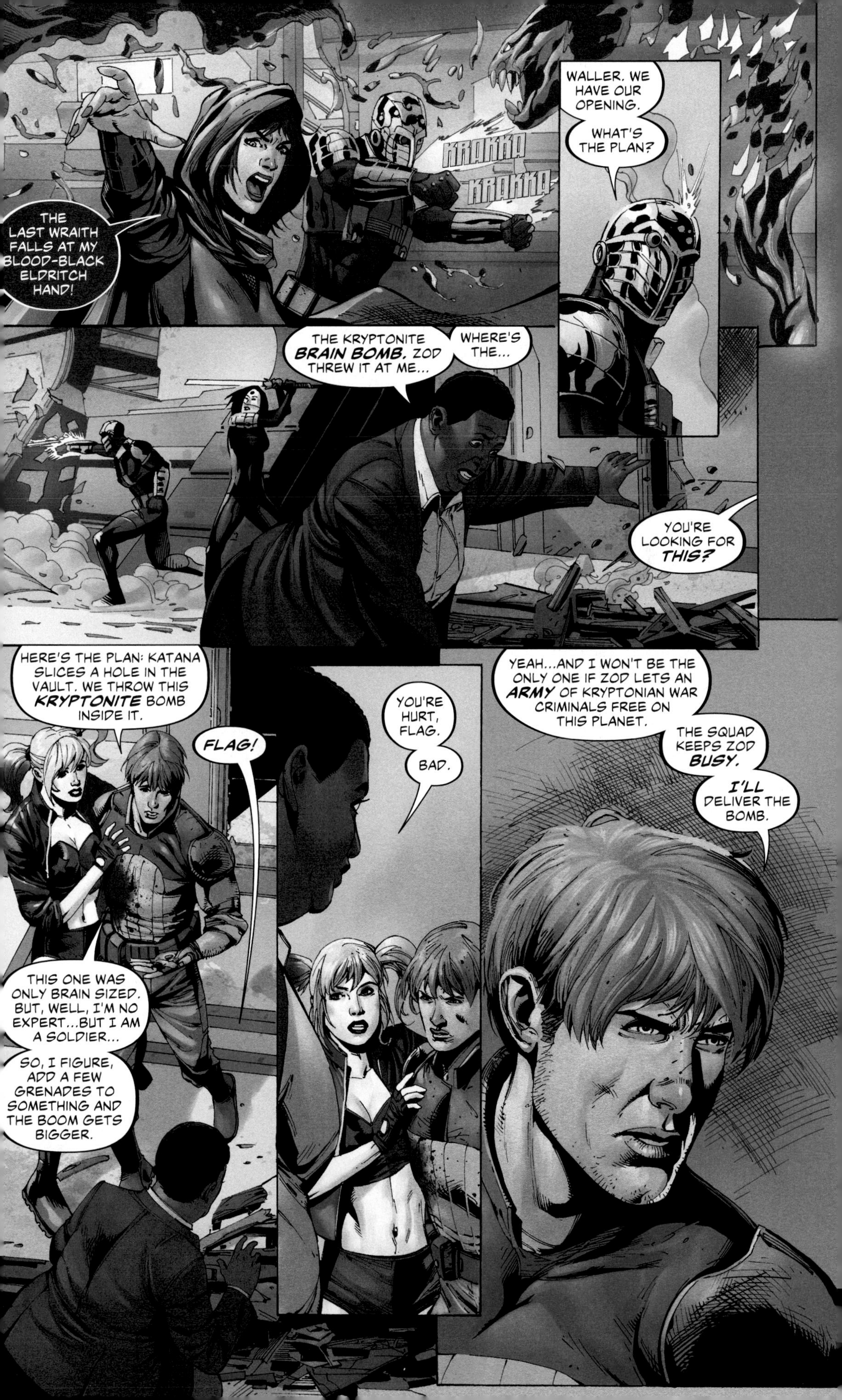
KRAKKA
KRAKKA
THE LAST WRAITH FALLS AT MY BLOOD-BLACK ELDRITCH HAND!
WALLER. WE HAVE OUR OPENING.
WHAT'S THE PLAN?
THE KRYPTONITE BRAIN BOMB. ZOD THREW IT AT ME...
WHERE'S THE...
YOU'RE LOOKING FOR THIS?
HERE'S THE PLAN: KATANA SLICES A HOLE IN THE VAULT. WE THROW THIS KRYPTONITE BOMB INSIDE IT.
THIS ONE WAS ONLY BRAIN SIZED. BUT, WELL, I'M NO EXPERT...BUT I AM A SOLDIER...
SO, I FIGURE, ADD A FEW GRENADES TO SOMETHING AND THE BOOM GETS BIGGER.
FLAG!
YOU'RE HURT, FLAG.
BAD.
YEAH...AND I WON'T BE THE ONLY ONE IF ZOD LETS AN ARMY OF KRYPTONIAN WAR CRIMINALS FREE ON THIS PLANET.
THE SQUAD KEEPS ZOD BUSY.
I'LL DELIVER THE BOMB.

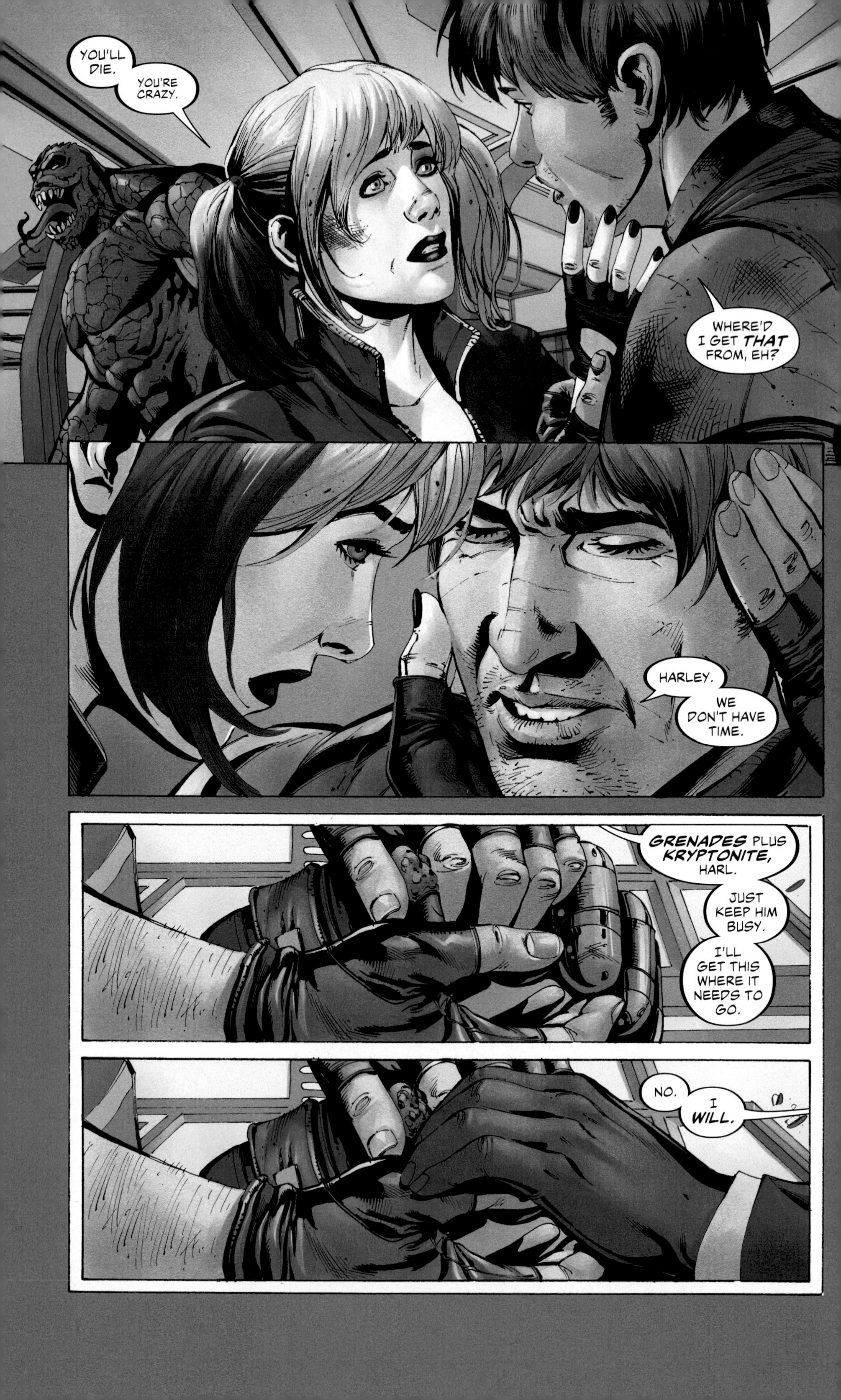
YOU'LL DIE.
YOU'RE CRAZY.
WHERE'D I GET THAT FROM, EH?
HARLEY.
WE DON'T HAVE TIME.
GRENADES PLUS KRYPTONITE, HARL.
JUST KEEP HIM BUSY.
I'LL GET THIS WHERE IT NEEDS TO GO.
NO.
I WILL.

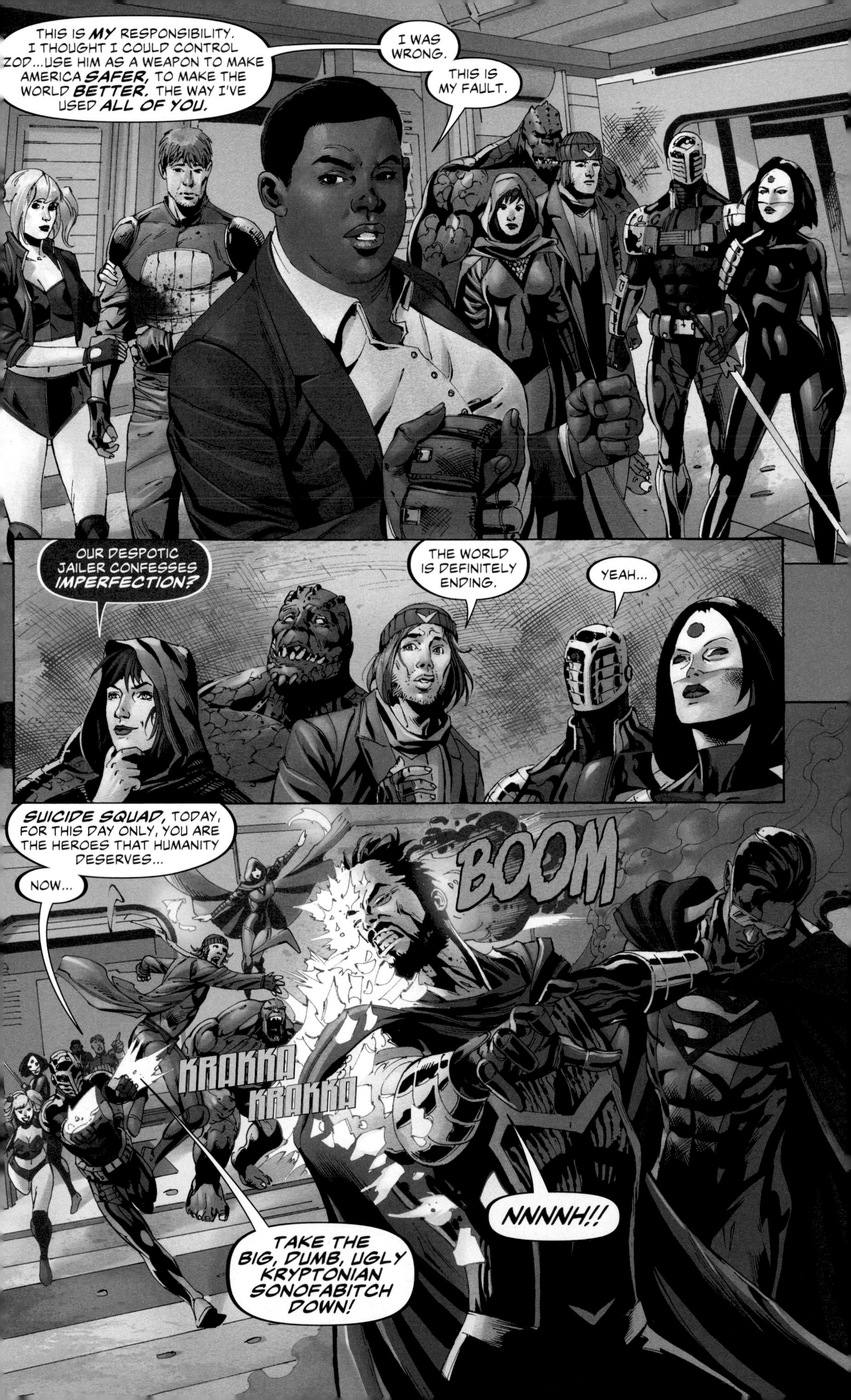

THIS IS MY RESPONSIBILITY. I THOUGHT I COULD CONTROL ZOD...USE HIM AS A WEAPON TO MAKE AMERICA SAFER, TO MAKE THE WORLD BETTER. THE WAY I'VE USED ALL OF YOU.
I WAS WRONG.
THIS IS MY FAULT.
OUR DESPOTIC JAILER CONFESSES IMPERFECTION?
THE WORLD IS DEFINITELY ENDING.
YEAH...
SUICIDE SQUAD, TODAY, FOR THIS DAY ONLY, YOU ARE THE HEROES THAT HUMANITY DESERVES...
NOW...
BOOM
KRAKKA
KRAKKA
NNNNH!!
TAKE THE BIG, DUMB, UGLY KRYPTONIAN SONOFABITCH DOWN!

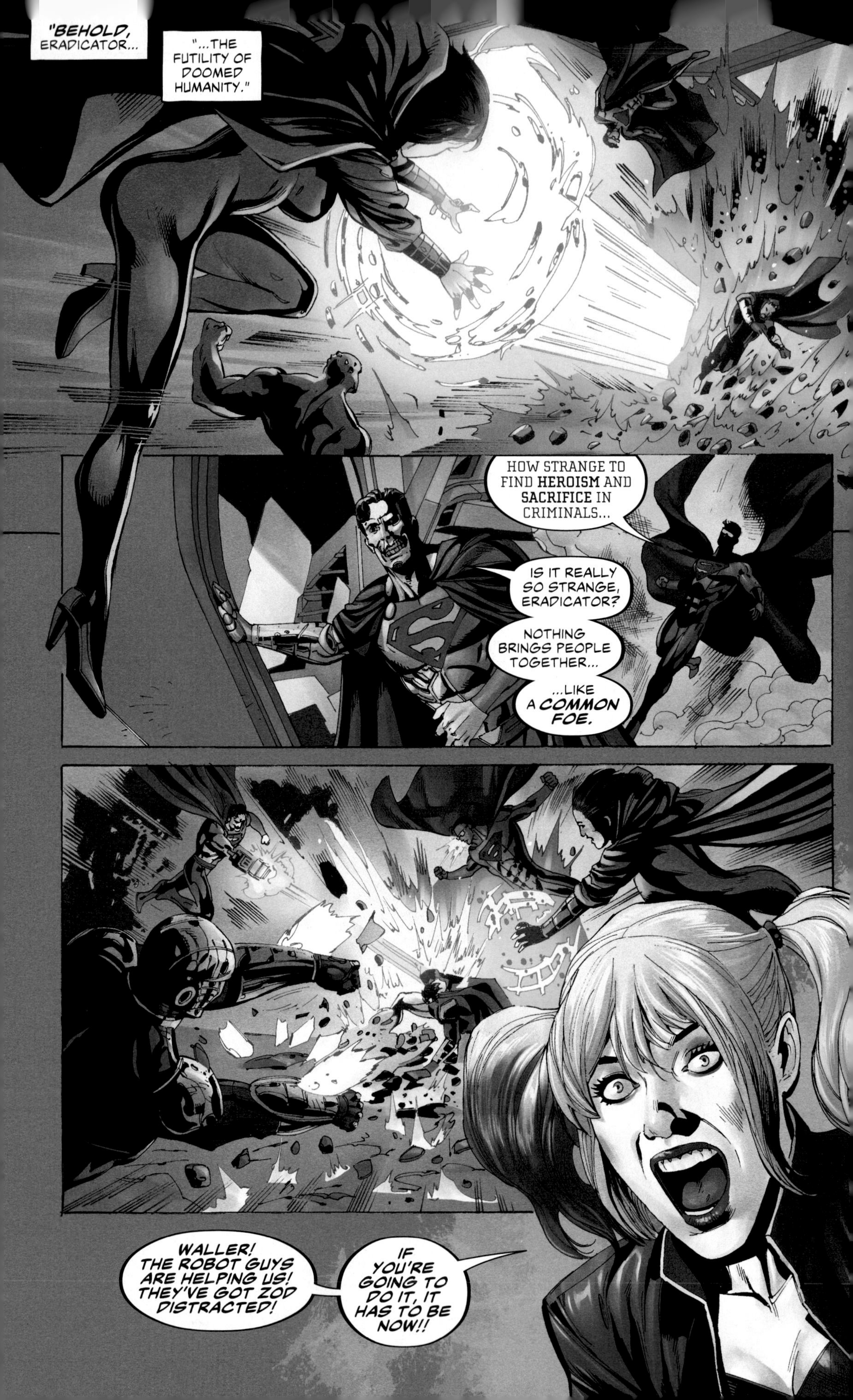
"BEHOLD, ERADICATOR...
"...THE FUTILITY OF DOOMED HUMANITY."
HOW STRANGE TO FIND HEROISM AND SACRIFICE IN CRIMINALS...
IS IT REALLY SO STRANGE, ERADICATOR?
NOTHING BRINGS PEOPLE TOGETHER...
...LIKE A COMMON FOE.
WALLER! THE ROBOT GUYS ARE HELPING US! THEY'VE GOT ZOD DISTRACTED!
IF YOU'RE GOING TO DO IT, IT HAS TO BE NOW!!

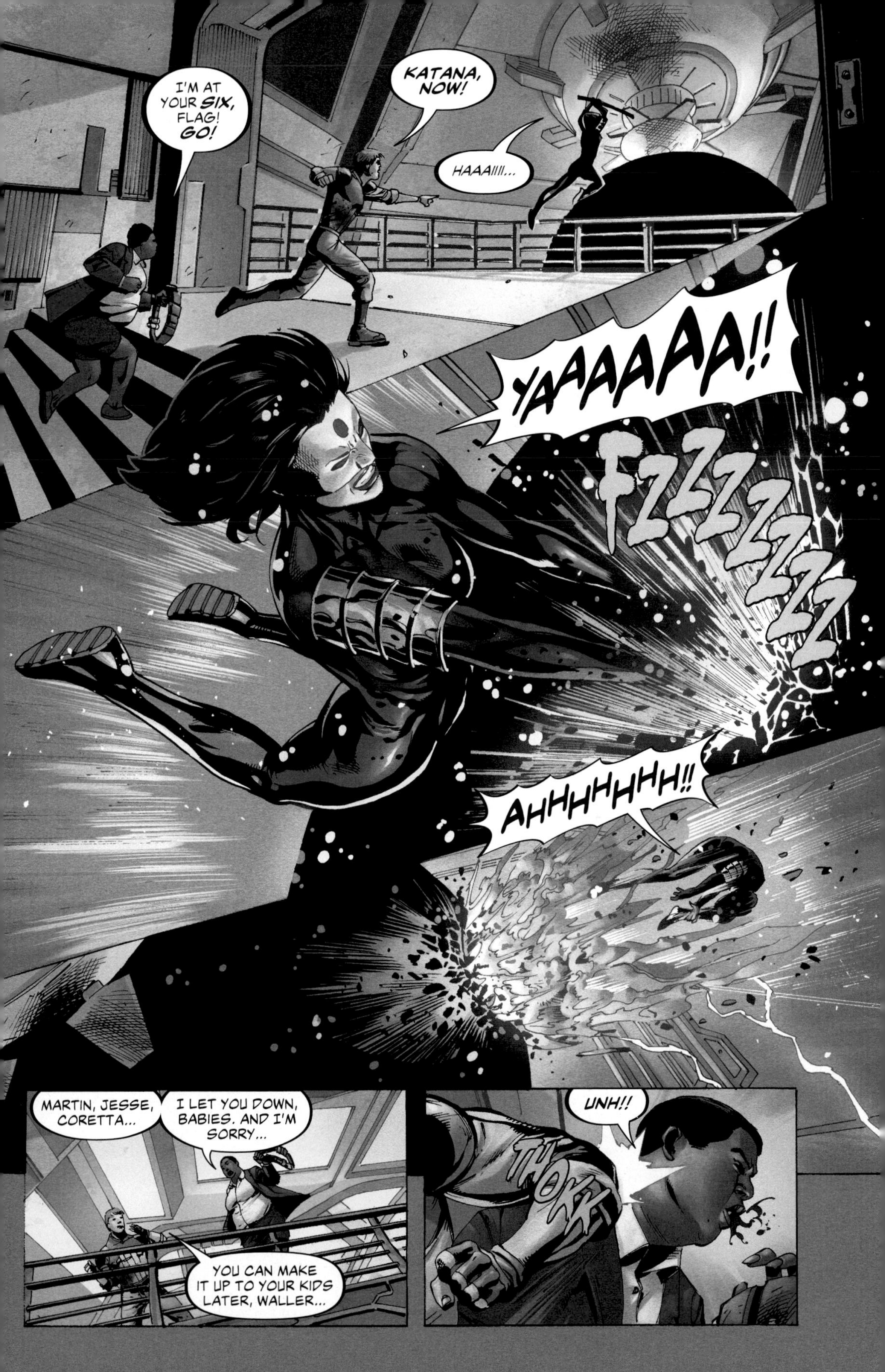
I'M AT YOUR SIX, FLAG! GO!
KATANA, NOW!
HAAAIIII...
YAAAAAA!!
FZZZZZZZ
AHHHHHHH!!
MARTIN, JESSE, CORETTA...
I LET YOU DOWN, BABIES. AND I'M SORRY...
YOU CAN MAKE IT UP TO YOUR KIDS LATER, WALLER...
UNH!!
THOKK

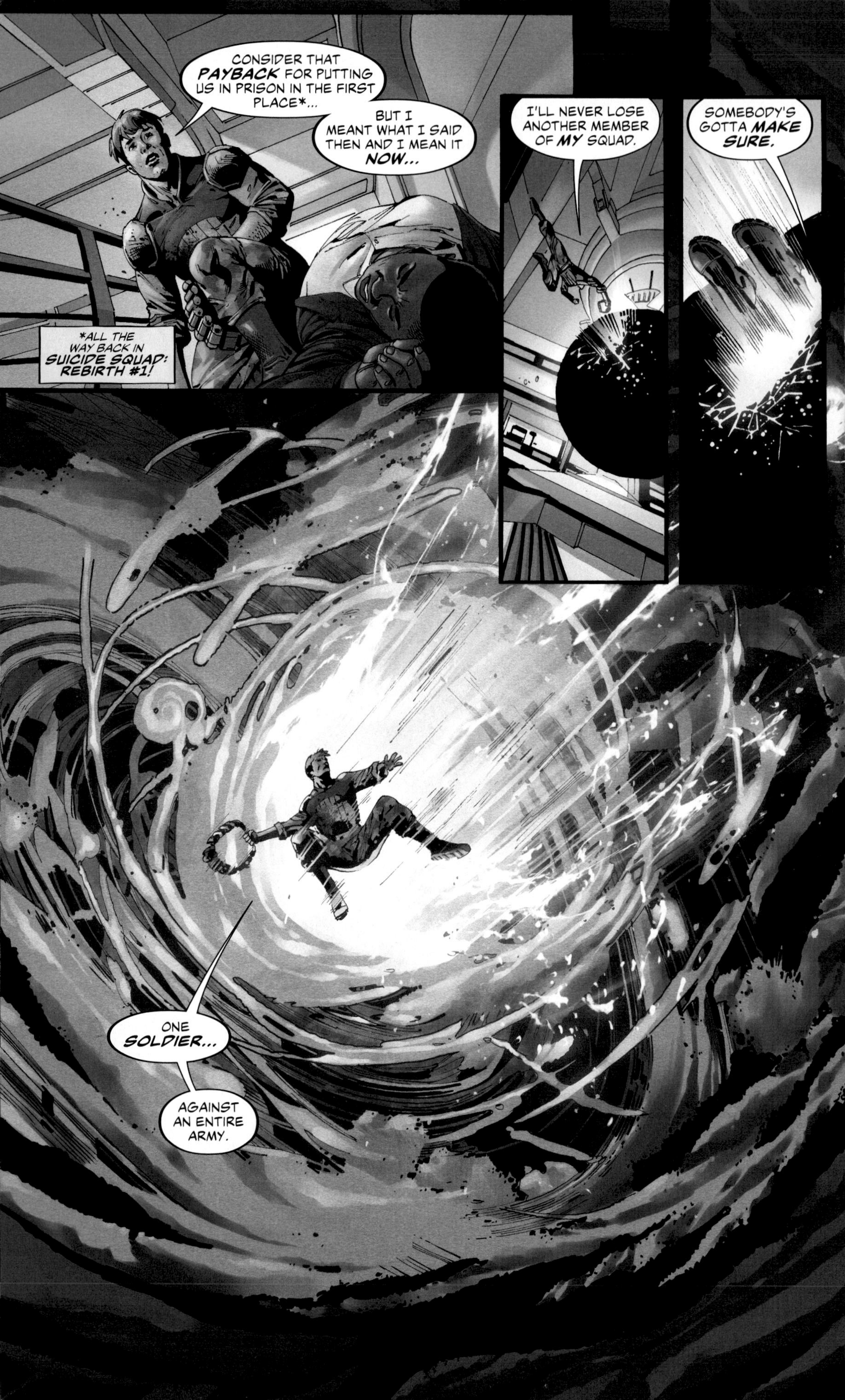
CONSIDER THAT PAYBACK FOR PUTTING US IN PRISON IN THE FIRST PLACE*...
BUT I MEANT WHAT I SAID THEN AND I MEAN IT NOW...
*ALL THE WAY BACK IN SUICIDE SQUAD: REBIRTH #1!
I'LL NEVER LOSE ANOTHER MEMBER OF MY SQUAD.
SOMEBODY'S GOTTA MAKE SURE.
ONE SOLDIER...
AGAINST AN ENTIRE ARMY.

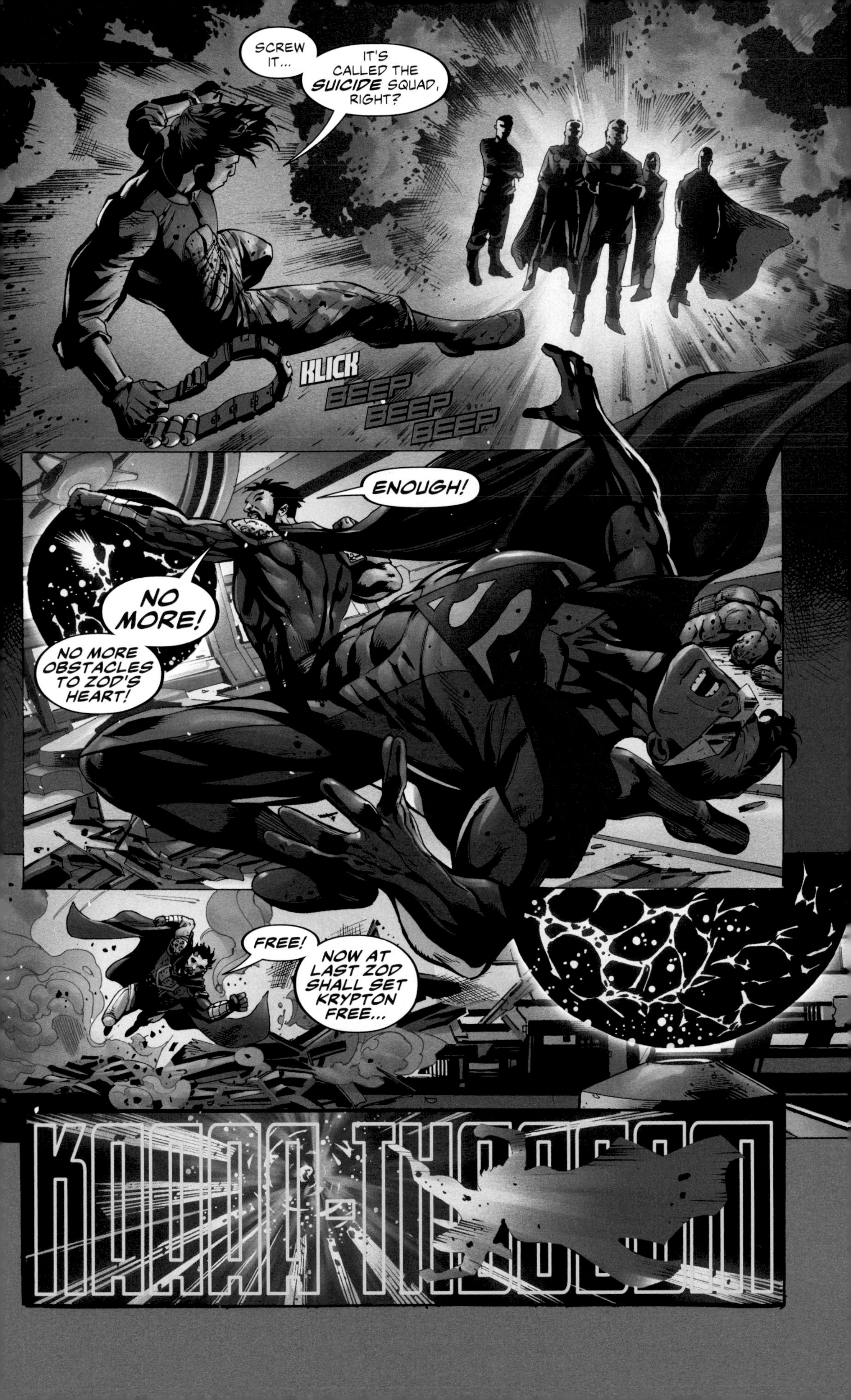
SCREW IT...
IT'S CALLED THE SUICIDE SQUAD, RIGHT?
KLICK
BEEP BEEP BEEP
ENOUGH!
NO MORE!
NO MORE OBSTACLES TO ZOD'S HEART!
FREE!
NOW AT LAST ZOD SHALL SET KRYPTON FREE...

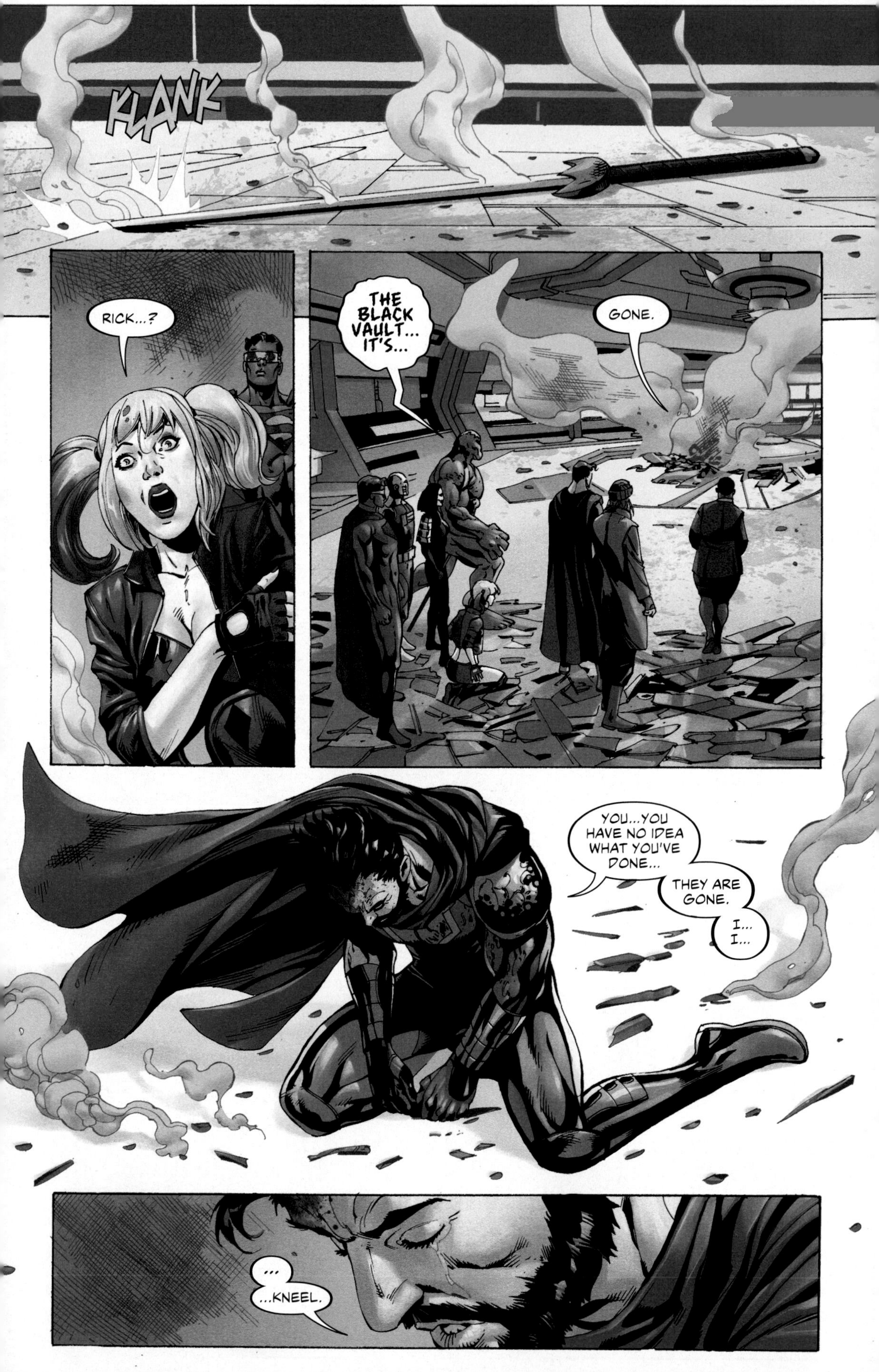
KLANK
RICK...?
THE BLACK VAULT... IT'S...
GONE.
YOU...YOU HAVE NO IDEA WHAT YOU'VE DONE...
THEY ARE GONE.
I... I...
...
...KNEEL.

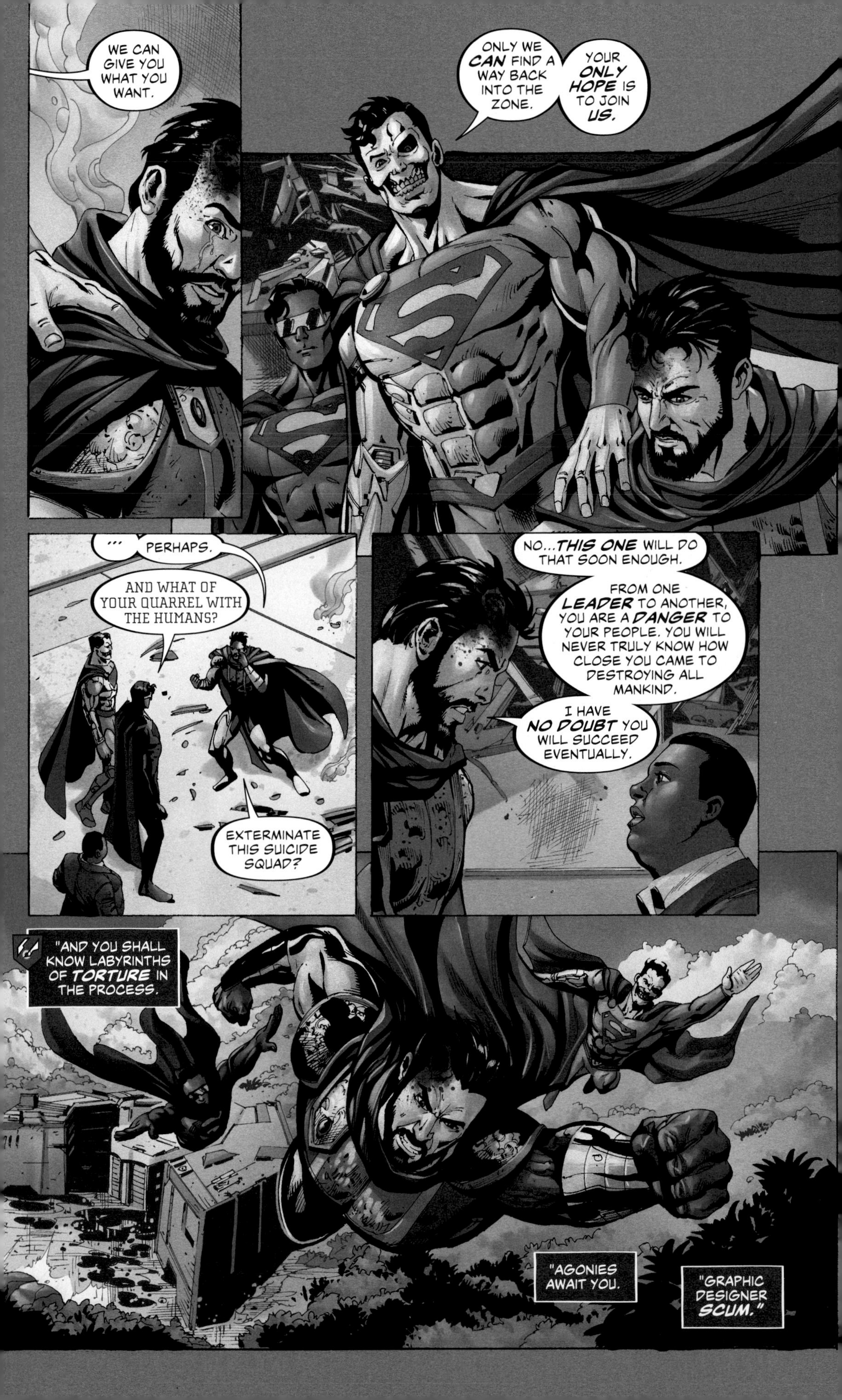

WE CAN GIVE YOU WHAT YOU WANT.
ONLY WE CAN FIND A WAY BACK INTO THE ZONE.
YOUR ONLY HOPE IS TO JOIN US.
... PERHAPS.
AND WHAT OF YOUR QUARREL WITH THE HUMANS?
EXTERMINATE THIS SUICIDE SQUAD?
NO...THIS ONE WILL DO THAT SOON ENOUGH.
FROM ONE LEADER TO ANOTHER, YOU ARE A DANGER TO YOUR PEOPLE. YOU WILL NEVER TRULY KNOW HOW CLOSE YOU CAME TO DESTROYING ALL MANKIND.
I HAVE NO DOUBT YOU WILL SUCCEED EVENTUALLY.
"AND YOU SHALL KNOW LABYRINTHS OF TORTURE IN THE PROCESS.
"AGONIES AWAIT YOU.
"GRAPHIC DESIGNER SCUM."

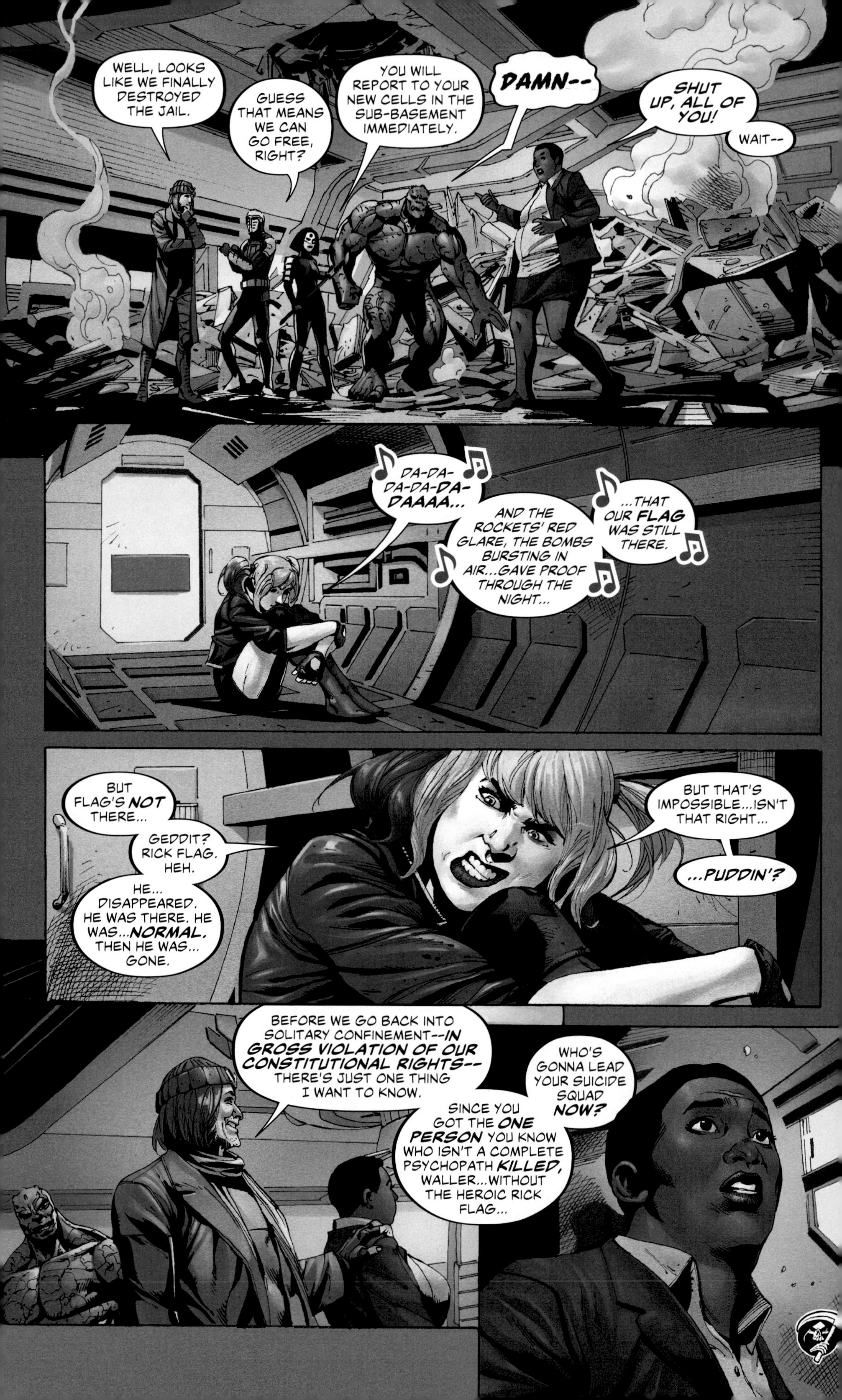
WELL, LOOKS LIKE WE FINALLY DESTROYED THE JAIL.
GUESS THAT MEANS WE CAN GO FREE, RIGHT?
YOU WILL REPORT TO YOUR NEW CELLS IN THE SUB-BASEMENT IMMEDIATELY.
DAMN--
SHUT UP, ALL OF YOU!
WAIT--
DA-DA-DA-DA-DA-DAAAA...
AND THE ROCKETS' RED GLARE, THE BOMBS BURSTING IN AIR...GAVE PROOF THROUGH THE NIGHT...
...THAT OUR FLAG WAS STILL THERE.
BUT FLAG'S NOT THERE...
GEDDIT? RICK FLAG. HEH.
HE... DISAPPEARED. HE WAS THERE. HE WAS...NORMAL. THEN HE WAS... GONE.
BUT THAT'S IMPOSSIBLE...ISN'T THAT RIGHT...
...PUDDIN'?
BEFORE WE GO BACK INTO SOLITARY CONFINEMENT--IN GROSS VIOLATION OF OUR CONSTITUTIONAL RIGHTS--THERE'S JUST ONE THING I WANT TO KNOW.
SINCE YOU GOT THE ONE PERSON YOU KNOW WHO ISN'T A COMPLETE PSYCHOPATH KILLED, WALLER...WITHOUT THE HEROIC RICK FLAG...
WHO'S GONNA LEAD YOUR SUICIDE SQUAD NOW?

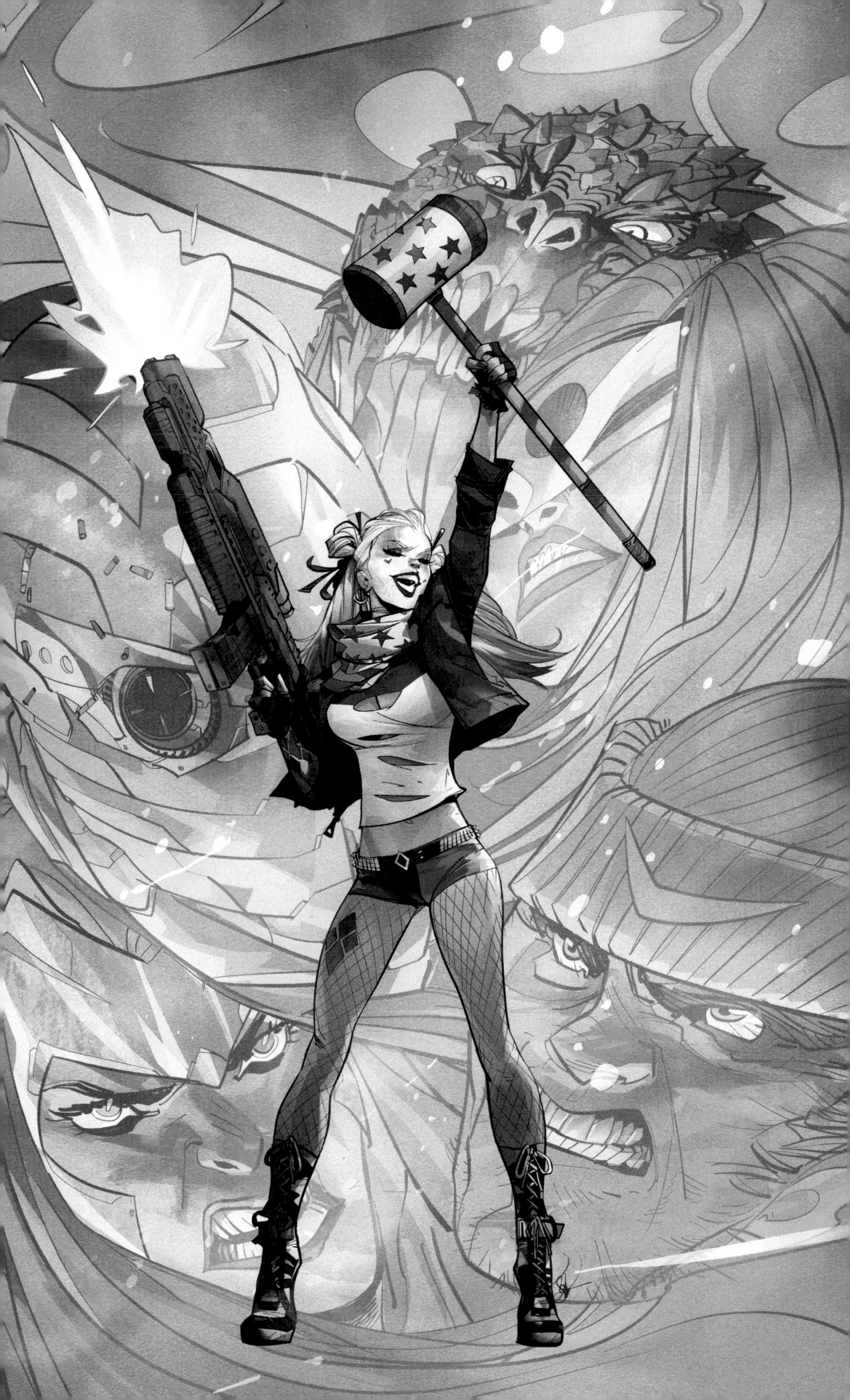

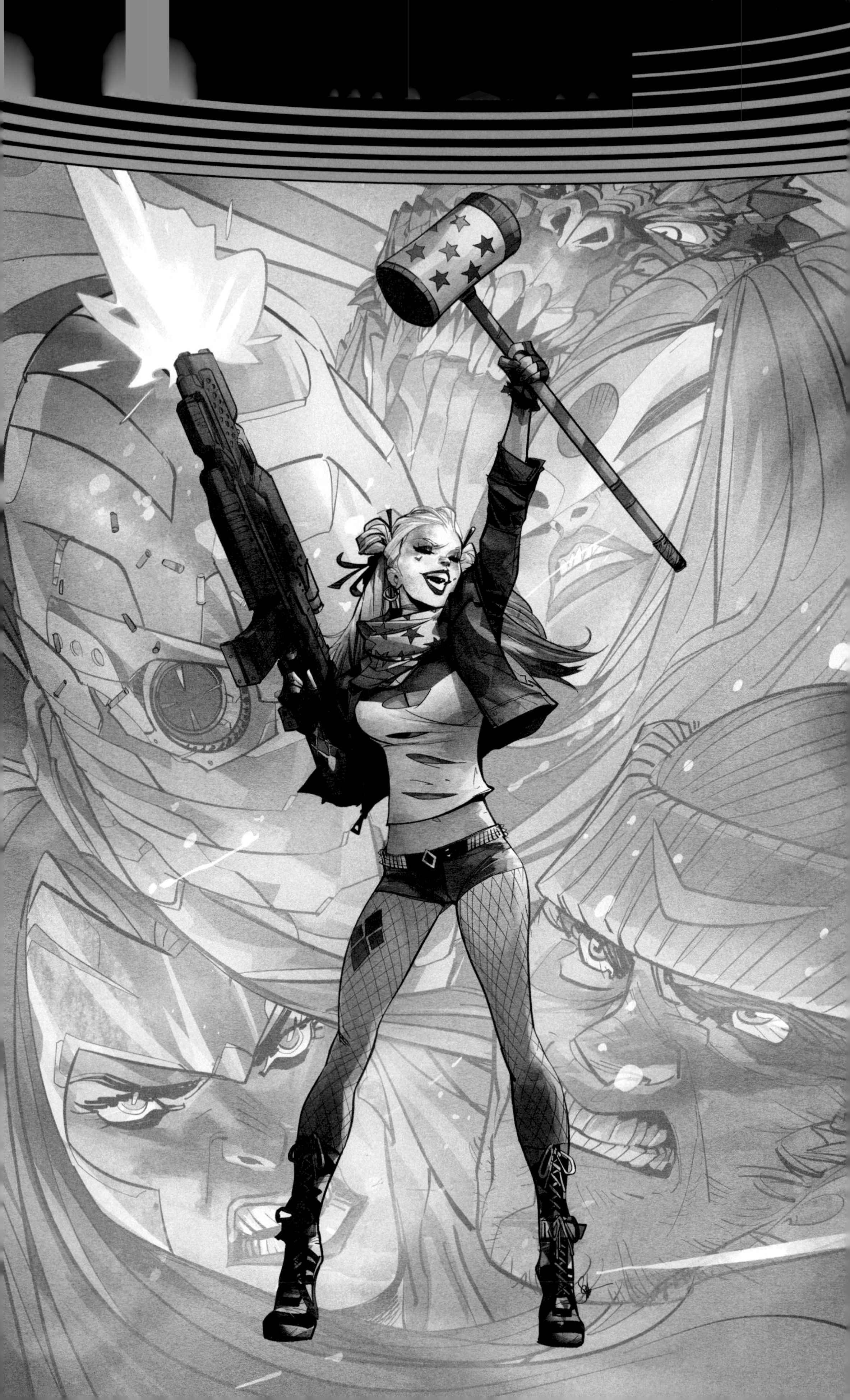

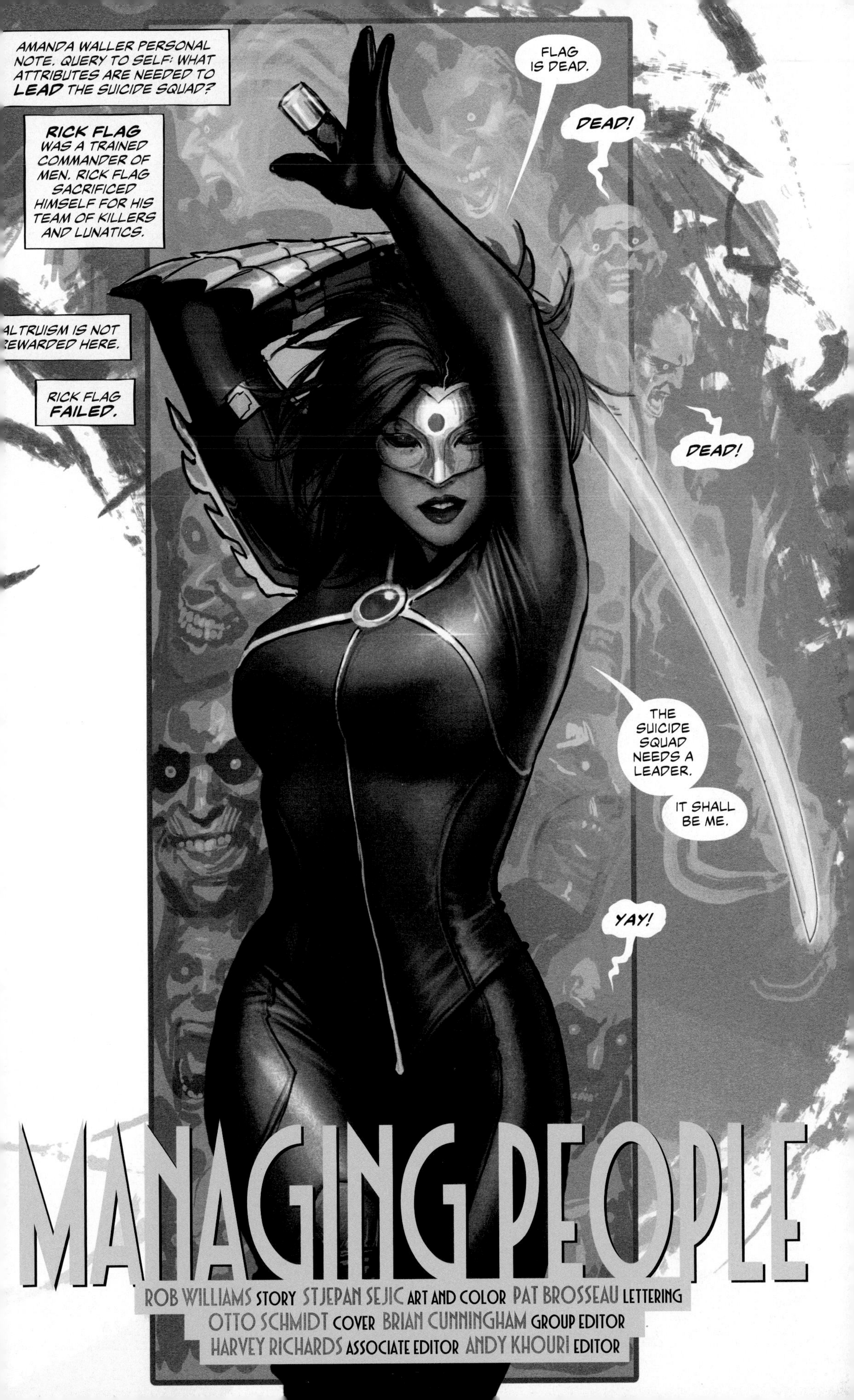
AMANDA WALLER PERSONAL NOTE. QUERY TO SELF: WHAT ATTRIBUTES ARE NEEDED TO LEAD THE SUICIDE SQUAD?
RICK FLAG WAS A TRAINED COMMANDER OF MEN. RICK FLAG SACRIFICED HIMSELF FOR HIS TEAM OF KILLERS AND LUNATICS.
FLAG IS DEAD.
DEAD!
ALTRUISM IS NOT REWARDED HERE.
RICK FLAG FAILED.
DEAD!
THE SUICIDE SQUAD NEEDS A LEADER.
IT SHALL BE ME.
YAY!
MANAGING PEOPLE
ROB WILLIAMS STORY STJEPAN SEJIC ART AND COLOR PAT BROSSEAU LETTERING
OTTO SCHMIDT COVER BRIAN CUNNINGHAM GROUP EDITOR
HARVEY RICHARDS ASSOCIATE EDITOR ANDY KHOURI EDITOR

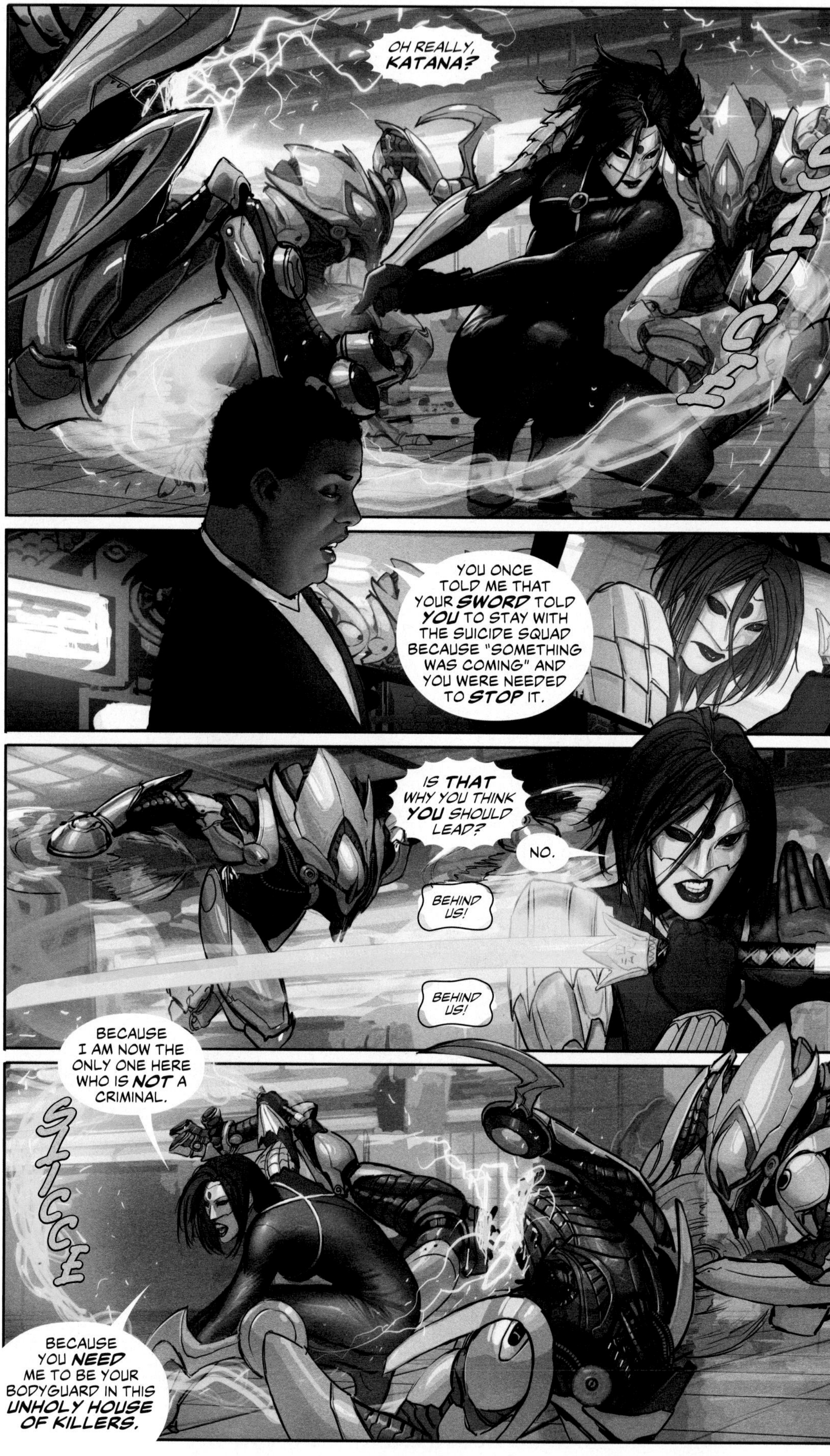
OH REALLY, KATANA?
SLICE
YOU ONCE TOLD ME THAT YOUR SWORD TOLD YOU TO STAY WITH THE SUICIDE SQUAD BECAUSE "SOMETHING WAS COMING" AND YOU WERE NEEDED TO STOP IT.
IS THAT WHY YOU THINK YOU SHOULD LEAD?
NO.
BEHIND US!
BEHIND US!
BECAUSE I AM NOW THE ONLY ONE HERE WHO IS NOT A CRIMINAL.
SLICE
BECAUSE YOU NEED ME TO BE YOUR BODYGUARD IN THIS UNHOLY HOUSE OF KILLERS.

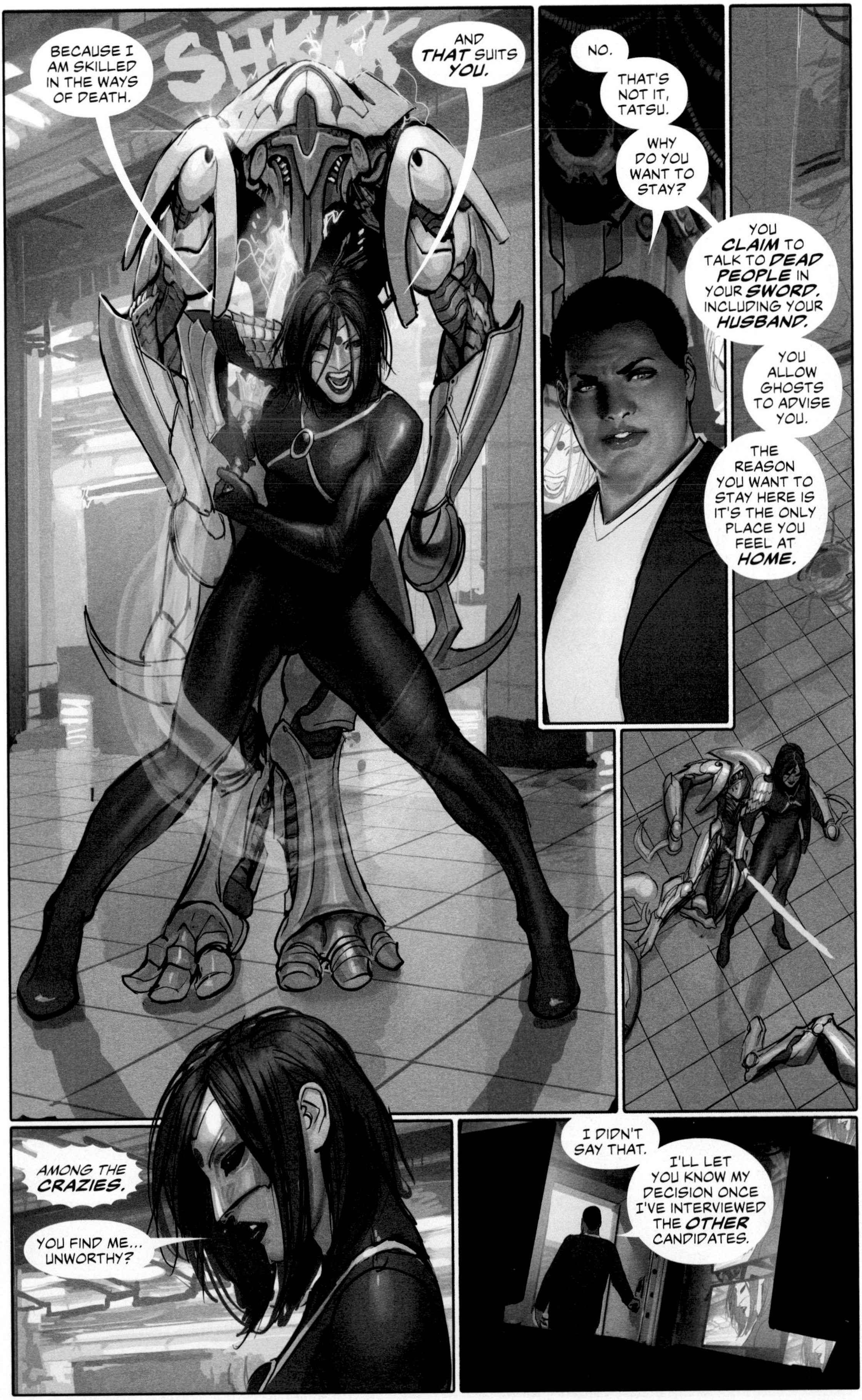
SHKKK
BECAUSE I AM SKILLED IN THE WAYS OF DEATH.
AND THAT SUITS YOU.
NO.
THAT'S NOT IT, TATSU.
WHY DO YOU WANT TO STAY?
YOU CLAIM TO TALK TO DEAD PEOPLE IN YOUR SWORD. INCLUDING YOUR HUSBAND.
YOU ALLOW GHOSTS TO ADVISE YOU.
THE REASON YOU WANT TO STAY HERE IS IT'S THE ONLY PLACE YOU FEEL AT HOME.
AMONG THE CRAZIES.
YOU FIND ME... UNWORTHY?
I DIDN'T SAY THAT.
I'LL LET YOU KNOW MY DECISION ONCE I'VE INTERVIEWED THE OTHER CANDIDATES.

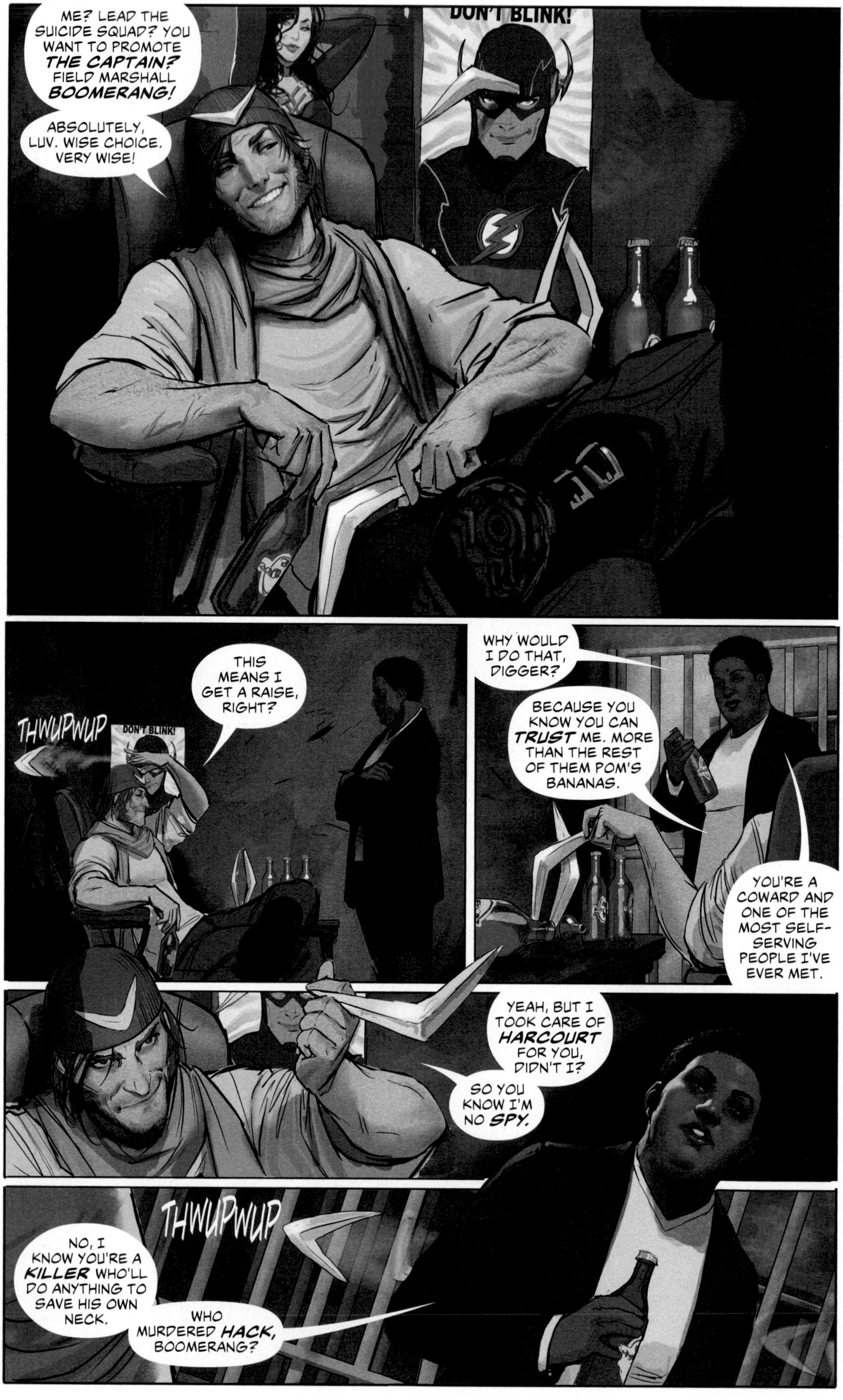
DON'T BLINK!
ME? LEAD THE SUICIDE SQUAD? YOU WANT TO PROMOTE THE CAPTAIN? FIELD MARSHALL BOOMERANG!
ABSOLUTELY, LUV. WISE CHOICE. VERY WISE!
THWUPWUP
DON'T BLINK!
THIS MEANS I GET A RAISE, RIGHT?
WHY WOULD I DO THAT, DIGGER?
BECAUSE YOU KNOW YOU CAN TRUST ME. MORE THAN THE REST OF THEM POM'S BANANAS.
YOU'RE A COWARD AND ONE OF THE MOST SELF-SERVING PEOPLE I'VE EVER MET.
YEAH, BUT I TOOK CARE OF HARCOURT FOR YOU, DIDN'T I?
SO YOU KNOW I'M NO SPY.
THWUPWUP
NO, I KNOW YOU'RE A KILLER WHO'LL DO ANYTHING TO SAVE HIS OWN NECK.
WHO MURDERED HACK, BOOMERANG?

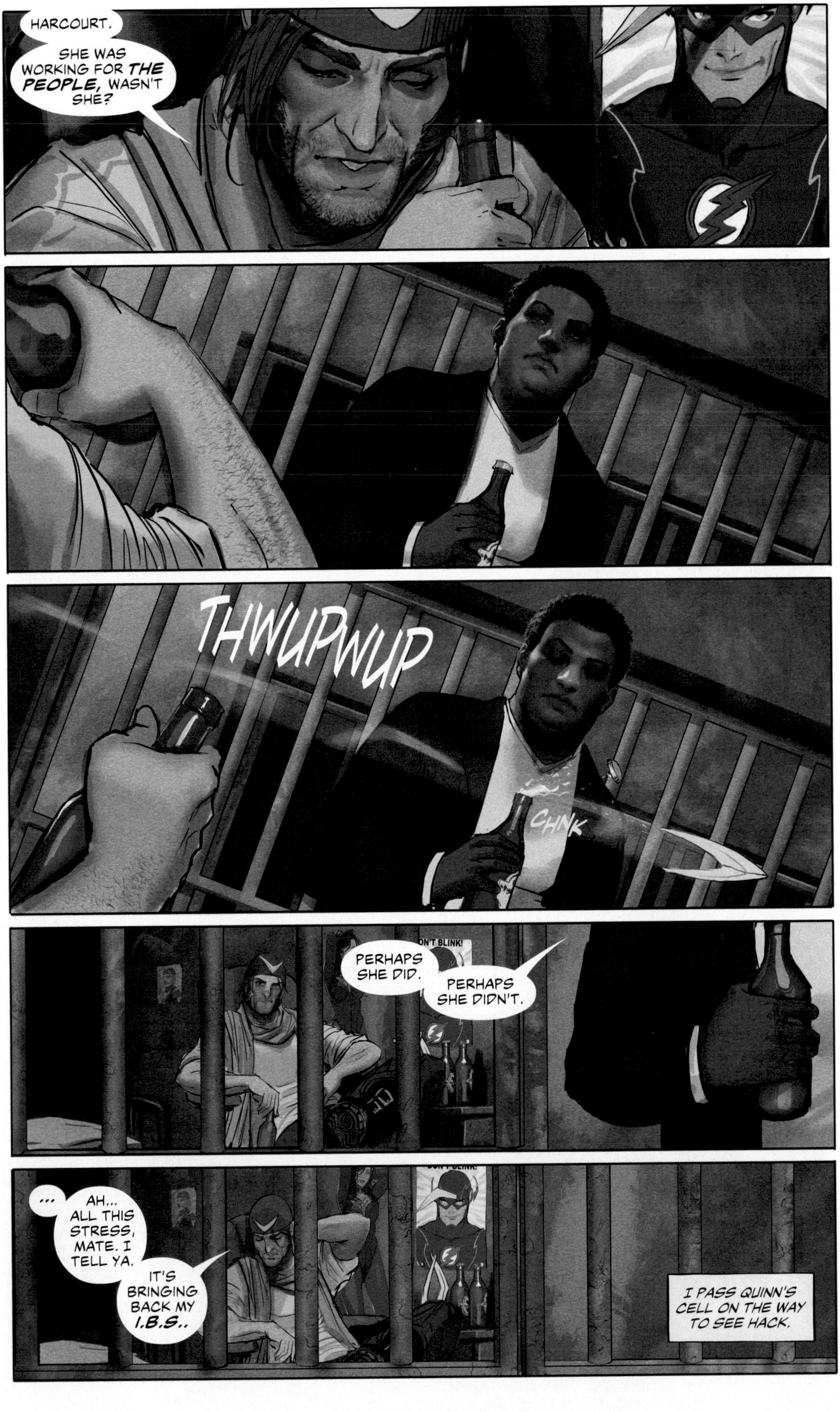
HARCOURT.
SHE WAS WORKING FOR **THE PEOPLE,** WASN'T SHE?
THWUPWUP
CHNK
PERHAPS SHE DID.
PERHAPS SHE DIDN'T.
...
AH... ALL THIS STRESS, MATE. I TELL YA.
IT'S BRINGING BACK MY ***I.B.S.***..
I PASS QUINN'S CELL ON THE WAY TO SEE HACK.

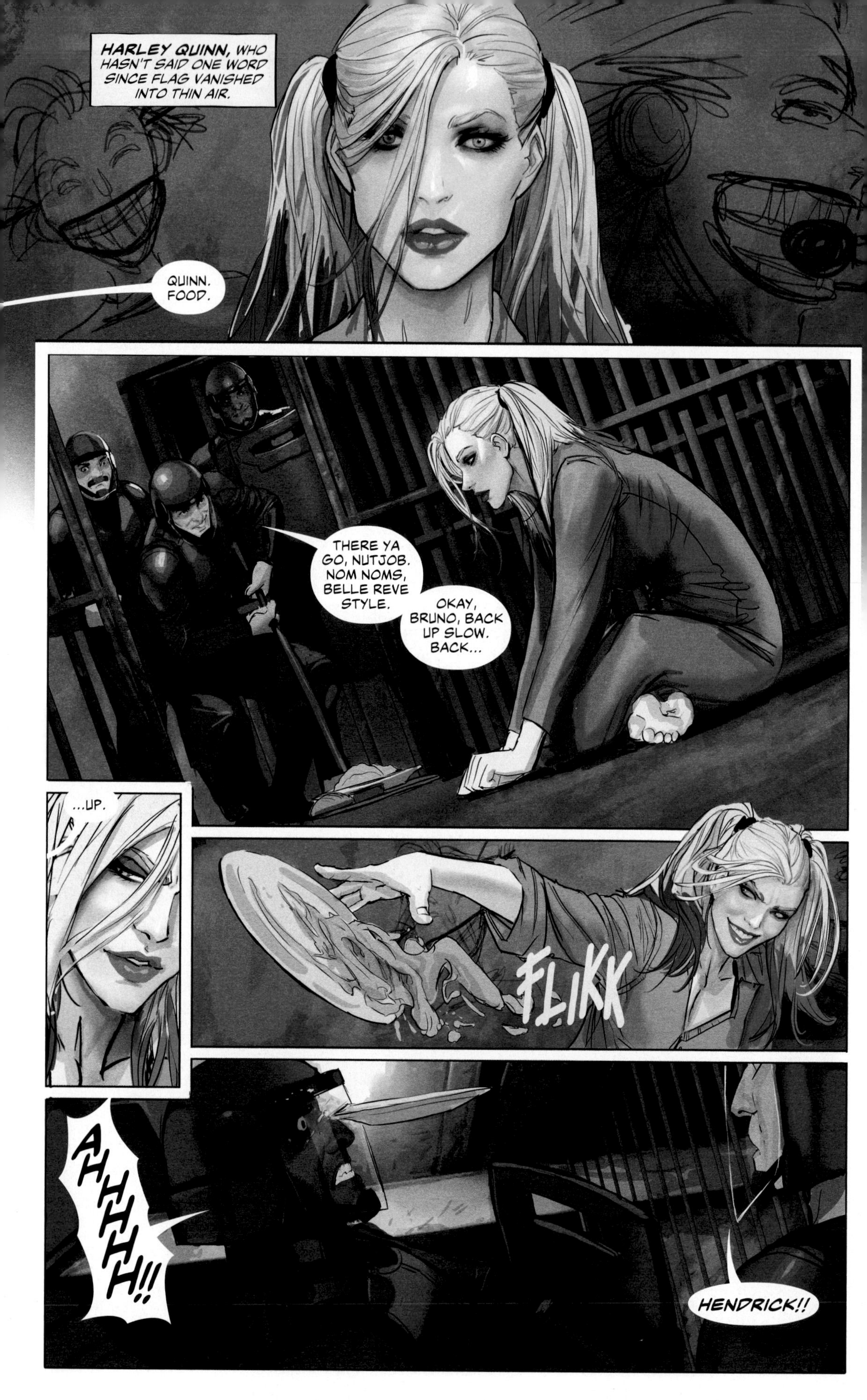
HARLEY QUINN, WHO HASN'T SAID ONE WORD SINCE FLAG VANISHED INTO THIN AIR.
QUINN. FOOD.
THERE YA GO, NUTJOB. NOM NOMS, BELLE REVE STYLE.
OKAY, BRUNO, BACK UP SLOW. BACK...
...UP.
FLIKK
AHHHHH!!
HENDRICK!!

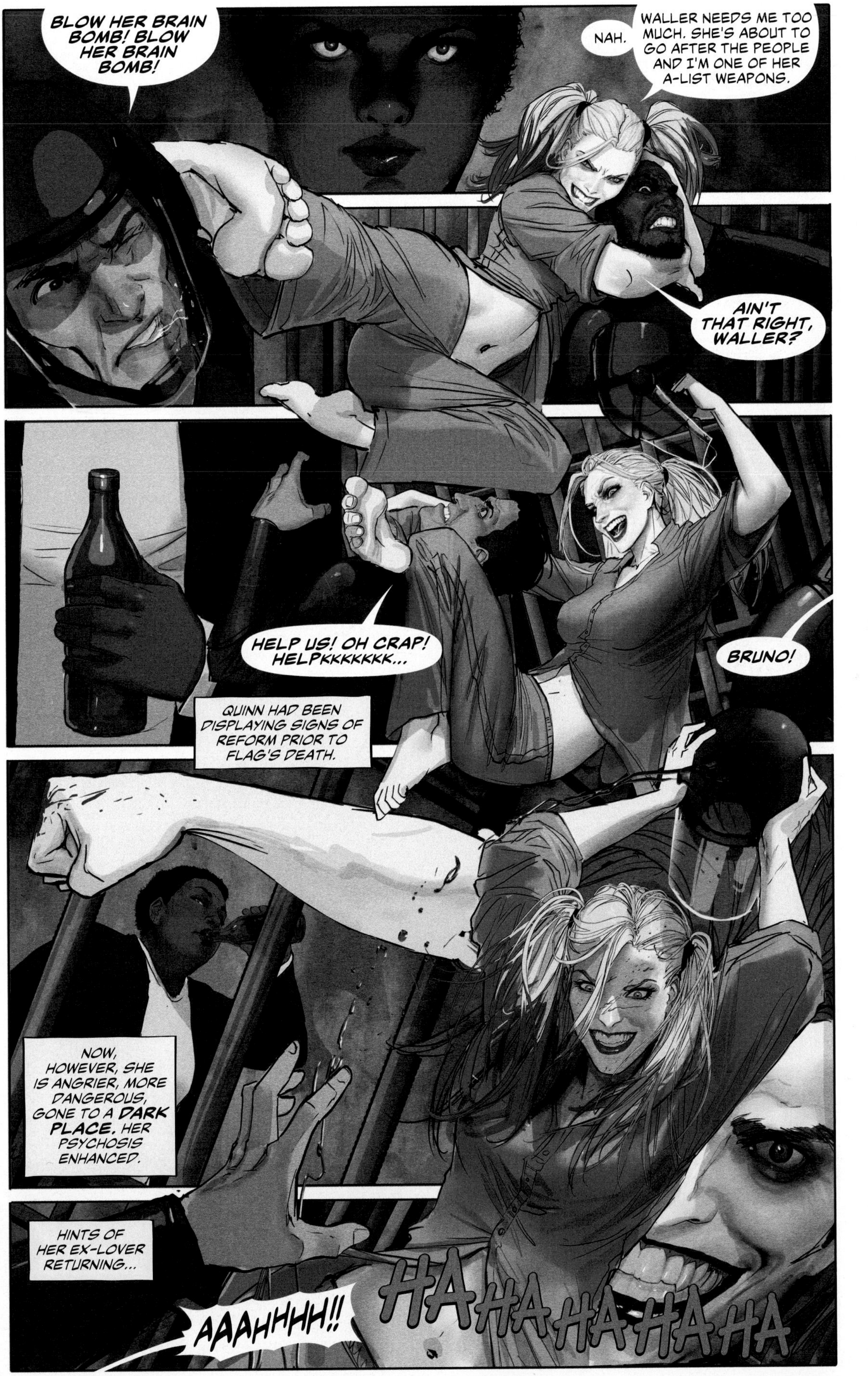
BLOW HER BRAIN BOMB! BLOW HER BRAIN BOMB!
NAH.
WALLER NEEDS ME TOO MUCH. SHE'S ABOUT TO GO AFTER THE PEOPLE AND I'M ONE OF HER A-LIST WEAPONS.
AIN'T THAT RIGHT, WALLER?
HELP US! OH CRAP! HELPKKKKKKK...
BRUNO!
QUINN HAD BEEN DISPLAYING SIGNS OF REFORM PRIOR TO FLAG'S DEATH.
NOW, HOWEVER, SHE IS ANGRIER, MORE DANGEROUS, GONE TO A DARK PLACE. HER PSYCHOSIS ENHANCED.
HINTS OF HER EX-LOVER RETURNING...
AAAHHHH!!
HAHAHAHAHAHA

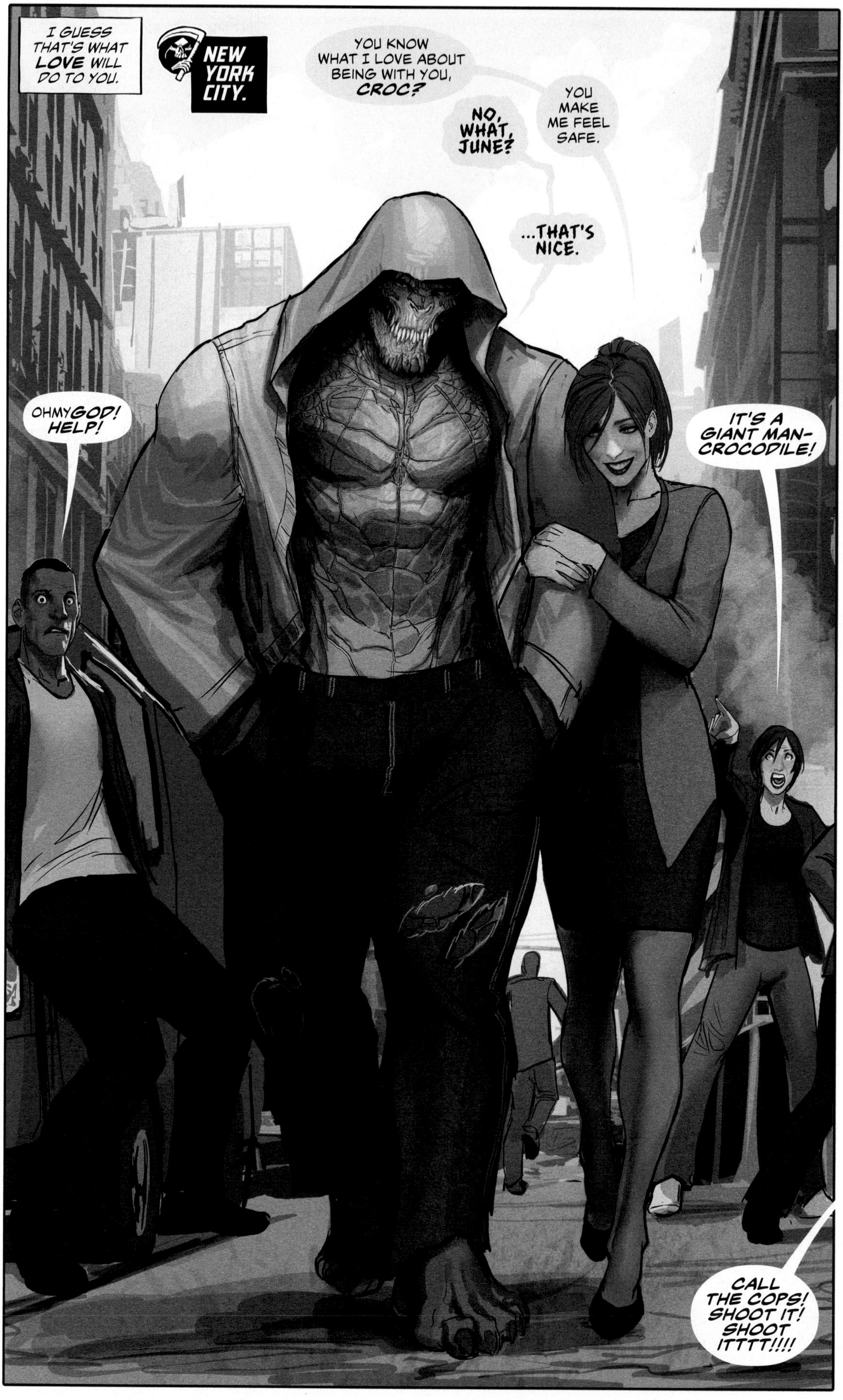
I GUESS THAT'S WHAT LOVE WILL DO TO YOU.
NEW YORK CITY.
YOU KNOW WHAT I LOVE ABOUT BEING WITH YOU, CROC?
NO, WHAT, JUNE?
YOU MAKE ME FEEL SAFE.
...THAT'S NICE.
OHMYGOD! HELP!
IT'S A GIANT MAN-CROCODILE!
CALL THE COPS! SHOOT IT! SHOOT ITTTT!!!!

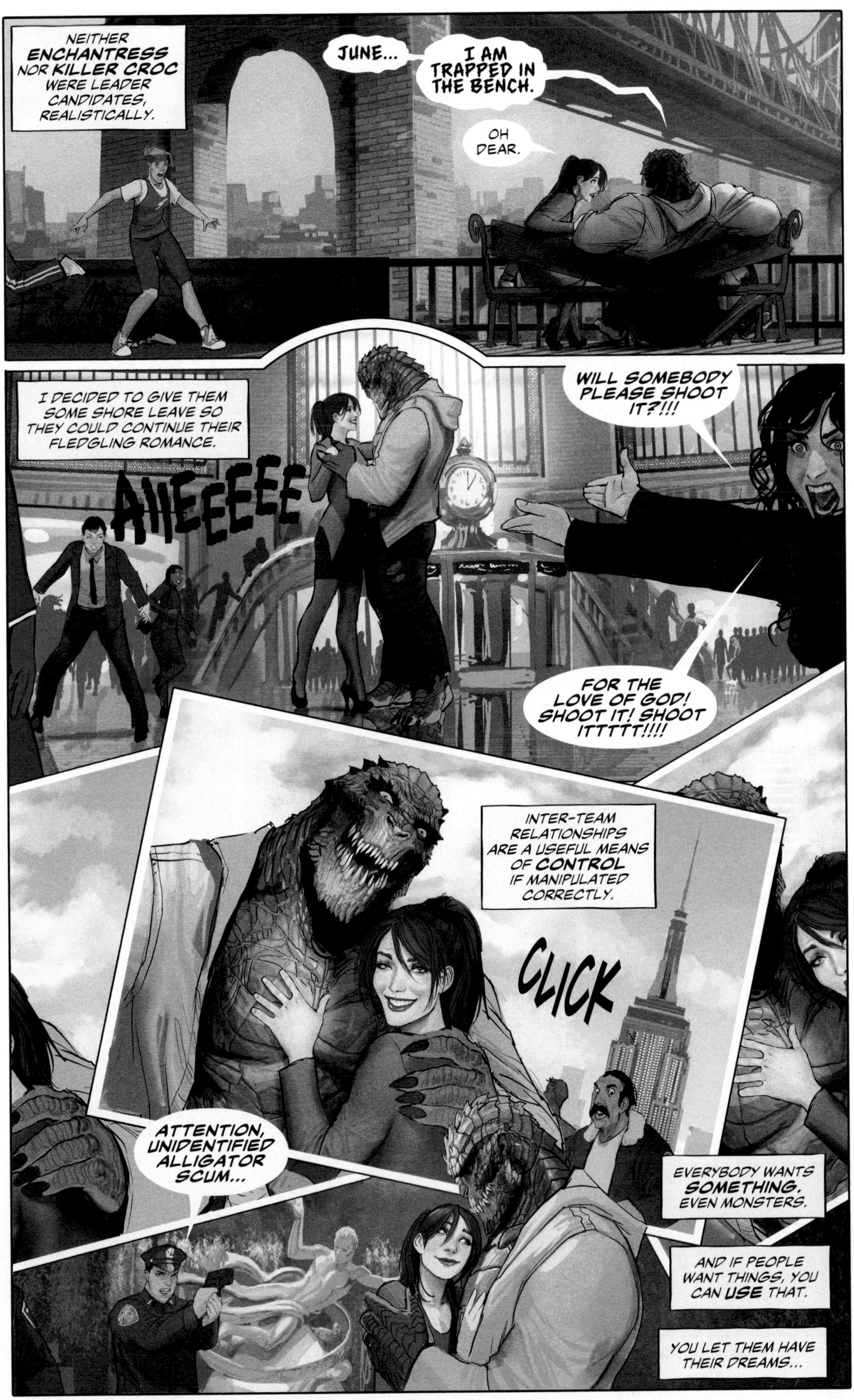
NEITHER ENCHANTRESS NOR KILLER CROC WERE LEADER CANDIDATES, REALISTICALLY.
JUNE...
I AM TRAPPED IN THE BENCH.
OH DEAR.
I DECIDED TO GIVE THEM SOME SHORE LEAVE SO THEY COULD CONTINUE THEIR FLEDGLING ROMANCE.
WILL SOMEBODY PLEASE SHOOT IT?!!!
AIIEEEEE
FOR THE LOVE OF GOD! SHOOT IT! SHOOT ITTTTT!!!!
INTER-TEAM RELATIONSHIPS ARE A USEFUL MEANS OF CONTROL IF MANIPULATED CORRECTLY.
CLICK
ATTENTION, UNIDENTIFIED ALLIGATOR SCUM...
EVERYBODY WANTS SOMETHING. EVEN MONSTERS.
AND IF PEOPLE WANT THINGS, YOU CAN USE THAT.
YOU LET THEM HAVE THEIR DREAMS...

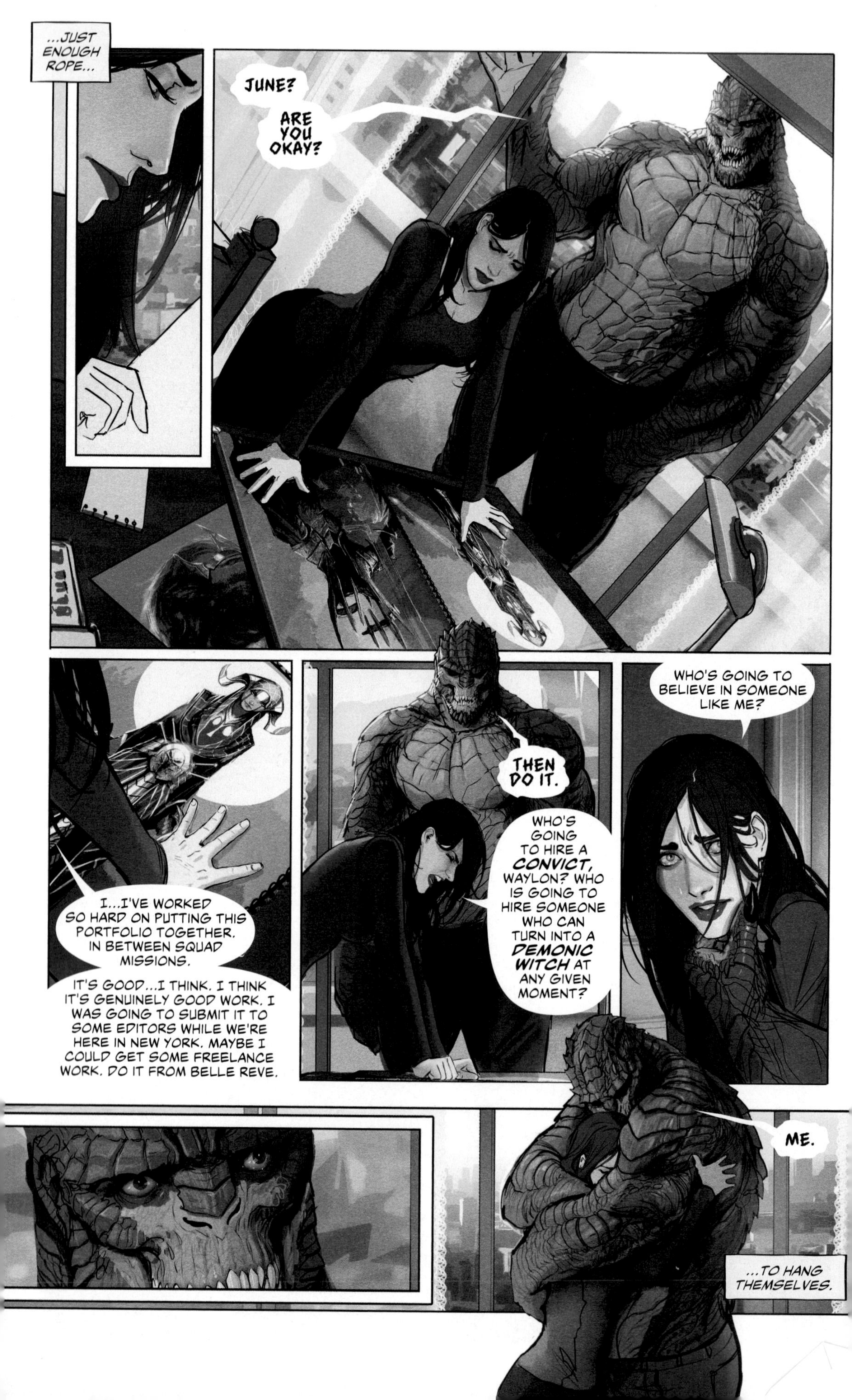
...JUST ENOUGH ROPE...
JUNE?
ARE YOU OKAY?
I...I'VE WORKED SO HARD ON PUTTING THIS PORTFOLIO TOGETHER. IN BETWEEN SQUAD MISSIONS.
IT'S GOOD...I THINK. I THINK IT'S GENUINELY GOOD WORK. I WAS GOING TO SUBMIT IT TO SOME EDITORS WHILE WE'RE HERE IN NEW YORK. MAYBE I COULD GET SOME FREELANCE WORK. DO IT FROM BELLE REVE.
THEN DO IT.
WHO'S GOING TO HIRE A CONVICT, WAYLON? WHO IS GOING TO HIRE SOMEONE WHO CAN TURN INTO A DEMONIC WITCH AT ANY GIVEN MOMENT?
WHO'S GOING TO BELIEVE IN SOMEONE LIKE ME?
ME.
...TO HANG THEMSELVES.

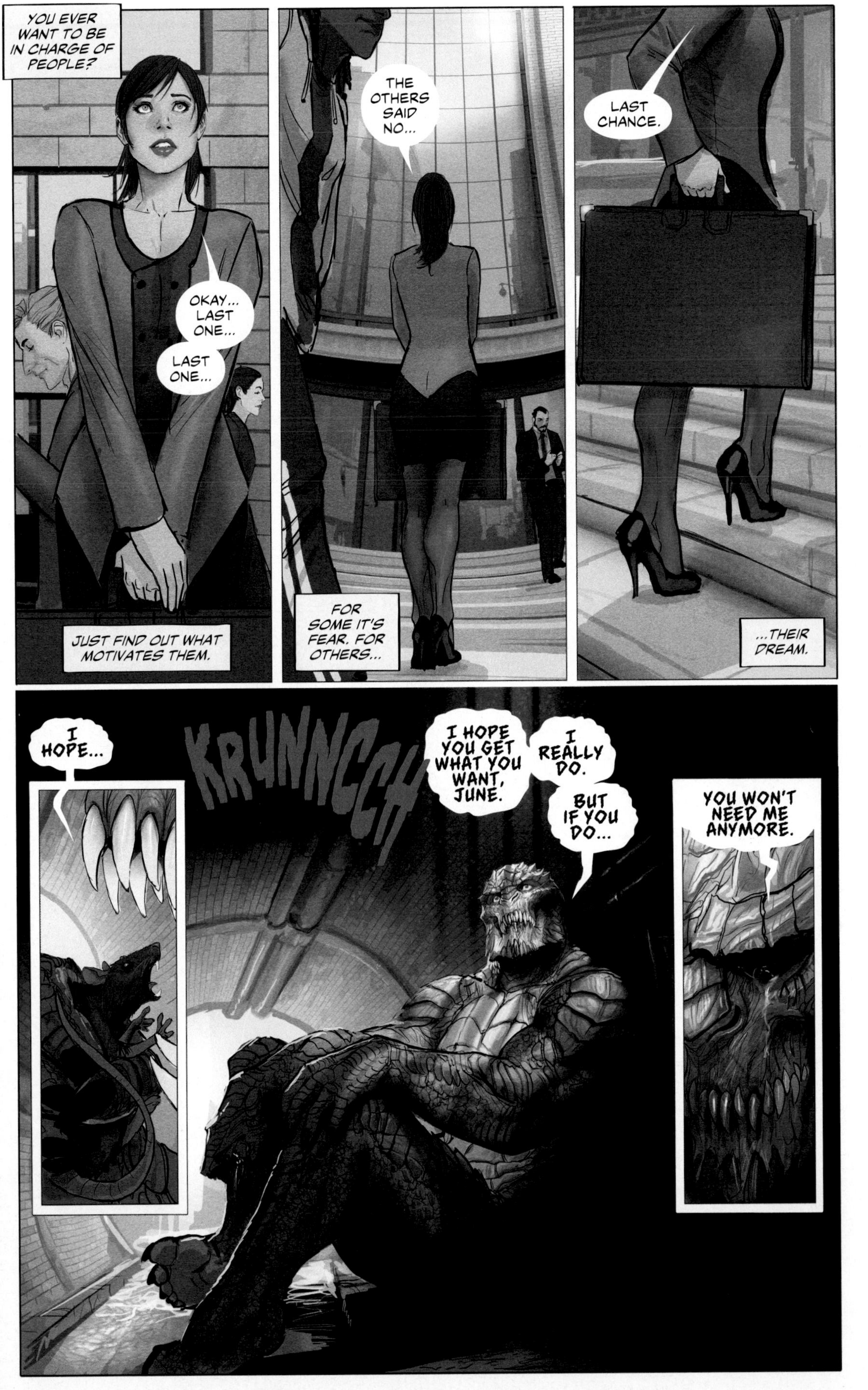
YOU EVER WANT TO BE IN CHARGE OF PEOPLE?
OKAY... LAST ONE...
LAST ONE...
JUST FIND OUT WHAT MOTIVATES THEM.
THE OTHERS SAID NO...
FOR SOME IT'S FEAR. FOR OTHERS...
LAST CHANCE.
...THEIR DREAM.
I HOPE...
KRUNNCCH
I HOPE YOU GET WHAT YOU WANT, JUNE.
I REALLY DO.
BUT IF YOU DO...
YOU WON'T NEED ME ANYMORE.

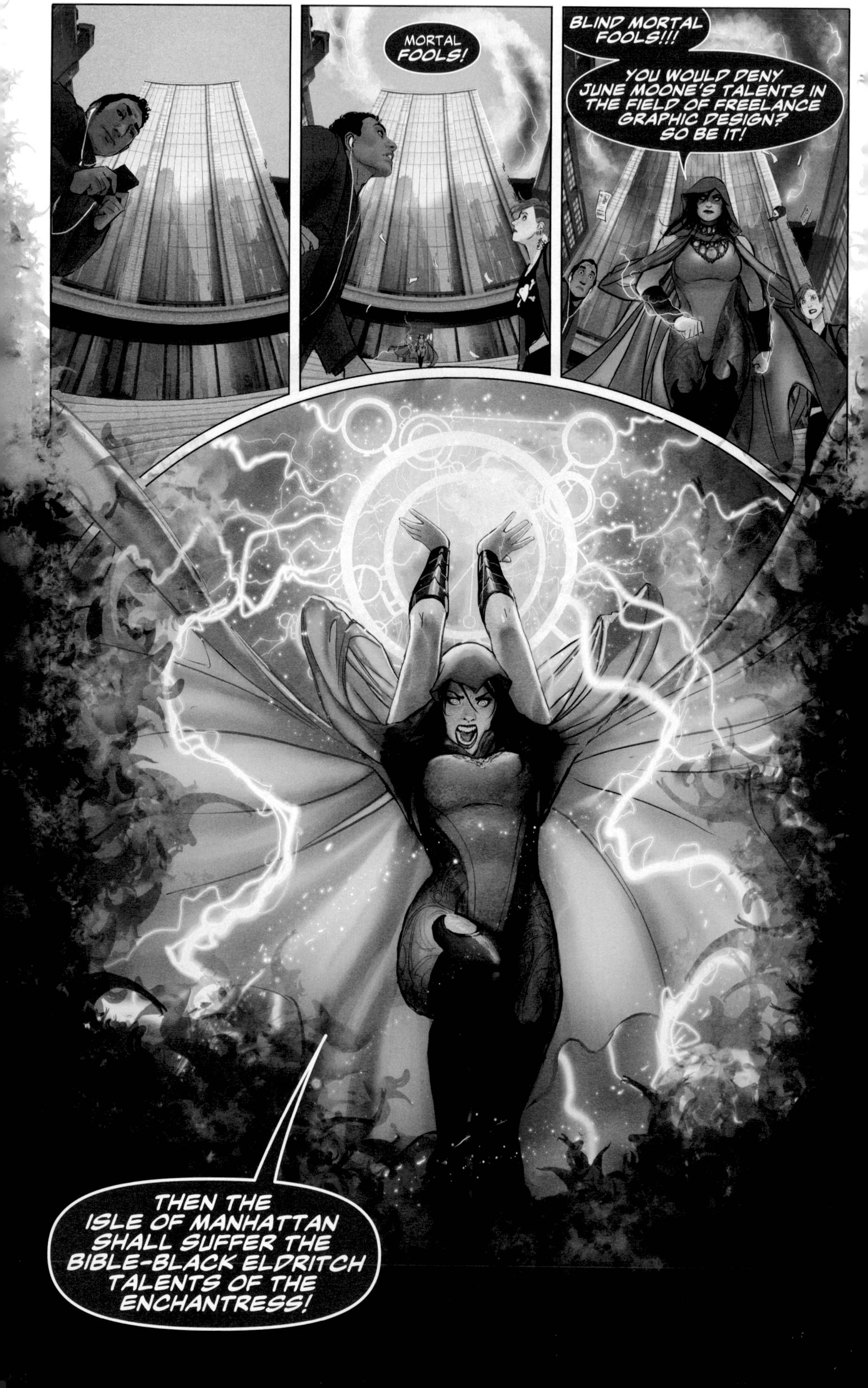
MORTAL FOOLS!
BLIND MORTAL FOOLS!!!
YOU WOULD DENY JUNE MOONE'S TALENTS IN THE FIELD OF FREELANCE GRAPHIC DESIGN? SO BE IT!
THEN THE ISLE OF MANHATTAN SHALL SUFFER THE BIBLE-BLACK ELDRITCH TALENTS OF THE ENCHANTRESS!

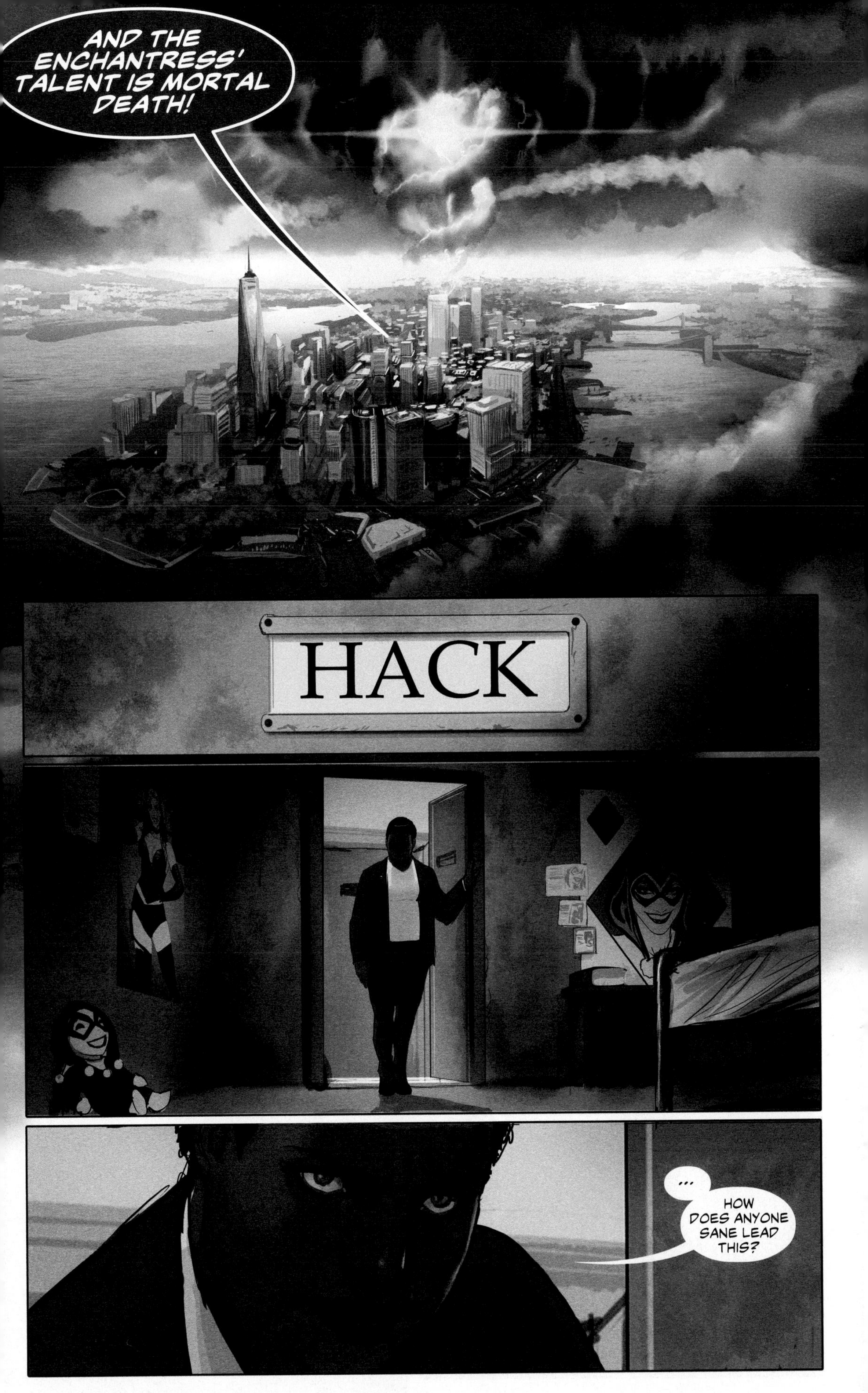
AND THE ENCHANTRESS' TALENT IS MORTAL DEATH!
HACK
...
HOW DOES ANYONE SANE LEAD THIS?

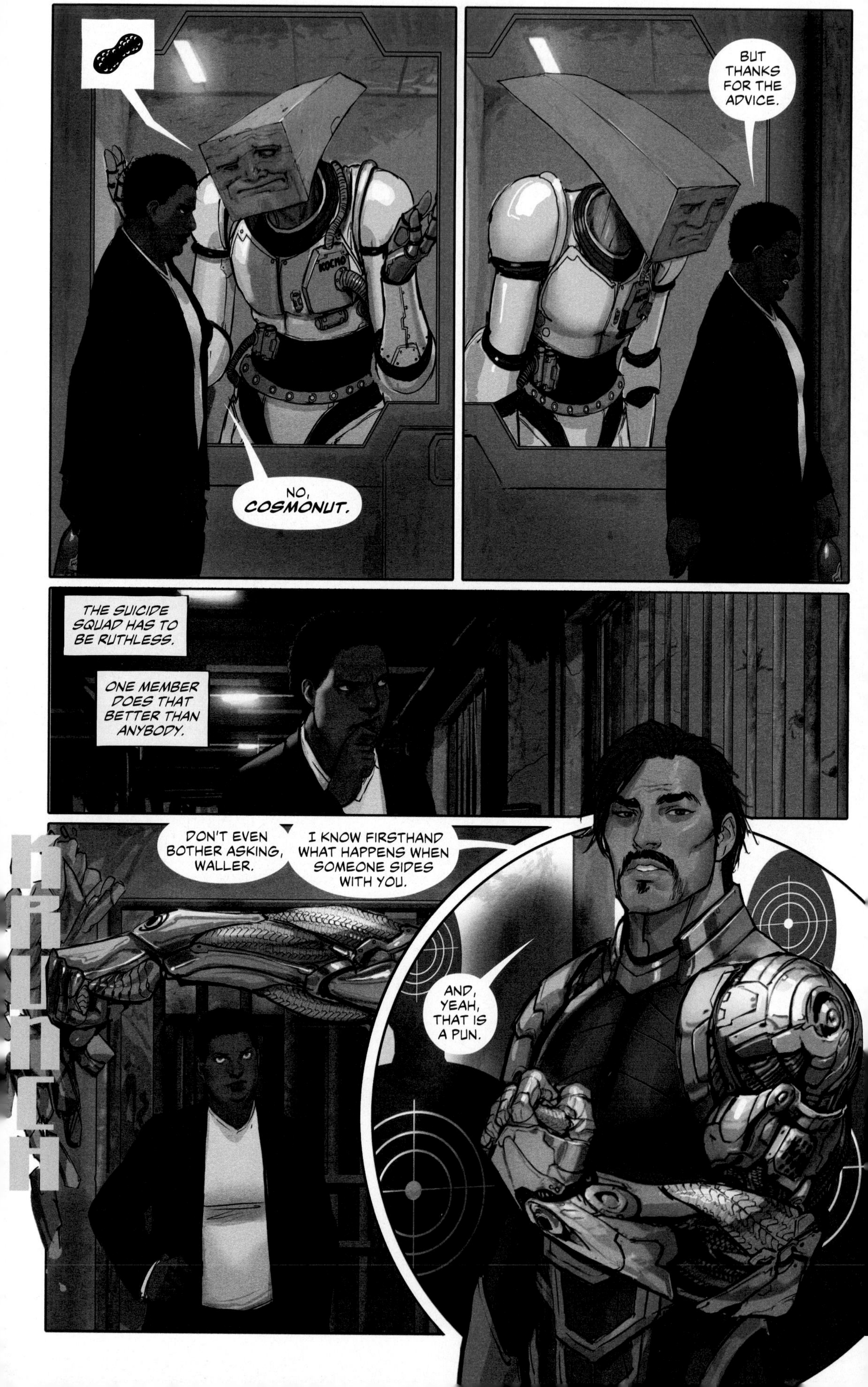

NO, COSMONUT.
BUT THANKS FOR THE ADVICE.
THE SUICIDE SQUAD HAS TO BE RUTHLESS.
ONE MEMBER DOES THAT BETTER THAN ANYBODY.
KRUNCH
DON'T EVEN BOTHER ASKING, WALLER.
I KNOW FIRSTHAND WHAT HAPPENS WHEN SOMEONE SIDES WITH YOU.
AND, YEAH, THAT IS A PUN.

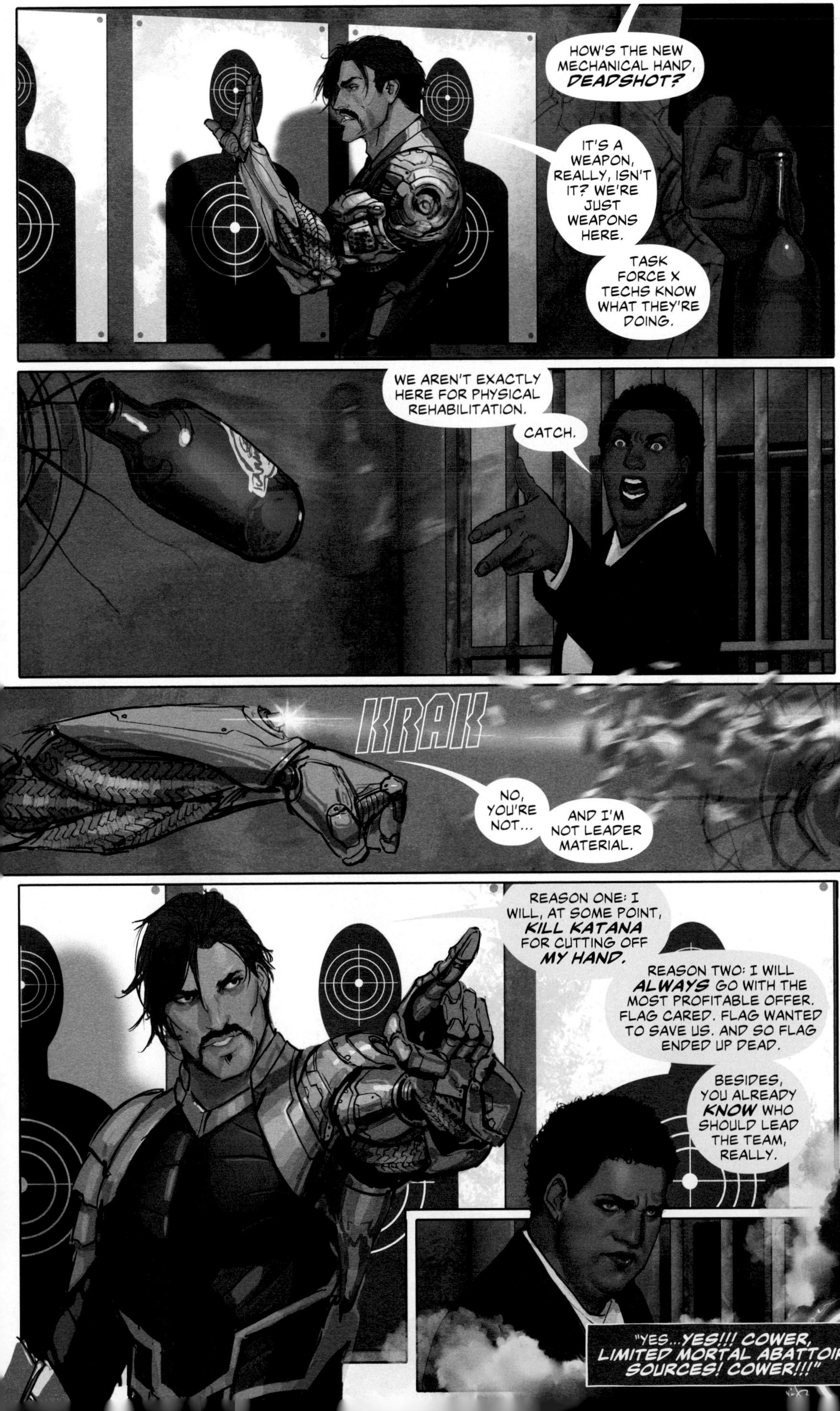
HOW'S THE NEW MECHANICAL HAND, DEADSHOT?
IT'S A WEAPON, REALLY, ISN'T IT? WE'RE JUST WEAPONS HERE.
TASK FORCE X TECHS KNOW WHAT THEY'RE DOING.
WE AREN'T EXACTLY HERE FOR PHYSICAL REHABILITATION.
CATCH.
KRAK
NO, YOU'RE NOT...
AND I'M NOT LEADER MATERIAL.
REASON ONE: I WILL, AT SOME POINT, KILL KATANA FOR CUTTING OFF MY HAND.
REASON TWO: I WILL ALWAYS GO WITH THE MOST PROFITABLE OFFER. FLAG CARED. FLAG WANTED TO SAVE US. AND SO FLAG ENDED UP DEAD.
BESIDES, YOU ALREADY KNOW WHO SHOULD LEAD THE TEAM, REALLY.
"YES...YES!!! COWER, LIMITED MORTAL ABATTOIR SOURCES! COWER!!!"

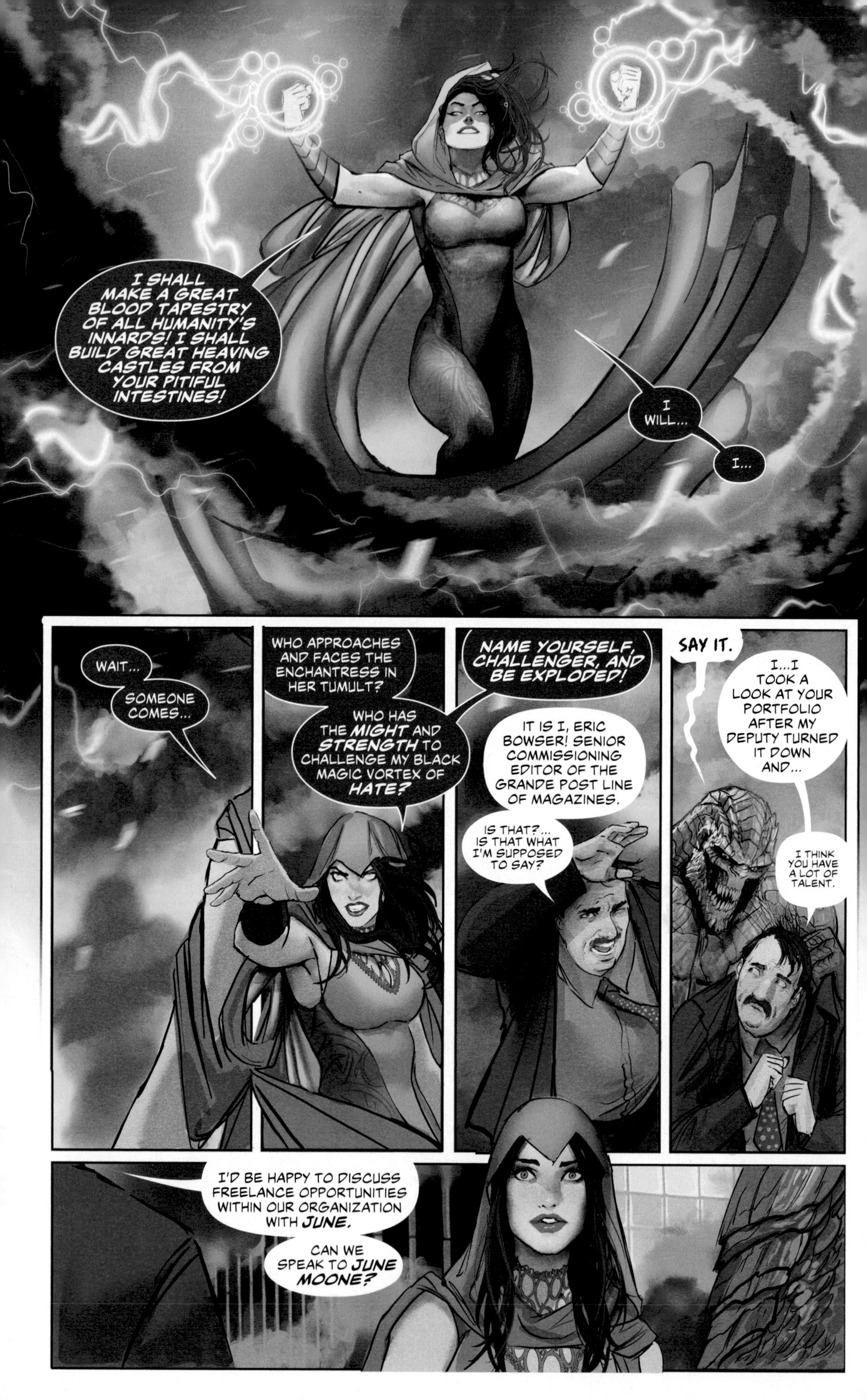
I SHALL MAKE A GREAT BLOOD TAPESTRY OF ALL HUMANITY'S INNARDS! I SHALL BUILD GREAT HEAVING CASTLES FROM YOUR PITIFUL INTESTINES!
I WILL...
I...
WAIT...
SOMEONE COMES...
WHO APPROACHES AND FACES THE ENCHANTRESS IN HER TUMULT?
WHO HAS THE MIGHT AND STRENGTH TO CHALLENGE MY BLACK MAGIC VORTEX OF HATE?
NAME YOURSELF, CHALLENGER, AND BE EXPLODED!
IT IS I, ERIC BOWSER! SENIOR COMMISSIONING EDITOR OF THE GRANDE POST LINE OF MAGAZINES.
IS THAT?... IS THAT WHAT I'M SUPPOSED TO SAY?
SAY IT.
I...I TOOK A LOOK AT YOUR PORTFOLIO AFTER MY DEPUTY TURNED IT DOWN AND...
I THINK YOU HAVE A LOT OF TALENT.
I'D BE HAPPY TO DISCUSS FREELANCE OPPORTUNITIES WITHIN OUR ORGANIZATION WITH JUNE.
CAN WE SPEAK TO JUNE MOONE?

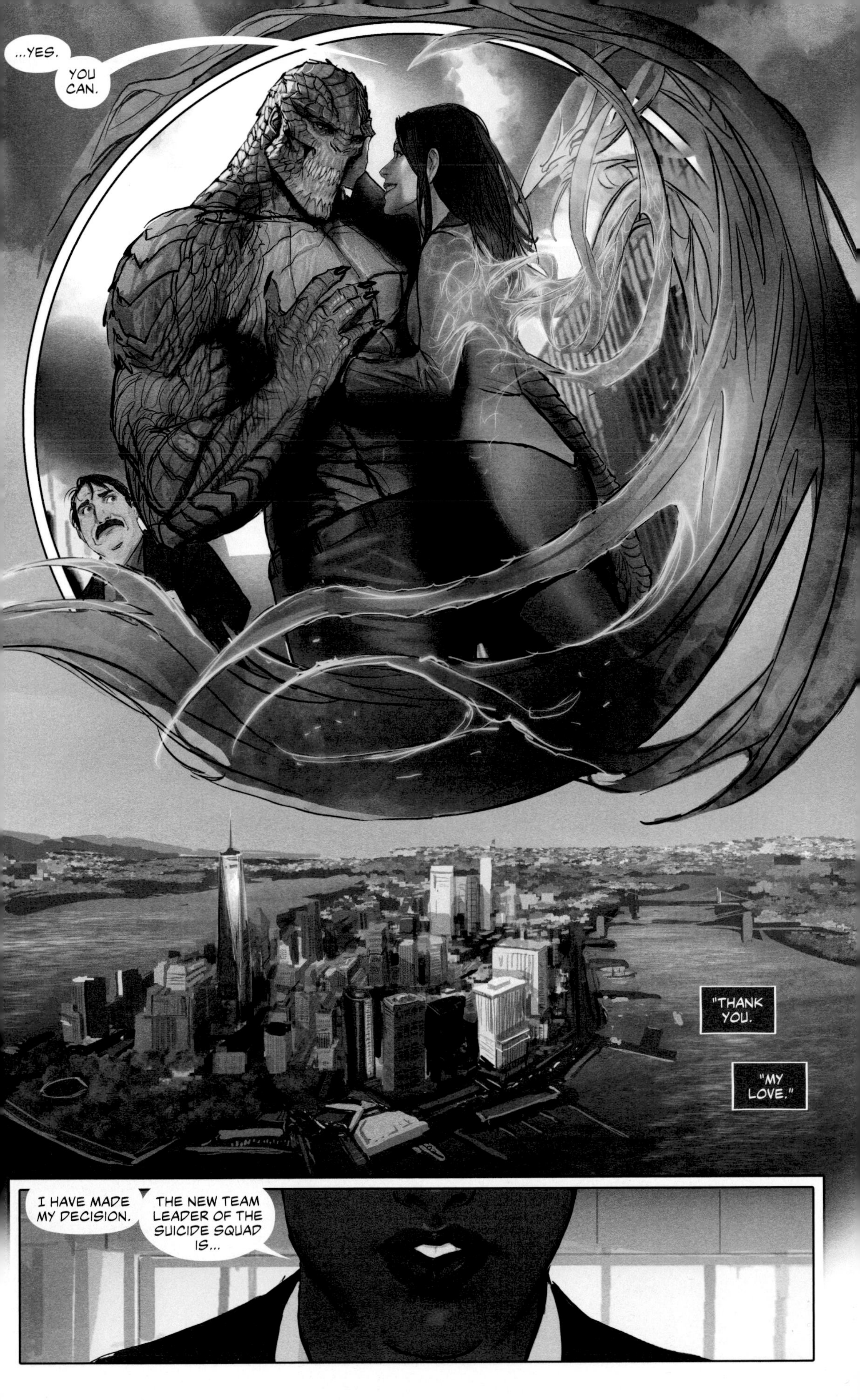
...YES.
YOU CAN.
"THANK YOU.
"MY LOVE."
I HAVE MADE MY DECISION.
THE NEW TEAM LEADER OF THE SUICIDE SQUAD IS...

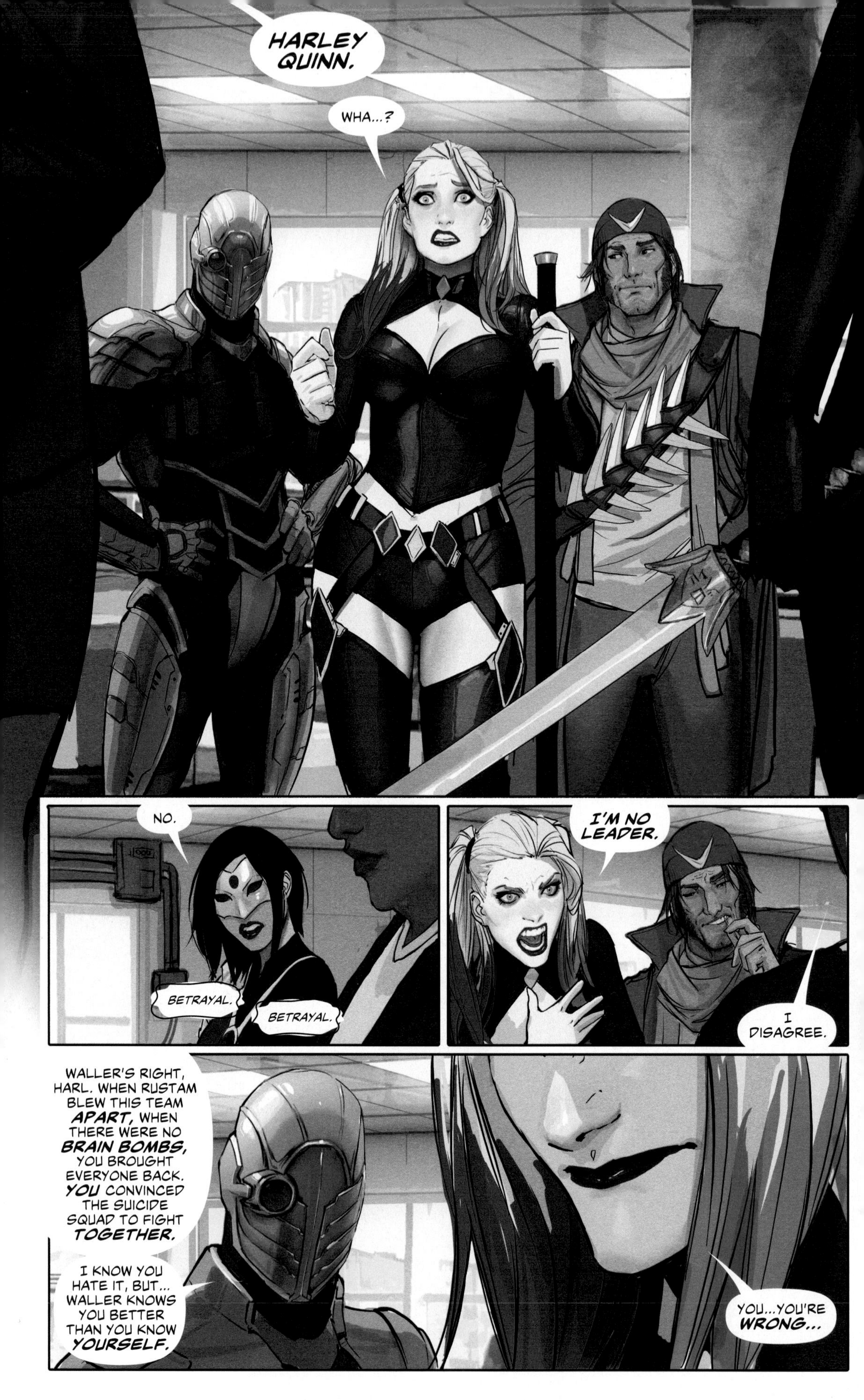
HARLEY QUINN.
WHA...?
NO.
BETRAYAL.
BETRAYAL.
I'M NO LEADER.
I DISAGREE.
WALLER'S RIGHT, HARL. WHEN RUSTAM BLEW THIS TEAM APART, WHEN THERE WERE NO BRAIN BOMBS, YOU BROUGHT EVERYONE BACK. YOU CONVINCED THE SUICIDE SQUAD TO FIGHT TOGETHER.
I KNOW YOU HATE IT, BUT... WALLER KNOWS YOU BETTER THAN YOU KNOW YOURSELF.
YOU...YOU'RE WRONG...

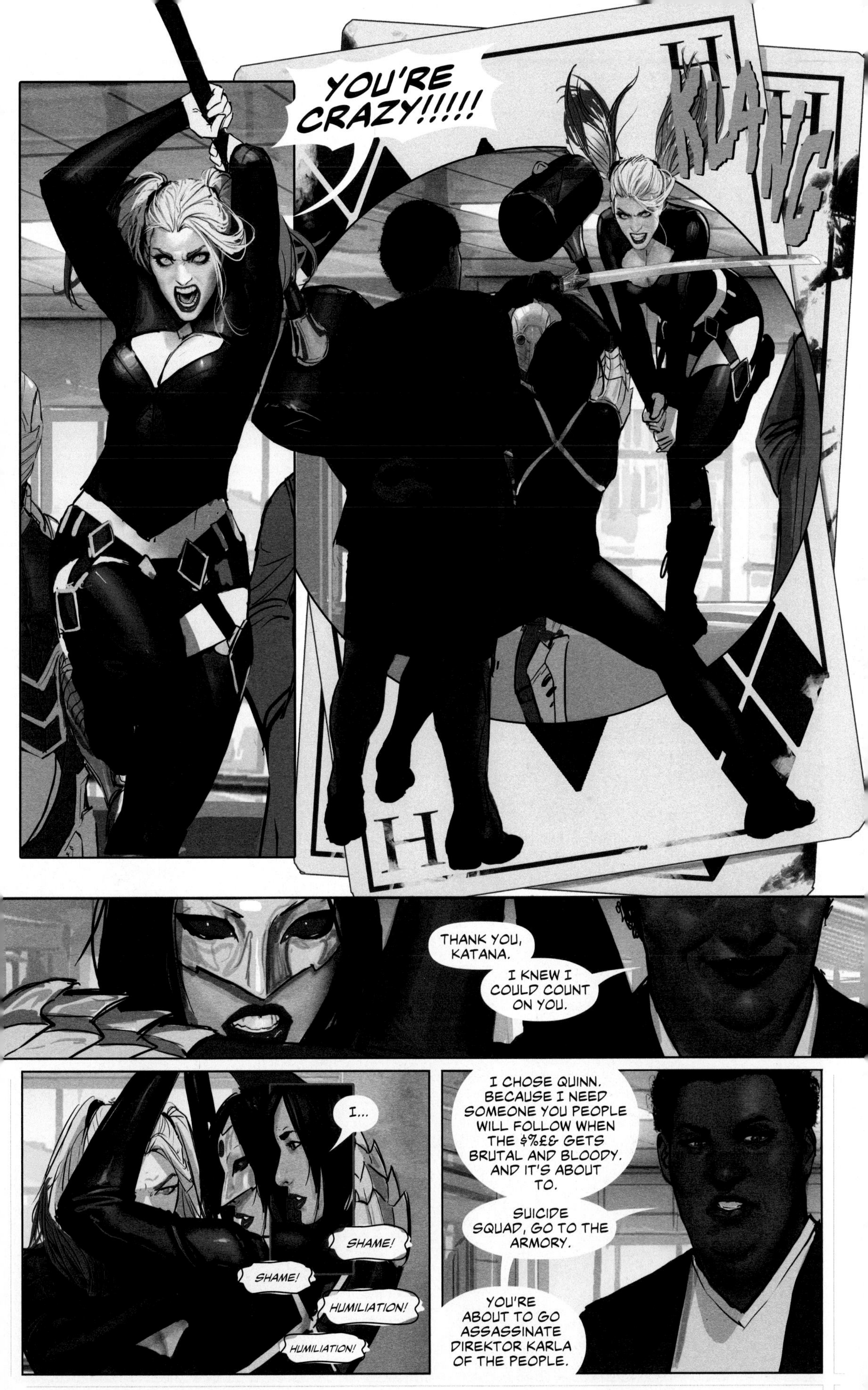
YOU'RE CRAZY!!!!!
KLANG
THANK YOU, KATANA.
I KNEW I COULD COUNT ON YOU.
I...
SHAME!
SHAME!
HUMILIATION!
HUMILIATION!
I CHOSE QUINN. BECAUSE I NEED SOMEONE YOU PEOPLE WILL FOLLOW WHEN THE $%£& GETS BRUTAL AND BLOODY. AND IT'S ABOUT TO.
SUICIDE SQUAD, GO TO THE ARMORY.
YOU'RE ABOUT TO GO ASSASSINATE DIREKTOR KARLA OF THE PEOPLE.

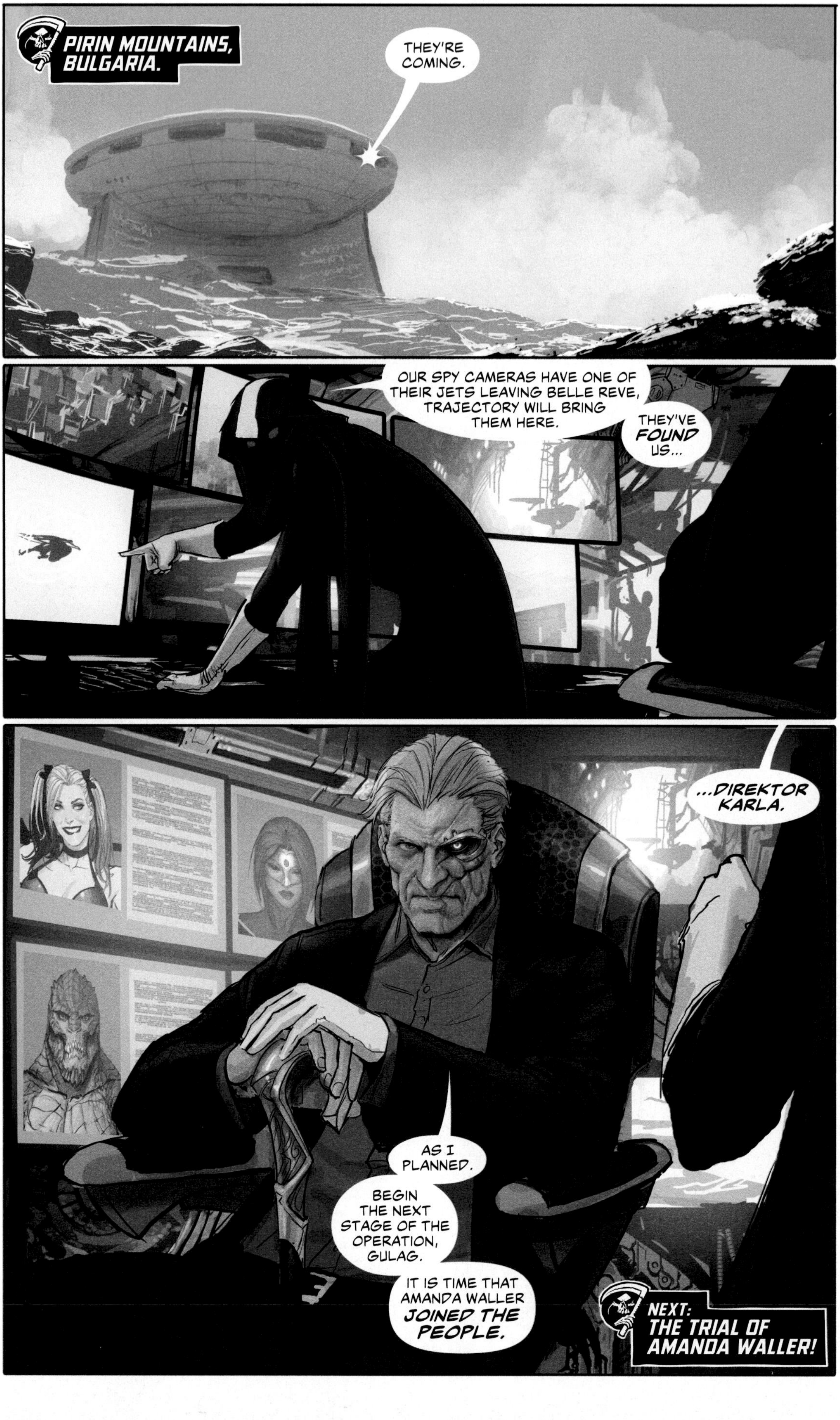
PIRIN MOUNTAINS, BULGARIA.
THEY'RE COMING.
OUR SPY CAMERAS HAVE ONE OF THEIR JETS LEAVING BELLE REVE, TRAJECTORY WILL BRING THEM HERE.
THEY'VE FOUND US...
...DIREKTOR KARLA.
AS I PLANNED.
BEGIN THE NEXT STAGE OF THE OPERATION, GULAG.
IT IS TIME THAT AMANDA WALLER JOINED THE PEOPLE.
NEXT: THE TRIAL OF AMANDA WALLER!

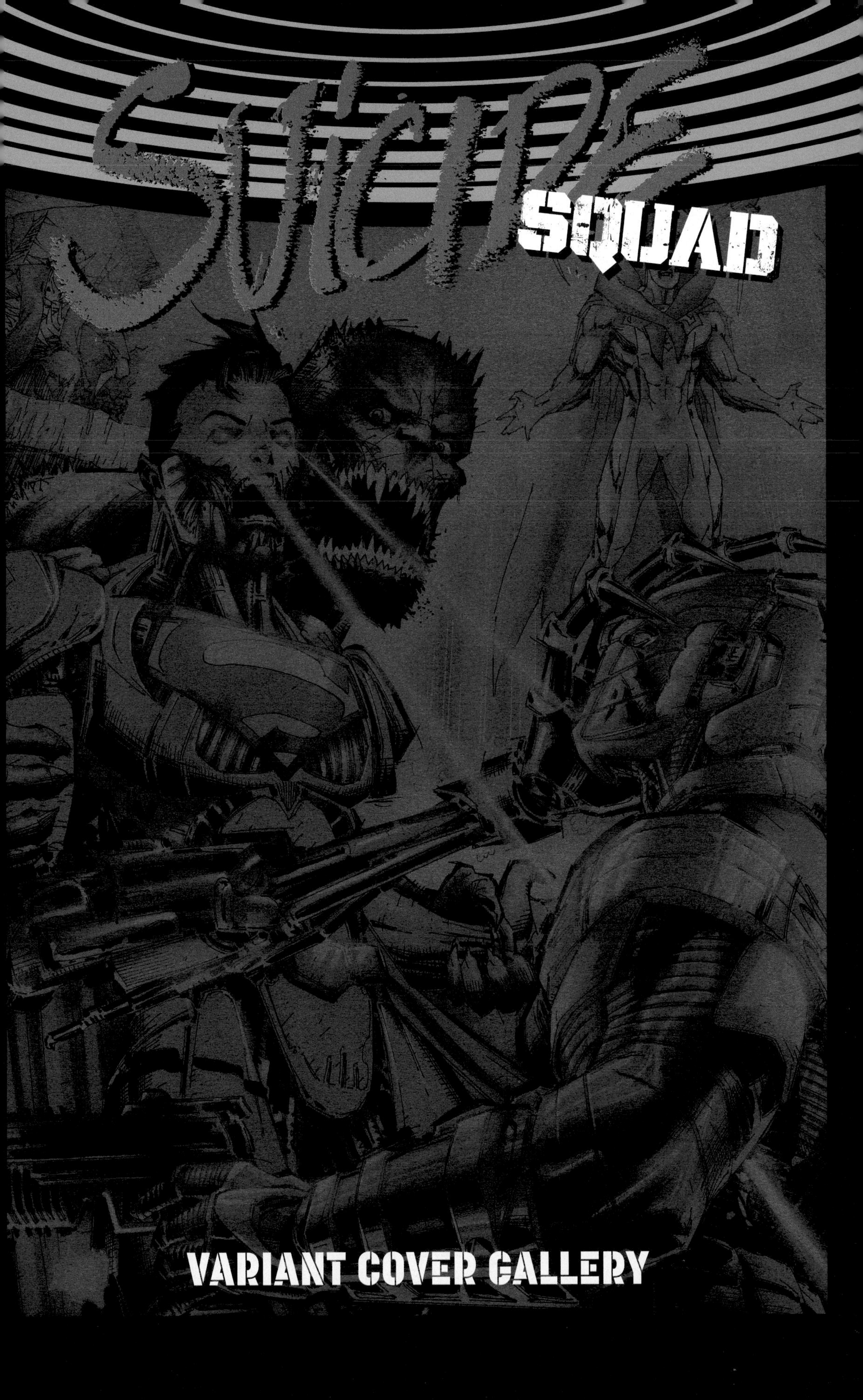
SUICIDE SQUAD

VARIANT COVER GALLERY

Variant cover art for SUICIDE SQUAD #16 by LEE BERMEJO

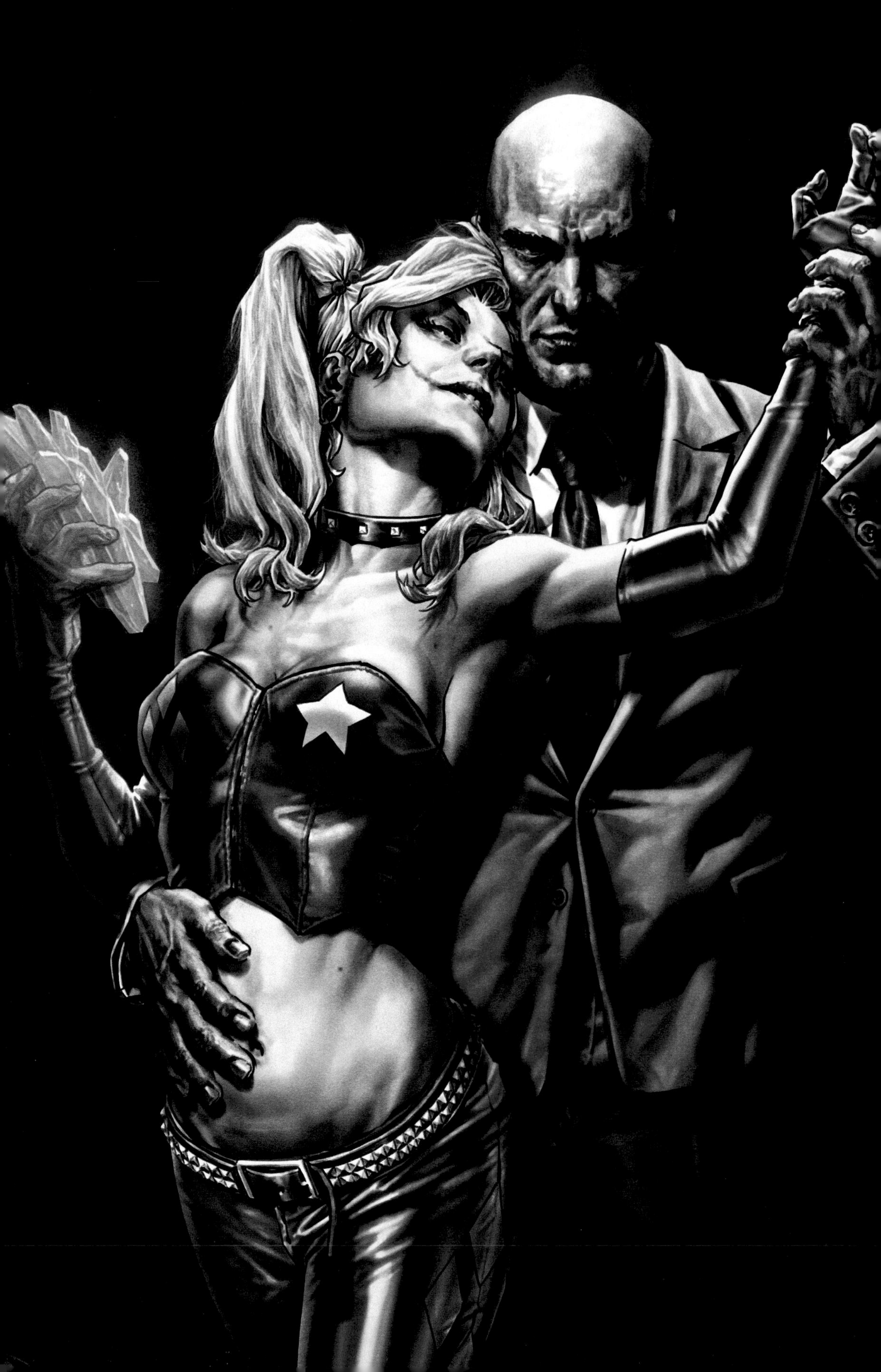

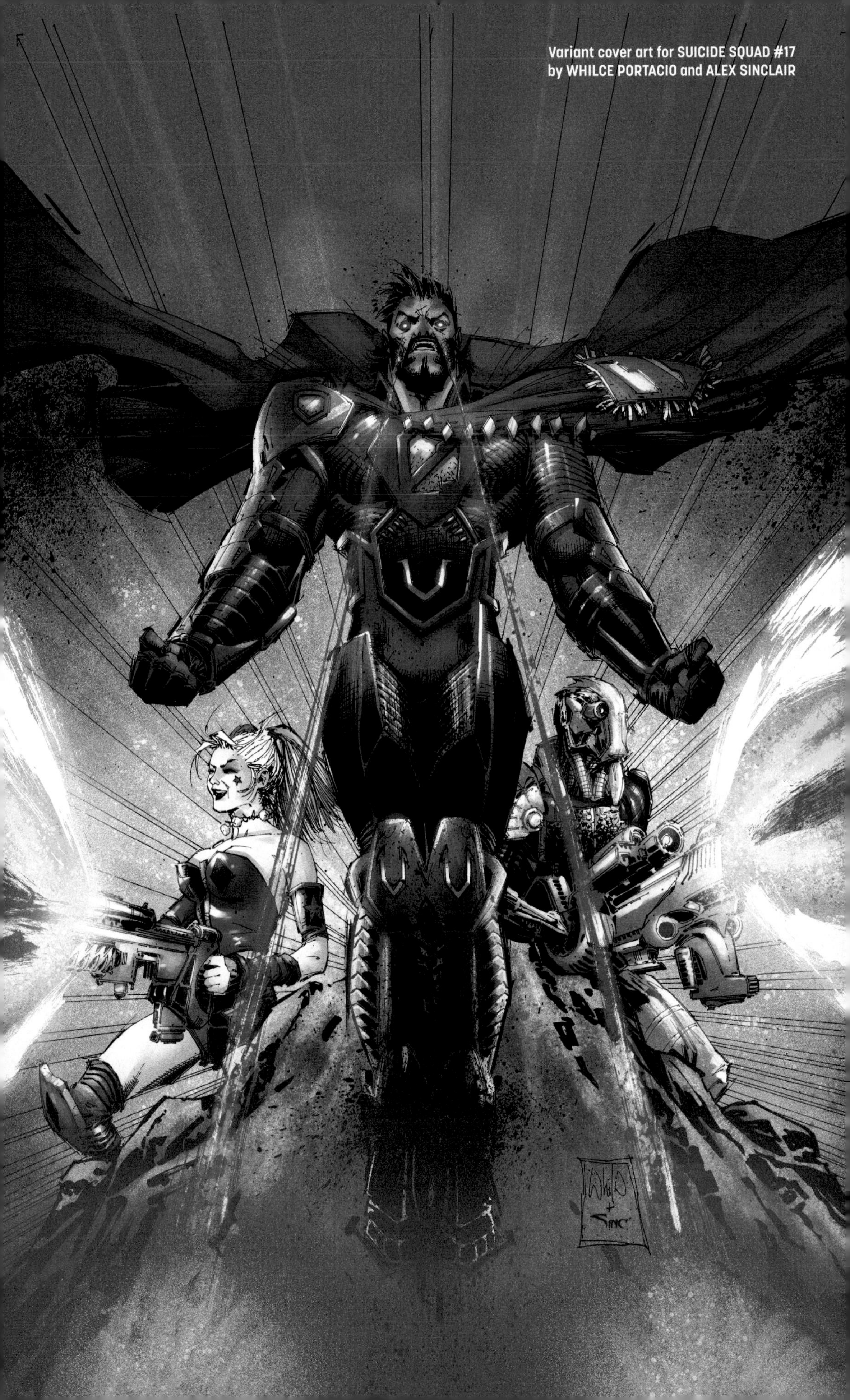

Variant cover art for SUICIDE SQUAD #17
by WHILCE PORTACIO and ALEX SINCLAIR

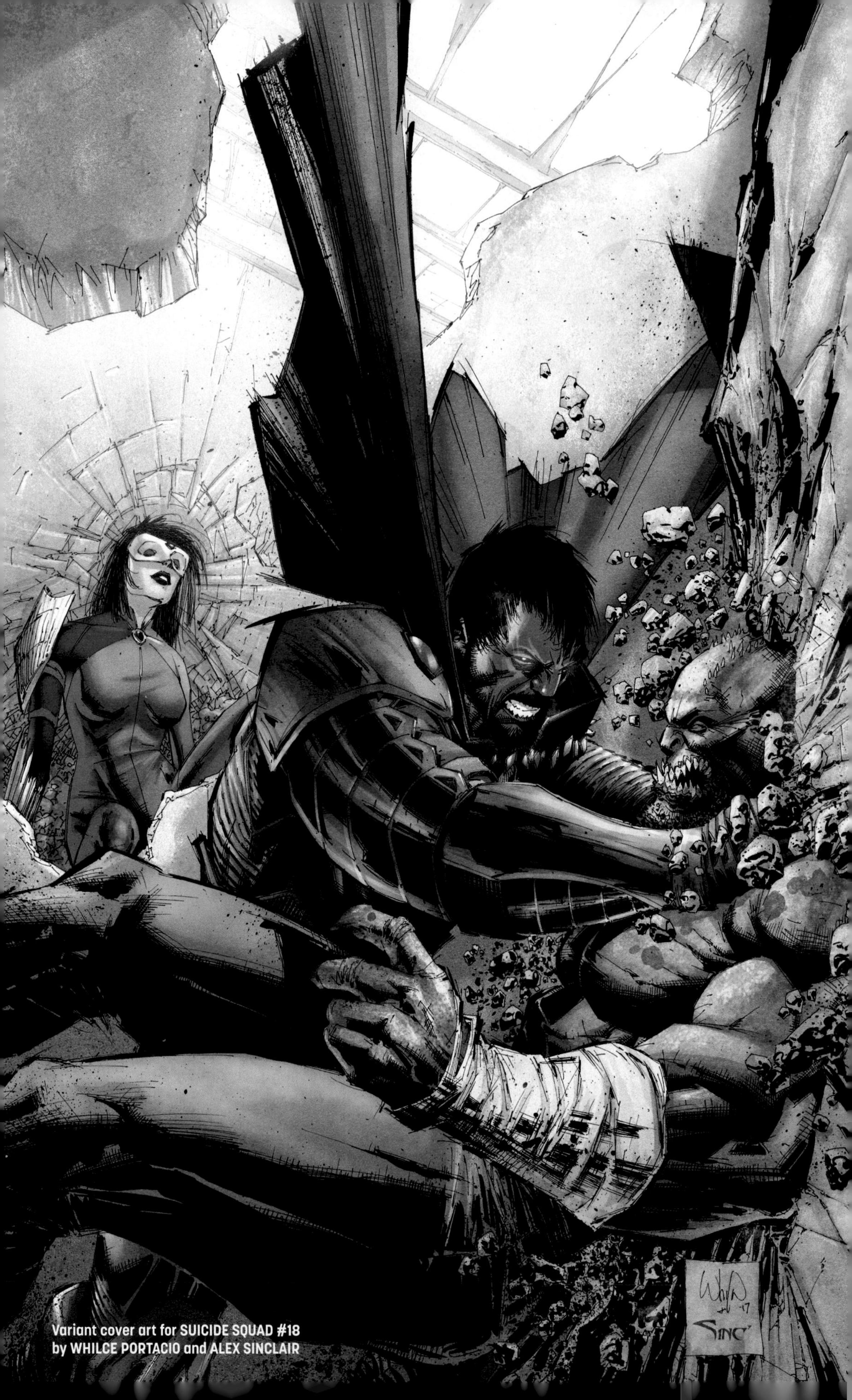

Variant cover art for SUICIDE SQUAD #18
by WHILCE PORTACIO and ALEX SINCLAIR

Variant cover art for SUICIDE SQUAD #19
by WHILCE PORTACIO and ALEX SINCLAIR

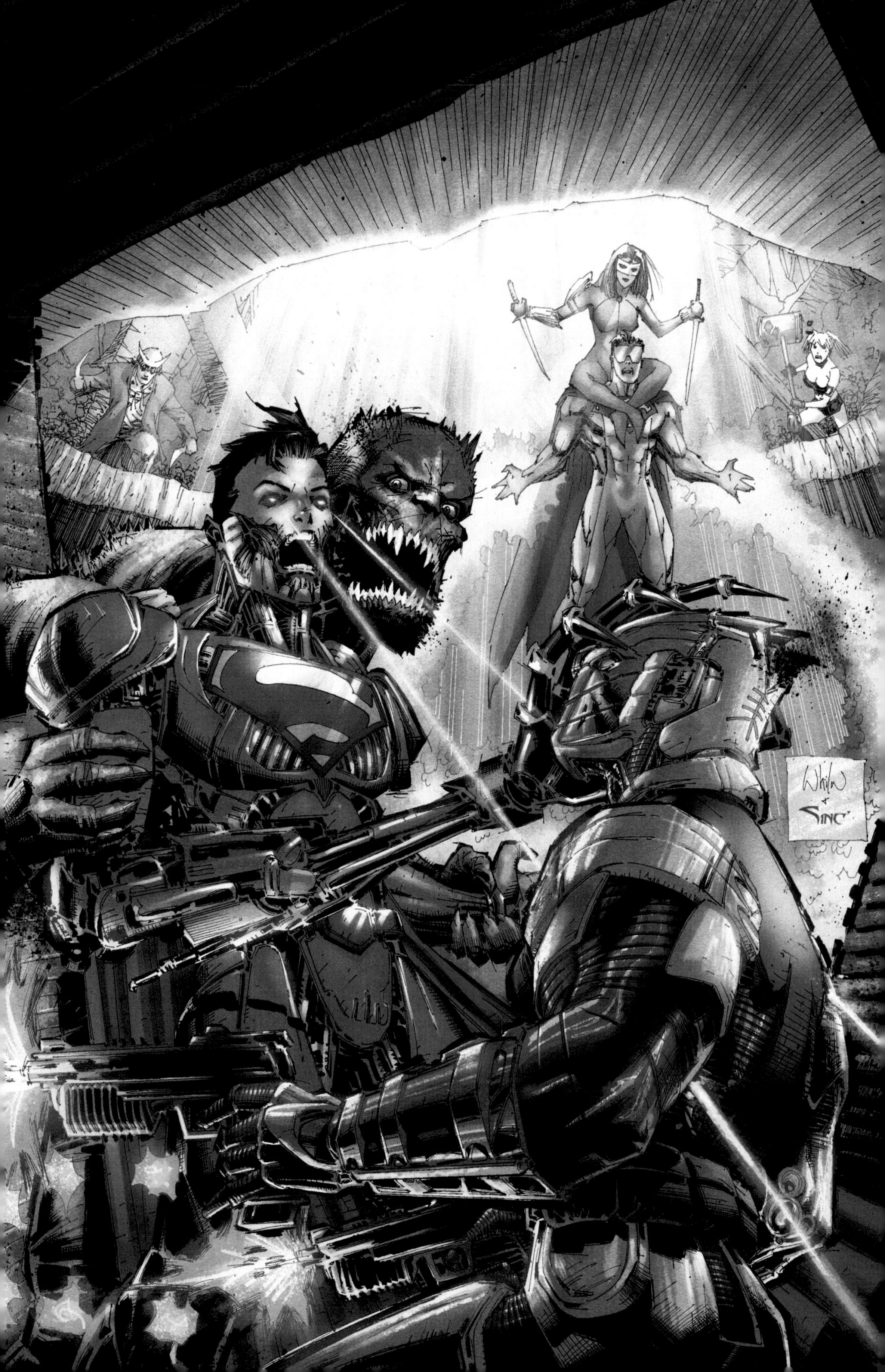

Variant cover art for SUICIDE SQUAD #20
by WHILCE PORTACIO and ALEX SINCLAIR

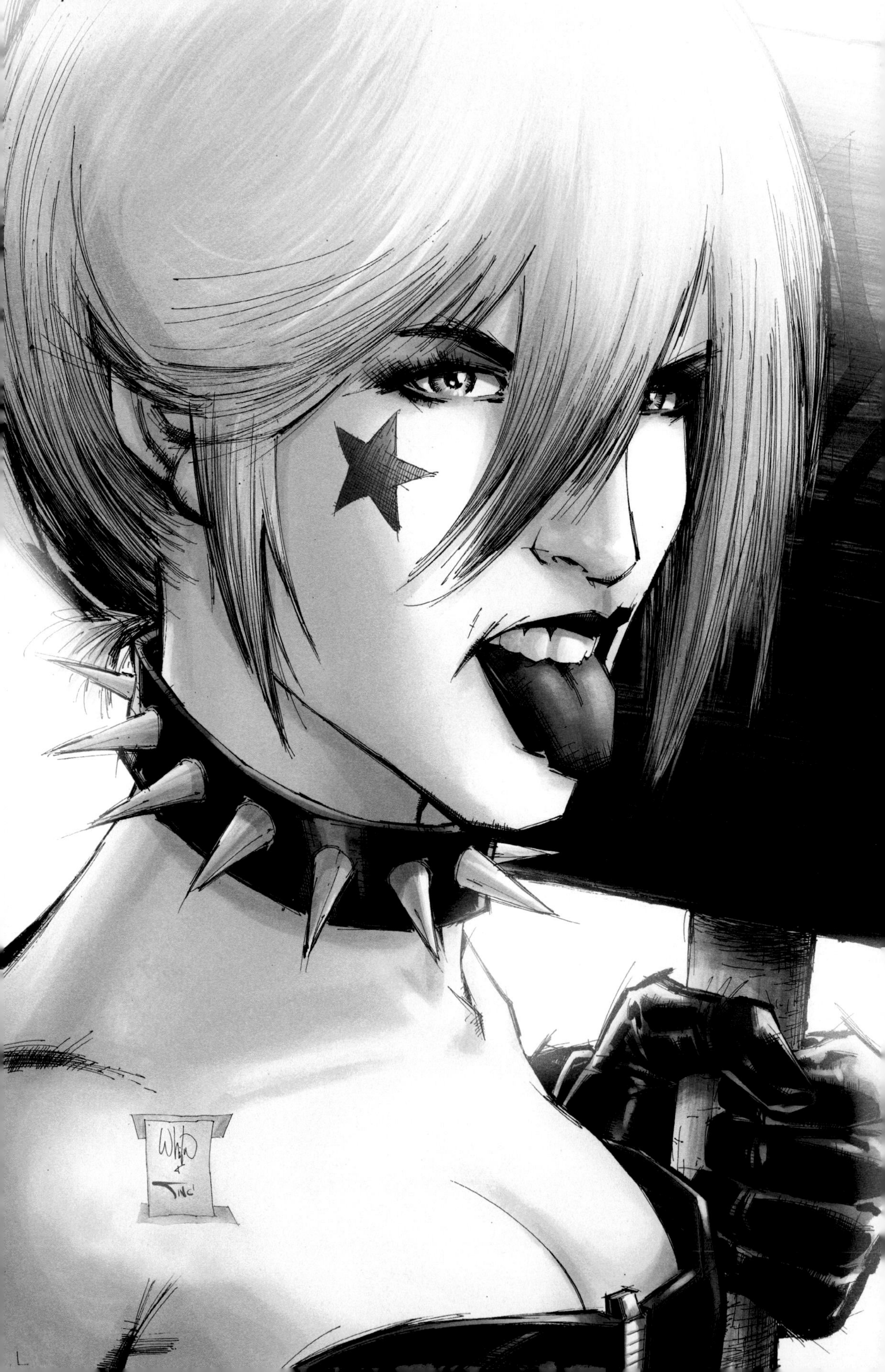

RED SONS RISING

Pencils by TONY S. DANIEL

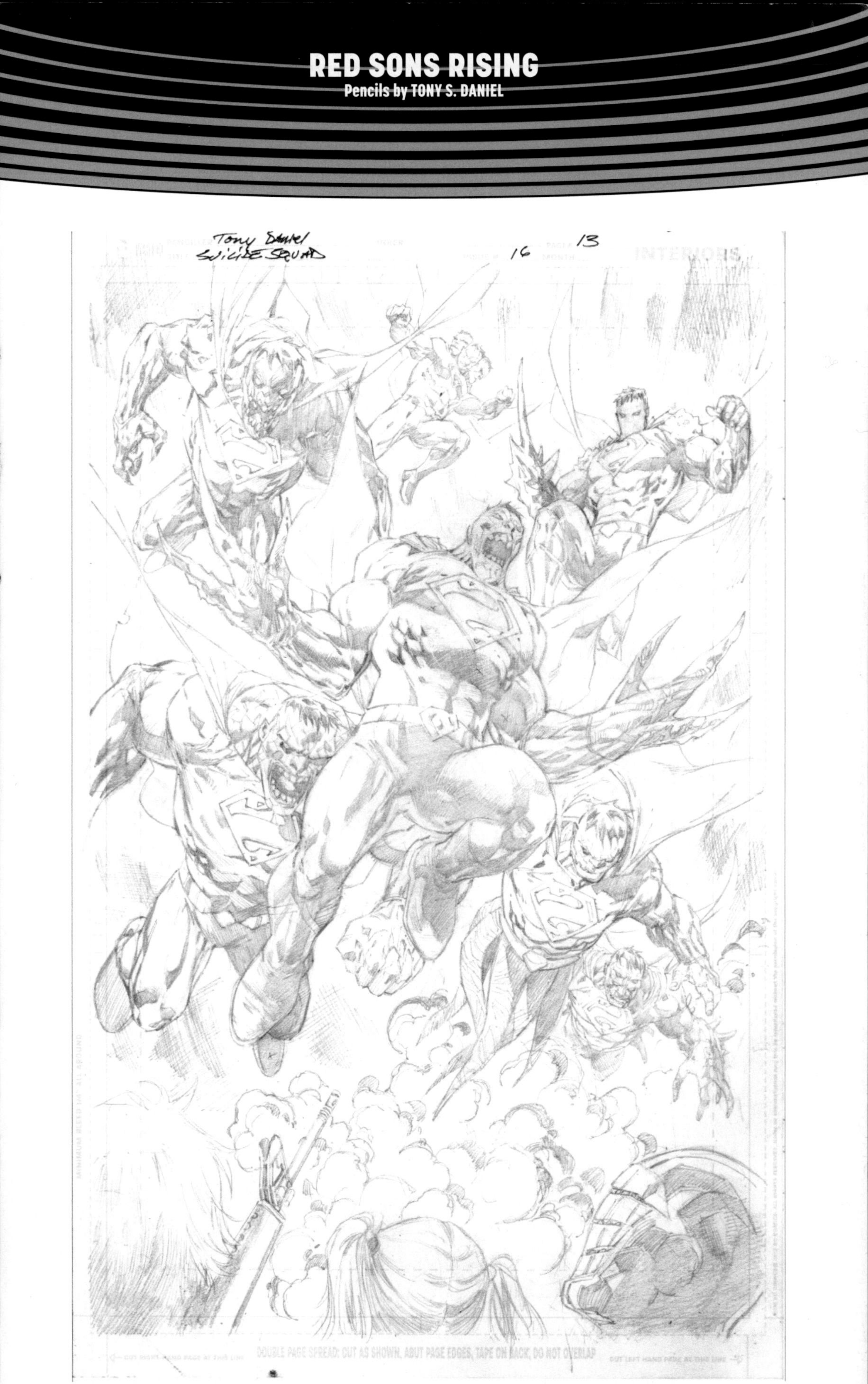

Tony Daniel
Suicide Squad
16
13
INTERIORS
DOUBLE PAGE SPREAD: CUT AS SHOWN, ABUT PAGE EDGES, TAPE ON BACK, DO NOT OVERLAP

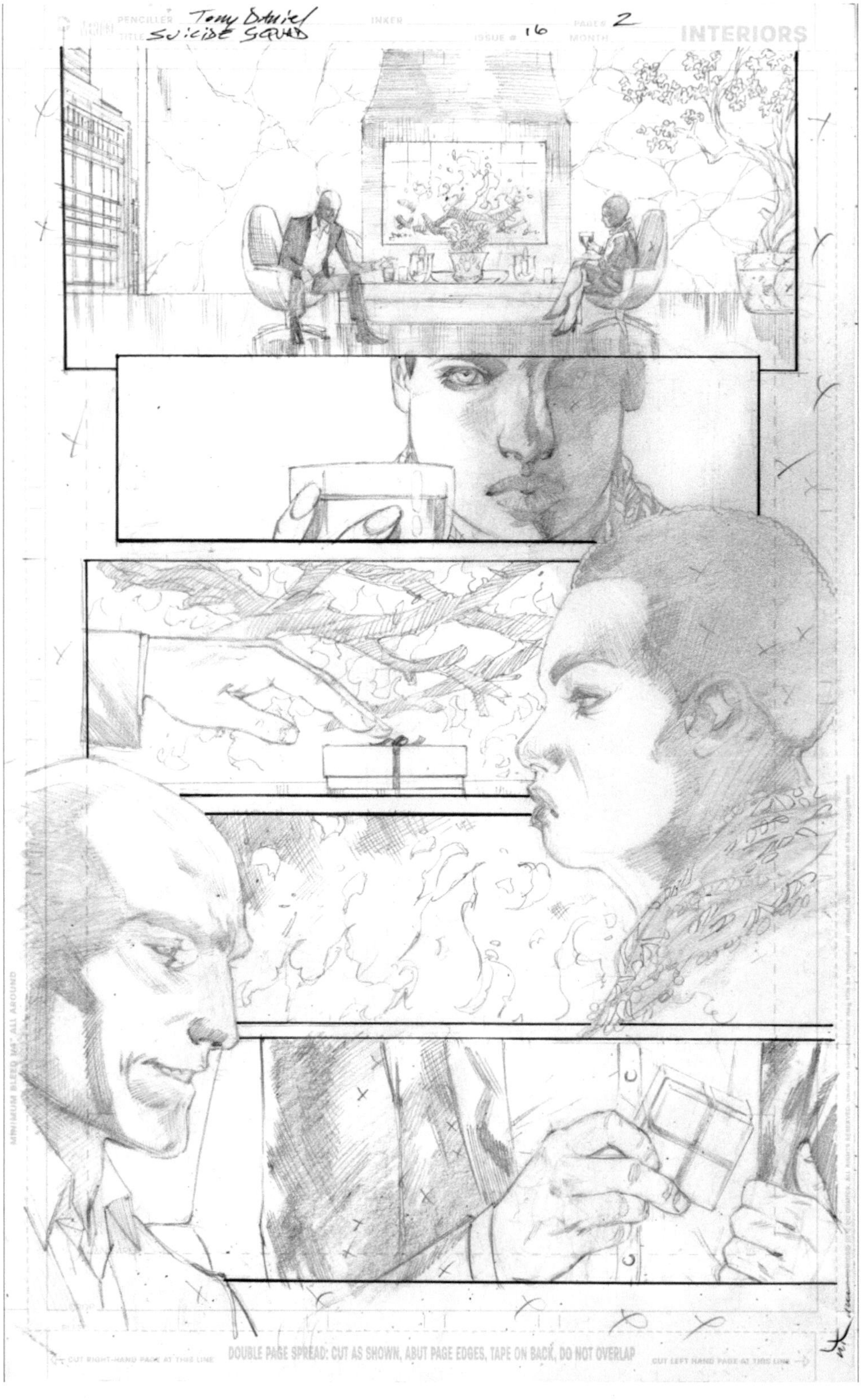
PENCILLER Tony Daniel
TITLE SUICIDE SQUAD
INKER
ISSUE # 16
PAGES 2
MONTH
INTERIORS
DOUBLE PAGE SPREAD: CUT AS SHOWN, ABUT PAGE EDGES, TAPE ON BACK, DO NOT OVERLAP

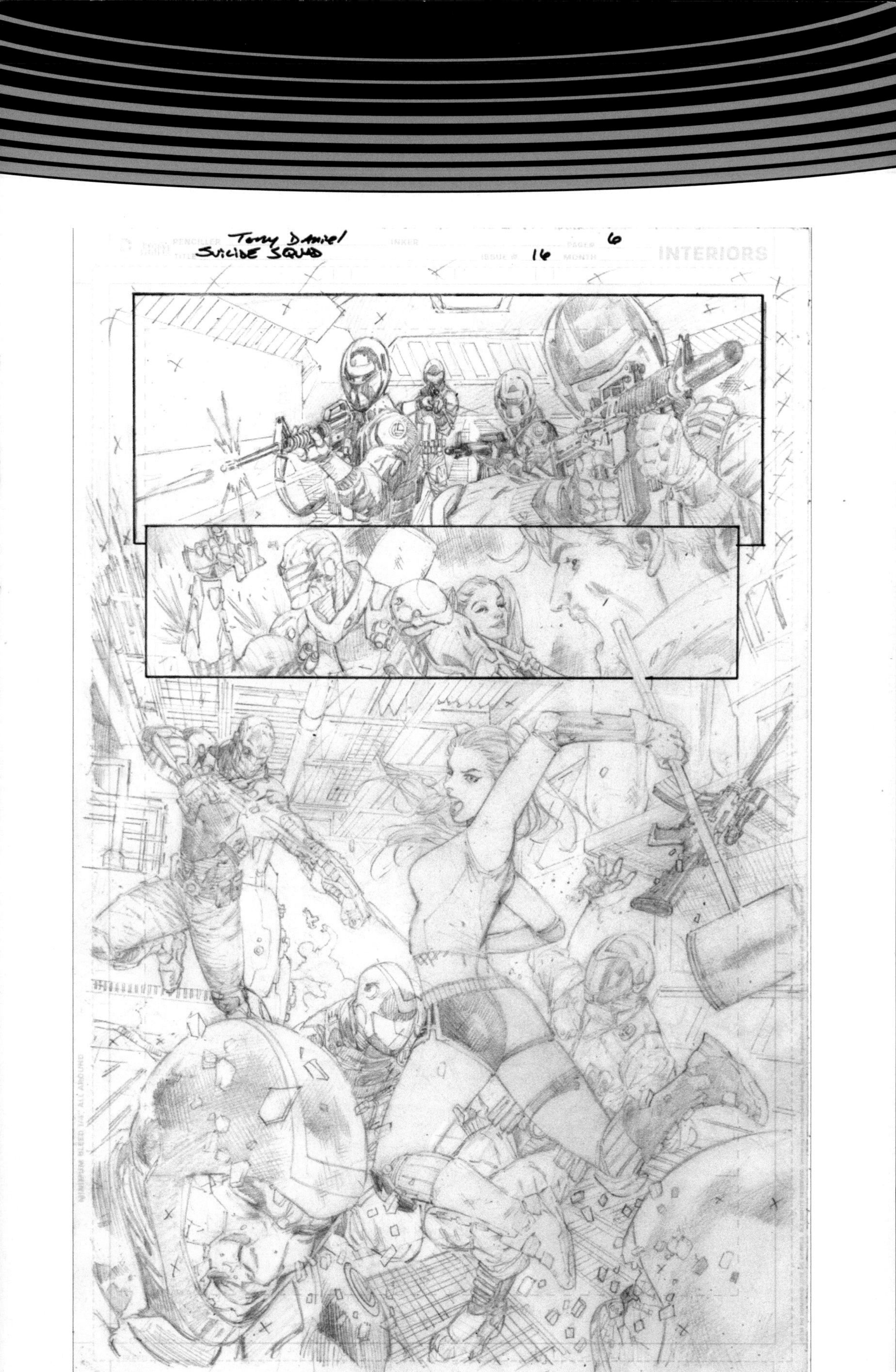

PENCILLER Tony Daniel
INKER
PAGE# 6
TITLE SUICIDE SQUAD
ISSUE # 16
MONTH
INTERIORS
DOUBLE PAGE SPREAD: CUT AS SHOWN, ABUT PAGE EDGES, TAPE ON BACK, DO NOT OVERLAP

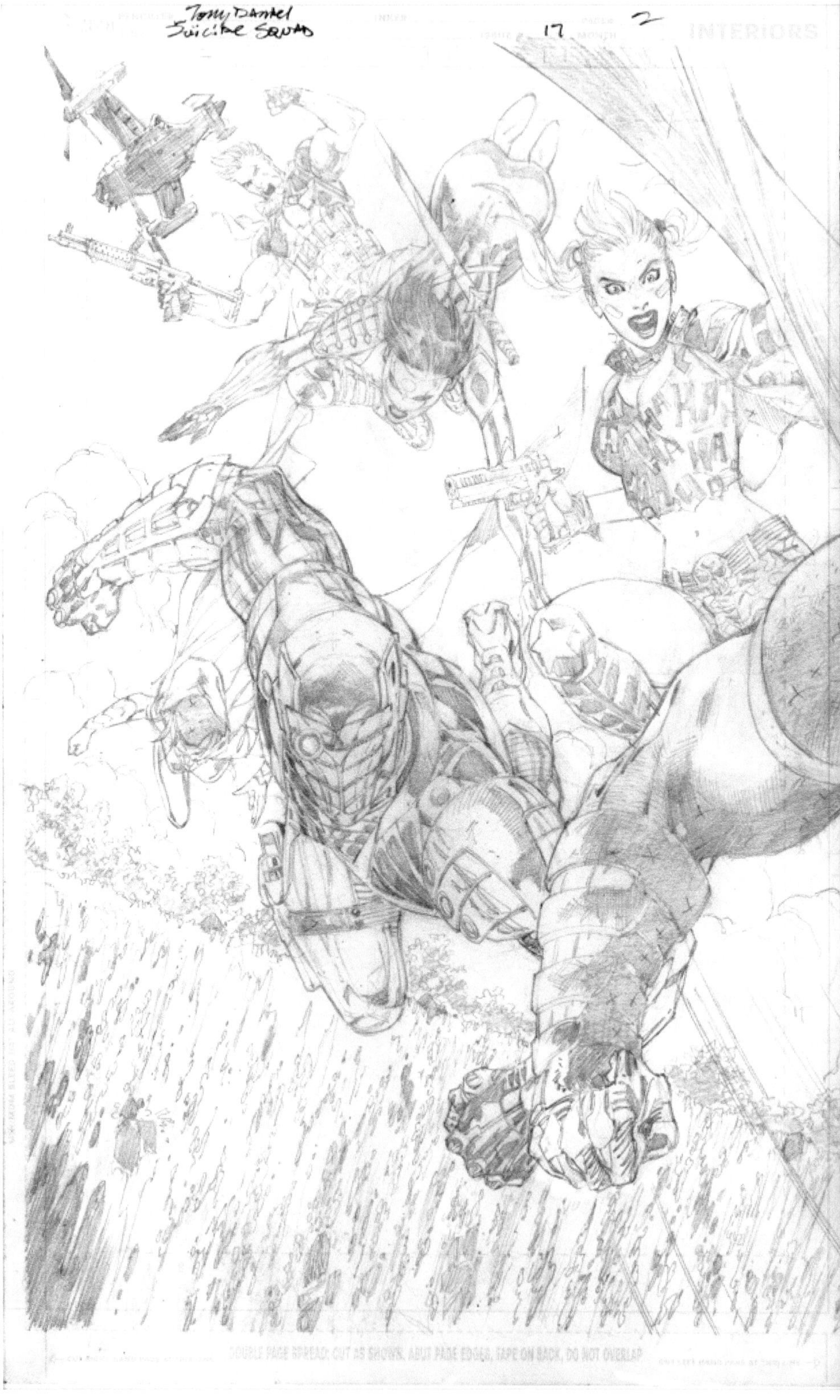
Tony Daniel
Suicide Squad
17
2
INTERIORS
DOUBLE PAGE SPREAD: CUT AS SHOWN. ABUT PAGE EDGES, TAPE ON BACK, DO NOT OVERLAP

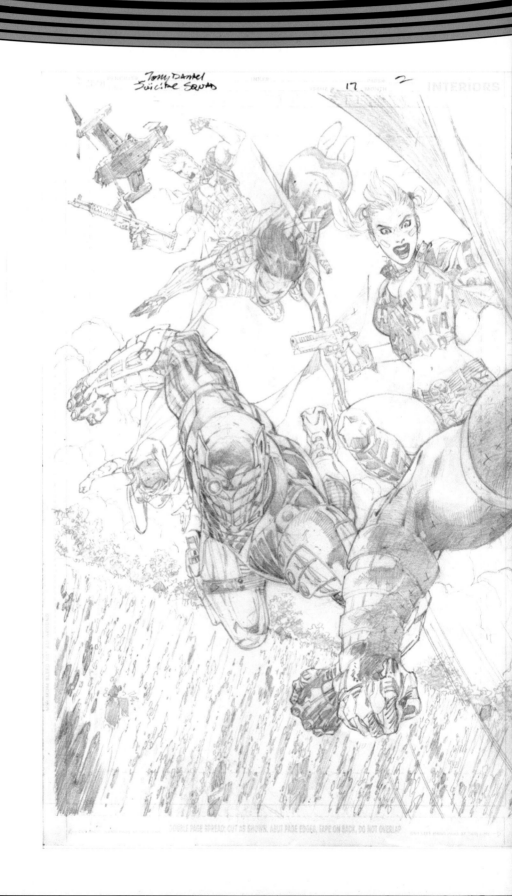

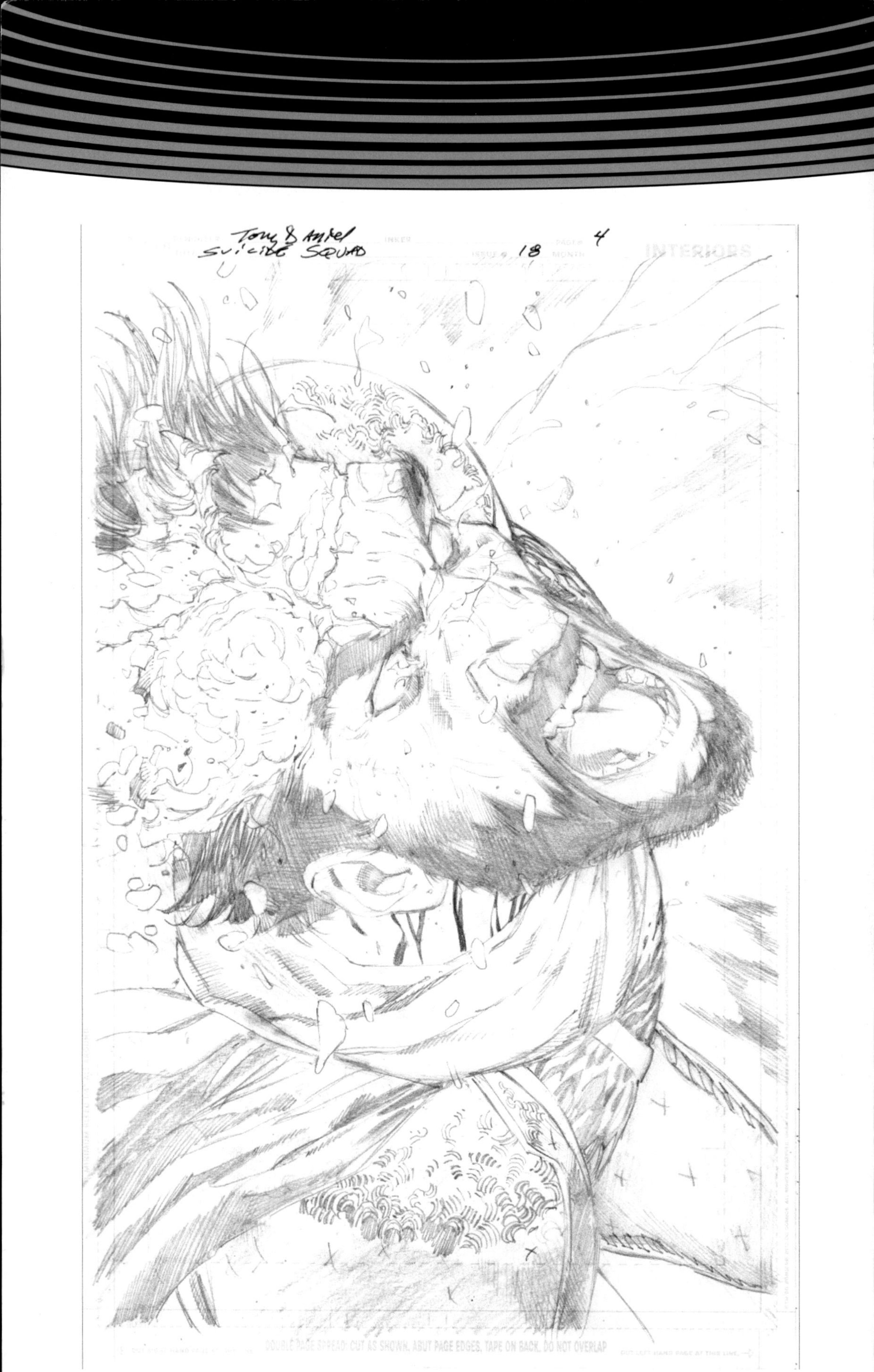
Tony S Daniel
SUICIDE SQUAD
INKER
ISSUE # 18
PAGE # 4
MONTH
INTERIORS
DOUBLE PAGE SPREAD: CUT AS SHOWN, ABUT PAGE EDGES, TAPE ON BACK, DO NOT OVERLAP

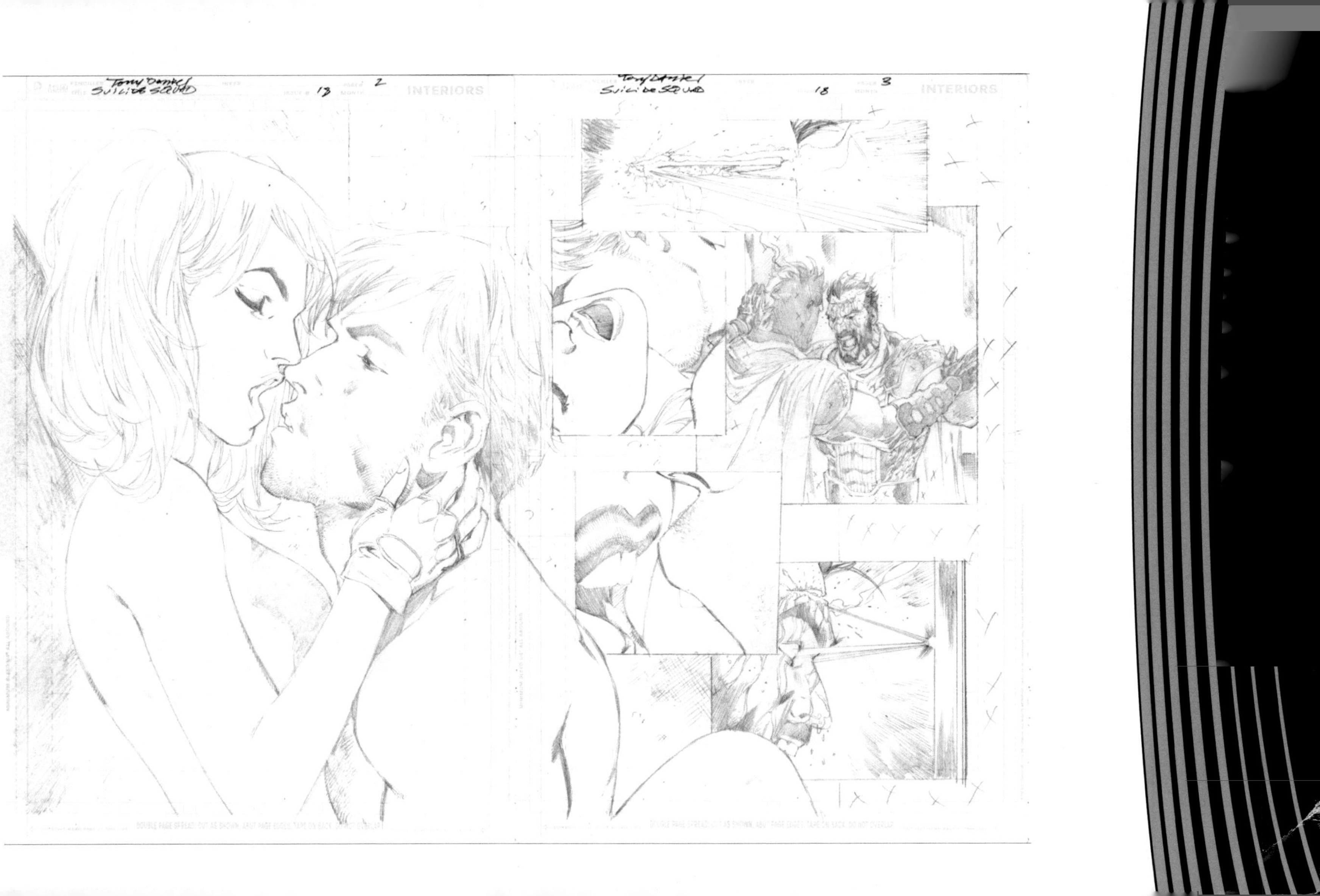
Tony Daniel
Suicide Squad
13
2
INTERIORS
Tony Daniel
Suicide Squad
18
3
INTERIORS

"It's nice to see one of the best comics of the late '80s return so strongly."
– Comic Book Resources

"It's high energy from page one through to the last page." **– BATMAN NEWS**

DC UNIVERSE REBIRTH

SUICIDE SQUAD

VOL. 1: THE BLACK VAULT

ROB WILLIAMS
with JIM LEE and others

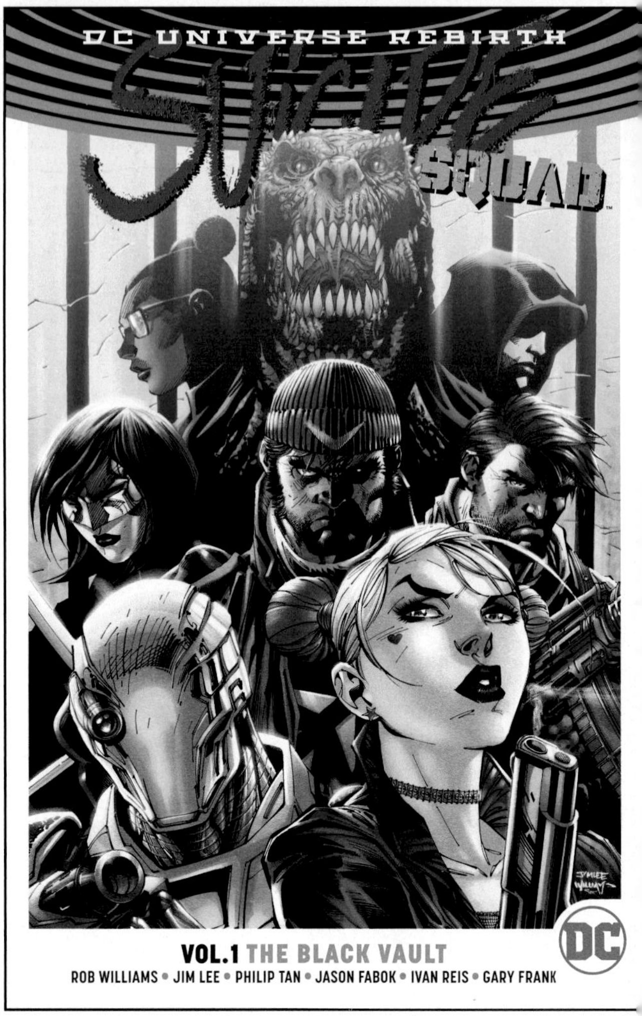
DC UNIVERSE REBIRTH
SUICIDE SQUAD
VOL.1 THE BLACK VAULT
ROB WILLIAMS • JIM LEE • PHILIP TAN • JASON FABOK • IVAN REIS • GARY FRANK

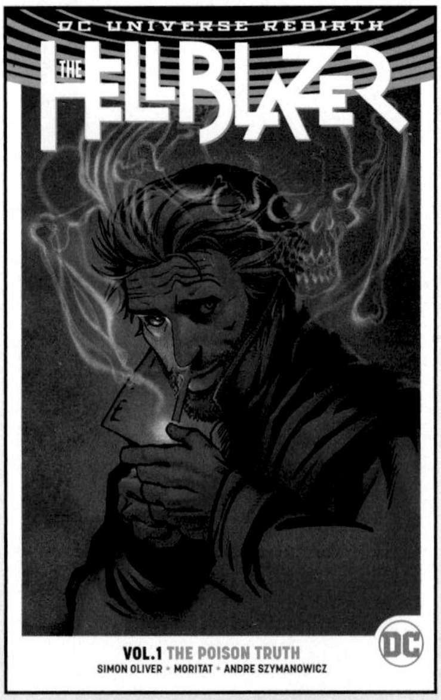
DC UNIVERSE REBIRTH
THE HELLBLAZER
VOL.1 THE POISON TRUTH
SIMON OLIVER • MORITAT • ANDRE SZYMANOWICZ

THE HELLBLAZER VOL. 1: THE POISON TRUTH

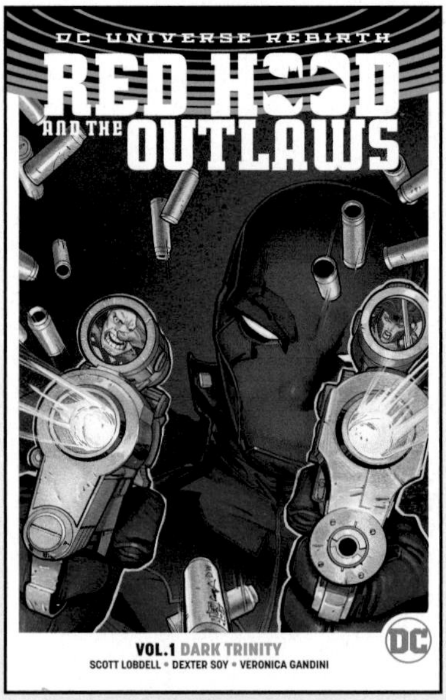
DC UNIVERSE REBIRTH
RED HOOD AND THE OUTLAWS
VOL.1 DARK TRINITY
SCOTT LOBDELL • DEXTER SOY • VERONICA GANDINI

RED HOOD AND THE OUTLAWS VOL. 1: DARK TRINITY

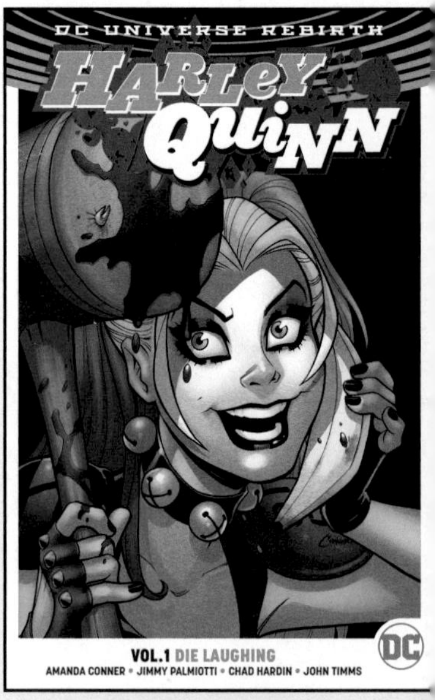
DC UNIVERSE REBIRTH
HARLEY QUINN
VOL.1 DIE LAUGHING
AMANDA CONNER • JIMMY PALMIOTTI • CHAD HARDIN • JOHN TIMMS

HARLEY QUINN VOL. 1: DIE LAUGHING

Get more DC graphic novels wherever comics and books are sold!

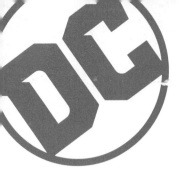